"It is heartening to find a textbook  managerial cognition in understar approach, sometimes called 'beha\ constraints on the time and comp organizations even supplemented with powerful computers.

Rich A. Bettis, *The University of North Carolina at Chapel Hill, USA*

"This is a much needed and long-awaited textbook. A behavioral approach brings to strategy a fresh new perspective that will definitely enhance scholars' and managers' understanding of how individuals, groups, and organizations make decisions, the impact that cognitive biases have on those decisions, and the corresponding performance implications. This theoretically rich and empirically grounded textbook is a first important step in that direction. It will contribute a more realistic description of how organizations behave and manage some of the key trade-offs involved in strategic management."

Gino Cattani, *Leonard N. Stern School of Business,*
New York University, USA

"In this book, Bromiley and Rau provide a good introduction to the core topics in strategic management. By taking an explicitly behavioral perspective, the authors bring to the fore important issues in the actual performance of strategy, which are given short shrift in the typical analytical account of strategy making. The concepts are highlighted with several interesting examples and the style of writing is engaging and accessible."

Kannan Srikanth, *Singapore Management University, Singapore*

"Although there are many strategy textbooks on the market today, this one represents an especially welcome alternative. Students will appreciate its direct, engaging style and many faculty will appreciate its thoughtful incorporation of insights from behavioral research."

Daniel Forbes, *University of Minnesota, USA*

BEHAVIORAL STRATEGIC MANAGEMENT

This unique text examines strategic management and its implementation in the context of what we know about how individuals and organizations actually make decisions. Through this behavioral approach, students gain a richer, more realistic understanding of how to create coherent strategies that take advantage of their strengths and build their capabilities.

Integrating analytical tools found in a typical strategy textbook with cognitive and psychological insights into decision making, the book focuses on core issues that will help students understand the complexities inherent in making profitable decisions. Readers will learn about the purpose of organizations; consider how political, technological, and industry environments play into firm capabilities; how these capabilities are used in competition; and how to adapt strategies over time. The authors also cover important topics like managerial cognition, learning, and corporate strategy, which receive scant attention in other texts. Chapter summaries, experiential exercises, and "Food for Thought" boxes featuring plenty of discussion questions provide practical insight into how to utilize a successful strategy and maintain a consistent, long-term direction within a firm.

Succinct and well-written, *Behavioral Strategic Management* offers graduate students of strategy a deeper and broader understanding of the topic.

Philip Bromiley is a Dean's Professor in Strategic Management at the Merage School of Management, University of California at Irvine, USA.

Devaki Rau is a Professor specializing in strategic management at the College of Business, Northern Illinois University, USA.

BEHAVIORAL STRATEGIC MANAGEMENT

**Philip Bromiley
and Devaki Rau**

Routledge
Taylor & Francis Group

NEW YORK AND LONDON

First published 2018
by Routledge
711 Third Avenue, New York, NY 10017

and by Routledge
2 Park Square, Milton Park, Abingdon, Oxon, OX14 4RN

Routledge is an imprint of the Taylor & Francis Group, an informa business

Library of Congress Cataloging-in-Publication Data
A catalog record for this book has been requested

ISBN: 978-1-138-29235-2 (hbk)
ISBN: 978-1-138-29236-9 (pbk)
ISBN: 978-1-315-23298-0 (ebk)

Typeset in Minion Pro and Helvetica
by Florence Production Ltd, Stoodleigh, Devon, UK

Visit the companion website:
www.routledge.com/cw/bromiley

To our spouses and children

We would like to thank Ann Clark and the staff of Taylor & Francis for their assistance in preparing this book.

BRIEF CONTENTS

DETAILED CONTENTS

FIGURES

PREFACE

You may have noticed this book is shorter than many other textbooks. This is intentional. Rather than overloading you with long lists of things to consider or factors that matter in strategy, we will identify the core issues you need to worry about. Where we provide lists, they are to help you check that you have not forgotten something. We seriously doubt most students retain 500 pages' worth of information from 500-page textbooks.

You may find that strategic management does not have many clearly right answers. We can clearly identify some traps to avoid, things to consider, and guidelines on how to frame problems, but good strategy requires creativity. One of the most exciting and challenging parts of running a business is developing and implementing a coherent yet distinctive strategy. Well-informed individuals often disagree about strategy. Disagreement, if it stays on the substance of the issues rather than becoming personal, improves thinking and helps the organization develop better decisions.

Strategic management success usually depends on relative rather than absolute performance. There is a story about two hunters who run into a bear. Both start running away but one starts slowing down to put on his sneakers. The other hunter says, "You know you can't outrun a bear, don't you?" The hunter putting sneakers on says, "That's okay, I just have to outrun you." Likewise, in business, you need to be better than the competition to win, but "better" is relative, not absolute. A VP of Marketing once told one of the authors, "We're not very good at marketing. Luckily, no one in our industry is good at marketing."

Strategies also need to change over time. If you come up with a wonderful strategy, your competition will work on countering and potentially mimicking it. This means that even a firm with a wonderful strategy must periodically check whether the strategy's value has dissipated as other organizations either copy it or develop counters to it.

Generally, organizations win by having coherent strategies. Having a coherent strategy simplifies decisions and helps align efforts across the organization. Without a strategy, the organization's units do not know whether they are looking for low cost or high quality, how important customer service is compared to features, etc. Good strategies not only take advantage of what we do well relative to the competition but also help us build our capabilities. Good strategies reflect a sophisticated understanding of the firm's competitive environment and a realistic understanding of the firm's abilities, resulting in consistent long-term direction. However, good strategies are not enough; a strategy is only as good as its implementation.

Put in terms of your career, a good strategy takes advantage of what you are good at relative to your peers, while considering the market in which you compete. A good strategy helps you coordinate the different parts of your education and career activities. For example, how much importance should you give to getting a higher grade versus being active in a student group? In addition, a good strategy requires effective implementation. You might sign up for the right courses, but if you do not put in the effort to learn what is being taught, you will not get much out of them.

While, like all strategic management texts, this text attempts to give you an understanding of how to think about strategy and choose a strategy for a business, this text differentiates itself from most texts in three ways:

1. This text takes a behavioral approach. This means that we interpret findings and knowledge about strategic management in the context of what scholars know about how individuals and organizations actually behave.
2. This text provides both the conceptual models and principles underlying a given set of tools as well as the tools themselves.
3. This text consciously restricts the number of concepts and the length devoted to each of these concepts. Although this text might be useful in other classes, we have in mind a 10-week class. Many texts give students far too many ideas to absorb in each class. Instead of attempting to solve this problem by providing abundant examples, we will try to solve it by reducing the number of ancillary discussions.

Finally, this text covers several concepts and topics largely ignored in conventional textbooks including managerial cognition, learning, strategic planning, and strategy implementation.

The rest of the text is organized as follows. First, we discuss general issues associated with strategic behavior and the purpose of an organization. Next, we analyze the firm's environment—the macro-environment involving politics, technology, etc., and then the industry environment. We move from these environmental analyses to discuss some generic ways that firms compete. Following this, we talk about firm capabilities and the evolution of industries. Finally, we talk about corporate strategy, governance, and strategy implementation. The appendix at the end of the book provides some experiential exercises based on a behavioral approach.

CHAPTER 1

Cognition and Strategy

OVERVIEW OF STRATEGY

This text is about the strategic direction of an organization, which means its objectives, how it will measure or evaluate progress toward those objectives, and the firm's major activities and how it goes about doing those. In general, organizations do better when carefully designed around a given strategy. For ease, let us use some sports analogies.

Think about any competitive activity between groups, whether the mathematics Olympiad, high school basketball, or professional soccer. To develop a good strategy, we need to address several questions:

1. What does the team want to achieve? Some teams want to win championships, while others value comradery after games.
2. What rules govern the game, and what else do we know about the game? While we should know the formal rules, we should also know how those are enforced, as well as a wide variety of other things about the game such as the likelihood of certain outcomes, the amount of training or practice we would need to reach a desired skill level, and so on.
3. Who is our competition, and what do we know about them?
4. What are we better or worse at than the competition?

Given an intersection of these four, we can attempt to create a strategy to achieve our objectives. These considerations apply equally to sports teams, your career, and businesses.

Think about your career. First, you need to decide what you really want. Do you want to maximize your income above all else? Or, do you value living in a particular place to the extent that you would give up income and career advancement to live where you want to live? Note that none of these goals or values is intrinsically better than the others; people routinely make different choices about the extent to which they value work achievement, home life, leisure, and so on.

Second, you need to understand the rules of the game. How do firms recruit in your area of interest? What are firms looking for in recruits? What do career paths look like? What determines who gets ahead?

Third, you need to understand the competition in the domain in which you intend to compete. Potential employees in different areas of business usually differ radically in intelligence, technical skills, etc.

Fourth, what are you good or bad at? Do you love dealing with people or do you prefer dealing with numbers? Some people like variety, whereas others do best handling routine. Some people may be highly creative while others excel at tight logic.

Fifth, in light of all of the above—what you want, the structure of the game, the competition, and your abilities—you choose how you will compete.

No one gets to pick who they are from a blank slate, but we do get to choose both the extent to which our careers fit our abilities and preferences as well as how we train for those careers. Most of you have chosen a career in management, and usually business management, but you have focused beyond that. A good career strategy can guide your efforts and increases the chances of achieving your objectives.

These same issues matter to businesses.

While some of your courses may assume companies want to maximize the net present value of future earnings, this is not universally true. The owner-managers of many businesses value owning and running their own businesses; many want to pass these on to their children. Some entrepreneurs run their businesses with the intention of eventually selling out to a larger company. Management in some companies may feel pressured to grow the business rapidly; in others, modest growth is acceptable. Many corporations claim to balance the interests of shareholders and other stakeholders. In short, companies have some choice about their goals, subject to a need to maintain sufficient economic performance for survival.

The rules and structure of competition differ across industries. Some industries require continuous product innovation, but others have produced similar products for decades. In some, customer service drives profits, but in others, customer service matters little. Some industries are simply more competitive than others.

Competition varies across industries and even within industries. When it comes to trading stocks on larger companies, you face competition from thousands of individuals with immense resources who compete by trading a limited number of stocks. A small company's stock may attract much less attention. Someone owning the only gas station in a small town faces radically different competition than a gas station owner in a large city. Alternatively, some businesses produce products similar to those of competitors and others produce products or services that no one else produces.

Companies also differ in their abilities. For example, while large pharmaceutical companies invest heavily in the development of new drugs, generic drug producers invest in the low-cost production of off-patent drugs. The management team that excels running a fast food outlet would probably fail in fine dining. While companies can change their abilities somewhat, research shows that history and early experience shape organizations in ways that make a radical change in capabilities difficult.

Effective business strategy takes all of these factors and then adds some creativity. Strategy provides the umbrella within which all corporate activities operate. And, just like an umbrella, activities that do not fit the strategy often do not do well.

This book helps you think about all of these.

A BEHAVIORAL APPROACH

Traditional strategy textbooks emphasize the analytical aspects of the problem-solving process almost to the complete exclusion of the constraints surrounding an individual decision maker. Such texts assume that adopting a systematic, structured approach to examining and processing relevant information will ensure that management does not overlook any critical factors in their decision making. The decision maker will therefore come up with the best solution for the problem.

While a structured, analytical approach to problem solving has much to recommend it, strategies cannot come from analysis alone. Good strategies require some novelty—mimicking everyone else seldom produces high returns. Strategy therefore requires a combination of analysis and creativity. Further, any analysis is only as useful as the thought process underlying it; many of us have probably come across flawed analyses based on unrealistic assumptions, missing information, or illogical connections. Therefore, while this book explains the tools you can use to analyze a problem, it does so emphasizing the behavioral approach to strategic decision making.[1]

A behavioral approach recognizes that when confronted with a complex, real-world problem, people have a limited ability to process the enormous amount of information required to find the optimal solution. Consequently, when faced with these problems, people typically satisfice, that is, make do with a good enough solution, rather than optimize, that is, come up with the best possible solution to a problem. Stated differently, a behavioral approach recognizes that how people think and interact with others substantially influences the problem-solving process. Indeed, these human aspects of problem solving are often much more difficult to manage than the analytical aspects. Hence, understanding these aspects can lead to a better understanding of strategy. Let us explain this in more detail.

If we wish to help people engage in some activity, we need to start by realistically understanding their abilities and limitations. Advice on how to get along in France will be very different for someone who speaks fluent French than for someone who speaks no French. Perhaps the most important thing to understand is that humans have severe limitations in their abilities to process information.

LIMITATIONS IN INFORMATION PROCESSING ABILITY

People who study cognition divide memory into short and long term. Long term is essentially unlimited—humans can learn to remember enormous amounts of things. Short term, on the other hand, is exceedingly limited. Short-term memory acts like the RAM in your computer—it is a memory your mind uses when it needs to process information. Depending on how you estimate it, short-term memory only holds between three and seven chunks of information. You can see this easily. Most of you can multiply two two-digit numbers in your head—47×28. However, when you try to multiply two three-digit numbers in your head, you find that you cannot remember the intermediate results—you run into this limitation of short-term memory. Transferring information from short- to long-term memory and retrieving information from the long-term memory takes time and effort.

These limitations on information processing highlighted by a behavioral approach have a variety of implications in both strategy and management. For example, human decisions, if repeatedly made with a defined set of data, generally reflect three or four variables. This can be seen from studies that show that relatively simple three or four variable models largely replicate expert judgment in things such as risk assessment for commercial loans, graduate admissions, and so forth. From a strategy standpoint, this means that we know that we will never consider all the possibilities when we make critical decisions. Therefore, what we need, at least to some extent, from a strategy course are heuristics or short cuts that help us search for information and select our options more effectively, recognizing the limitations we face.

BELIEFS AND DECISION MAKING

A behavioral approach suggests another general limitation on decision making; everyone's decisions depend on what he or she believes. We all operate with an implicit (and sometimes explicit) model of the world. While, in many cases, managerial beliefs align nicely with reality, they appear not to do so in many other important areas. For example, managers often have misconceptions about customer preferences or employee attitudes and motivation. Many of us have had experiences where we have misunderstood the motivations of our closest friends and relatives. Furthermore, we often have biases that make it hard for us to adapt our belief systems to an external reality.

For example, for many years, the Polaroid Corporation had great success with a coherent strategy that emphasized technological advances that attempted to improve the quality of instant printing of photographs toward the quality provided by traditional 35mm film cameras. The firm profited mainly by selling the film rather than the camera itself. Most of the top management of the company spent their careers in an enormously successful corporation built on these assumptions.

However, these assumptions meant the company had great difficulty with digital cameras when film disappeared and the firm needed to profit on the cameras themselves. Even when Polaroid attempted to move into the digital age, the people it hired to lead that move became isolated from others in the company (and therefore, could not operate effectively in the company) because the belief structures of these new hires differed so greatly from the belief structures of the senior managers of the company.

Cognitive limitations appear in all organizations in many forms.
The greater investment in MBAs meant that American business schools saw themselves as producers of MBAs, while European equivalents had less history invested in the MBA. Consequently, non-American universities led the move to specialized master's programs in management, a move that American universities only followed reluctantly and after substantial delay.

Alternatively, consider the American auto industry. Starting after the oil shortages in the late 1970s, U.S. auto companies dabbled with small, fuel-efficient cars. However, the efforts of U.S. auto companies were always somewhat halfhearted. Partially, this reflected a top management that grew up in an industry where the ideal car was a large Cadillac or Lincoln. Small vehicles with few features were not considered attractive. With the exception of short periods of oil shortage, the companies made much more money on large vehicles including minivans and SUVs than they made on smaller vehicles. Consequently, these companies could not maintain a focus on the development of small vehicles.

You may have seen or experienced similar things in your industry.
A student in one of our MBA classes works in a company that had sold steel pipe for running water underground, in an industry that is moving to plastics. However, both the managers and the salespeople have spent the last 30 years telling themselves and consumers that plastic was not as good as steel. They have had difficulty changing to plastic pipes even as plastic begins to offer performance/cost superior to that offered by traditional steel piping. Firms and individuals have difficulty adapting their fundamental beliefs to new evidence.

WHERE DO BELIEFS COME FROM?

For much of what managers believe, they lack good data. Much of the information managers act on comes from what others have told them, often without explicit evidence supporting the assertions. Not that long ago, many U.S. managers had explicit discriminatory beliefs about the abilities of minorities and women. In previous eras, people had similar discriminatory beliefs regarding other ethnic groups such as Jews, Italians, and Irish. They could maintain such beliefs for several reasons.

To begin with, beliefs are often self-confirming. If we believe people X incapable of college, we never give them a chance, and so never see college graduates of type X. Alternatively, we give them a chance, but not a fair one.

This is equally true in business. If we believe the world operates in a particular way, then we will tend to see problems or opportunities through the lens of our beliefs, as well as take actions that make sense in that context. Even if we want to test our assumptions about how the world operates, we seldom offer a fair test. In one way or another, other members of the organization often sabotage efforts that contradict the organization's dominant mode of thinking.

Examples are legion. Polaroid's efforts in digital cameras offer one example. Xerox, through its research arm, developed many of the innovations underlying the modern computer (graphical user interfaces, the mouse, etc.), but made almost nothing on them. Xerox's focus on photocopying made capitalizing on technology unrelated to photocopying extremely difficult. Xerox also made its money on big, fast copiers and missed the movement to smaller copiers. That Tesla led the development of electric cars and Google self-driving vehicles, both industry outsiders, illustrates the strength of existing car manufacturers' dominant logics and their difficulty overcoming these logics.

Most people emphasize facts that fit their beliefs and downplay facts that conflict with their beliefs. For example, if someone holds a belief that engineers should not do a particular job, that individual will seize on examples of engineers in that job not succeeding while ignoring equivalent evidence on nonengineers failing in those positions. Likewise, a manager who believes the company should not be in a given business will tend to emphasize facts supporting that position while downplaying facts opposed to the position. Some of this may be strategic; we selectively use information to aid our careers. However, what makes it far more difficult to manage is that this appears to be a fundamental feature of human information processing. We do it even when we have no tangible incentives to bias facts in one way or another—we simply favor information that confirms our beliefs.

We design our organizations to give us data that aligns with particular ways of thinking. If we think about the world as a set of national markets, we organize that way, and get data that way. If we think about the world as a set of global product markets, we organize and get data that way. Our beliefs influence the structure of our company, and the structure of our company influences our beliefs. The structure heavily influences the data we get. The data we have defines what questions we can actually answer.

Organizations designed to change in specific ways often can readily do so. For example, many companies have well-developed procedures to develop product line extensions and bring them to market. However, they often have trouble with new products that require fundamentally different business models. For example, Gillette readily develops and markets product line extensions in the men's razor and razor blade markets, inventing new razors and new forms of razor blades while maintaining a relatively constant business model. This became a problem when Gillette bought Duracell batteries where the model was no longer selling the razor cheaply and making money on expensive razor blade replacements, but rather making profits on the entity itself. Gillette had substantial difficulty integrating and taking advantage of the Duracell acquisition.

We only operate with one organizational structure for the most part. This means we do not have good data on other structures. We operate with one set of rules for approving capital expenditures and a variety of other factors. This means we have no directly comparable experience from which we might decide something else is better. We may adopt management practices because we believe, often based on public discussion, that these practices are good, but it is hard to see how we would learn to use such practices from our own experience.

To summarize, we can have all the analytical tools you want for strategy analysis, but if individuals with a particular mindset wield those tools, the outcome of those tools will probably align with the mindsets of the users.

WHAT DOES THE BEHAVIORAL APPROACH IMPLY FOR THE STUDY OF STRATEGY?

Broadly speaking, the behavioral approach suggests that strategy does not have neat solutions. Instead of thinking of strategy as a chess game with clear rules and objectives, we should think of strategy more as a game of dice or a board game in which the rules may change mid-game, we sometimes play blindfolded, and we often have missing pieces—and to top it all, our competitors may cheat. In particular, we wish to make the following two points.

First, formulating a strategy is seldom as clear-cut as analytical approaches to strategy would imply. While the tools and frameworks we discuss in this book make the process easier, the fact remains that while we may intend that a firm follows a particular strategy, the realized strategy (i.e., the strategy the firm eventually follows) often looks very different from its intended strategy. In their 1985 paper, Mintzberg and Waters capture this idea with the terms "deliberate" and "emergent" strategies.[2] Perfectly deliberate strategies are strategies that unfold precisely as intended. In contrast, organizations with perfectly emergent strategies will show consistency in their actions over time (without consistency in actions there would be no strategy, only chaos), but there is no intended strategy underlying these actions. Most firms' strategies fall somewhere between these endpoints of deliberate and emergent strategies. The firm may come in with a plan, but changes in the environment, actions of its competitors, and reactions from its customers may cause the firm to modify the plan to a greater or lesser extent.

Second, people make and implement strategy. Hence, in addition to the effects of information processing limitations and beliefs, to understand strategy formulation and implementation, as well effectiveness of strategies, we need to understand a whole host of social and psychological concepts. These include how peoples' personalities and backgrounds (in particular, those of the CEO and others at the top) influence strategic decision making, how people interact with one another, handle conflict, and develop trust, how people react to incentives in ways that we do not necessarily anticipate, and so on. A number of studies, for example, demonstrate various aspects of CEO personality such as narcissism, hubris, charisma, and overconfidence influence firm outcomes.[3]

Our behavioral approach makes us skeptical of claims that firms optimize anything outside of a few operational details narrowly defined (e.g., optimizing truck routing for deliveries). To say a firm maximizes profits means that there is nothing whatsoever the firm could do differently that would result in higher profits. We have yet to see a firm that could not do something better. While managers may try to maximize profits, our understanding of people and organizations leads to a conclusion that they cannot really maximize profits.

HOW DO WE OPEN OUR MINDS TO BECOME BETTER STRATEGISTS?

Let us begin by reiterating that this is very difficult. For the reasons noted above, getting people to think more broadly and to give up some of their beliefs is exceedingly hard. However, we can offer some suggestions.[4]

Adding outsiders may help. Outsiders bring new ideas. Some evidence suggests entrepreneurial startups should include both people who have worked together before, as well as people who have worked in multiple companies. The individuals who have worked in multiple companies can provide examples that the company can attempt to integrate into its operations. These individuals can imagine more alternative ways to do the job.

However, outsiders have a downside. If the outsiders differ greatly from others in the company, the others may isolate and ignore them. Homogeneity has its benefits; we tend to trust people like ourselves more, and effective group decision making requires trust.

Adding good data may help. One old strategy professor claimed when he got to a company that said it was good at X he would immediately ask what real evidence the company had to support that conclusion. One of us knew a consultant who would interview a company's customers before meeting the top management team; he usually knew things about the customers that top management did not know. Our beliefs in what we are good at often deviate from the facts. Just ask your classmates how many of them are below-average drivers. Simply put, hard data or evidence can help us see things more broadly or differently.

Opening to input from lower levels may also help. Newer and lower-level employees have acclimatized less to the corporate way of seeing the world. Newer and lower-level employees also have different ongoing experiences. They often have more direct interactions with customers and/or suppliers than senior management. Dealing with customers face-to-face may generate data that differs greatly from a third hand report about what our customers think. That said, top management frequently ignores the inputs from lower level management.

We see this publicly following disasters or major product failures. After a major failure (e.g., G.M.'s product safety issues related to a faulty ignition switch[5]), old memos from lower-level employees often appear detailing the problem, but those memos and the issues they raised did not get to the top management team (or top management ignored them). Often, companies have fired low-level employees for raising the problem. However, we need a reality check. In many cases, when you have a disaster, you can find someone who warned of it. If you look carefully, though, you also will find warnings of a whole lot of disasters that did not occur. Consequently, management cannot pay full attention every time someone cries wolf. While mid-level employees usually warn of problems before disasters, too many mid-level employees warn of problems for managers to heed them all.

Organizational designs can encourage alternative mindsets. Many companies such as Johnson and Johnson use cross-functional teams to explore the development of new technologies and products across divisions. Others, such as Lockheed Martin, use skunkworks, or groups with a high degree of autonomy, to explore new ideas. Some explicitly hire employees from outside the company or industry to bring new perspectives. Companies such as Google and 3M give employees a certain percentage of time free to pursue pet projects independently. The Virgin group follows an extreme decentralization strategy encouraging employees to think on their own.

In addition to encouraging the development of alternative mindsets through organization recruiting and structure, many companies turn to other firms to explore new ideas. Pharmaceutical and technology firms, in particular, use corporate venturing projects, ranging from taking a financial stake in a start up to forming an alliance with a smaller partner to explore new business models.

A recent trend in management emphasizes the notion of "ambidexterity" where companies simultaneously or sequentially pursue their original or dominant business models and new ways of doing business. To achieve ambidexterity, firms often use cross-functional or cross-disciplinary teams, have divisions periodically switch between different modes of strategy, encourage individual efforts at ambidextrous thinking, develop a tension between exploration and exploitation, etc. PepsiCo, for example, has two groups of people in each division. One group works on implementing current strategy, while the other group looks for ways to disrupt it. However, such efforts can create organizational problems, and probably make more sense in larger firms.

SUMMARY

Strategy addresses how we compete—our objectives and how we hope to achieve them. Strategies typically rest on an analysis of the competition and of our capabilities relative to the competition. However, an overemphasis on analysis often neglects a key factor influencing strategic decision making: how the human aspects of problem solving influence not only what we see as problems but also the decisions we make to solve those problems. A behavioral approach to strategy recognizes the limitations and constraints imposed by these human aspects, particularly managers' cognition (thinking), beliefs, and information processing. In particular, we note that limitations in our memory lead to limitations in information processing, our belief structures strongly resist change, and the structure of the organizations we work in influences both what data we get and what we become good at doing. Overall, all of these factors influence the decisions we make. We conclude with some suggestions to overcome some of these constraints.

FOOD FOR THOUGHT

1. Organizations often use teams to make a variety of decisions. However, teams differ in effectiveness. Some teams quickly make excellent decisions, while others are synonymous with slow and ineffective decision making. Given our discussion on information processing constraints, why do you think organizations use teams? What makes teams effective or ineffective at decision making? How would the type of decision addressed influence the effectiveness of a team?

2. Premortem is a managerial tool in which a manager or decision-making team begins by imagining that a project or strategy under consideration has failed. The team then works backward to determine what could potentially cause the project or strategy to fail. Why do you think this tool works?

3. Observers often revile red tape or bureaucracy for slowing decision making in companies. However, almost all organizations use preset routines and procedures—in other words, some form of bureaucracy—to make any number of routine decisions. Why? How does the use of routines and procedures relate to our discussion of cognitive limitations during decision making?

4. Research finds that managers' willingness to take risks varies with situation. Assume you own a company. If your company currently meets its targets, how willing would you be to make risky business decisions? How would your willingness to take risks change if your company failed to meet targets? How would your willingness to take risks change if your business was in danger of bankruptcy? What factors would influence your decision in the three cases?

NOTES AND BIBLIOGRAPHY

1. For further reading, see Powell, T. C., Lovallo, D., and Fox, C. R., "Behavioral Strategy," *Strategic Management Journal* 32(13) (2011):1369–1386; Bromiley, P., *Behavioral Foundations of Strategic Management* (Oxford: Blackwell, 2005).
2. Mintzberg, H., and Waters, J. A., "Of Strategies, Deliberate and Emergent," *Strategic Management Journal* 6 (1985):257–272.
3. See Bromiley, P., and Rau, D., "Social, Behavioral, and Cognitive Influences on Upper Echelons during Strategy Process: A Literature Review," *Journal of Management* 42(1) (2016):174–202.
4. See also Hammond, J. S., Keeney, R. L., and Raiffa, H., "The Hidden Traps in Decision Making," *Harvard Business Review* (1998) 76(5):47–58; Lovallo, D., and Sibony, O., "The Case for Behavioral Strategy," *McKinsey Quarterly* (March 2010):30–43.
5. See www.npr.org/2014/03/31/297158876/timeline-a-history-of-gms-ignition-switch-defect

CHAPTER 2
Purpose

O rganizations are blunt objects. To get an organization moving consistently in some direction, generally somebody must decide and communicate what direction it needs to go in. Apart from stampedes, a herd of people seldom pushes in the same direction without guidance on direction.

Companies without a clear idea of their purpose, that is, what they want and do not want to do, often take on a variety of happenstance businesses and end up with a collection of activities that make little or no sense. If you read histories of companies, or even the cases you have studied in your business program, you will note an unpleasantly large number of statements such as this: "In the past, the organization got overly diversified. However, under financial pressure, the organization refocused on its core businesses." This parallels the student who picks courses because they appear easy or have entertaining instructors. At the end of the program, the student has not accumulated a useful, coherent body of knowledge. The firm that just grabs businesses that look good often ends with an unmanageable hodgepodge of units.

MISSION, GOALS, ETC.

The literature on corporate purpose suffers from an excess of jargon that people use in varying ways. Let us start with the jargon.

The terms you will hear, in roughly descending order of generality, are as follows:

- intent or vision;
- mission;
- purpose;
- principles;
- values;
- goals; and
- objectives.

We are not sure how the first three really differ. That said, many consultants and managers take these differences quite seriously.[1]

Graham Kenny, an Australian strategy consultant, argues the differences are as follows:

1. Vision describes what the organization wishes to be like at some future time.
2. Mission describes what business the organization is and is not in now and in the future.
3. Principles give employees a set of directions.
4. Values describe the desired culture.

Goals and objectives are things that the organization, the unit of the organization, or an individual is supposed to accomplish. Good goals and objectives are usually tangible, measurable, and time constrained, even if the criteria used to measure these goals and objectives are subjective.

One of the least useful debates that occur in companies is over the definition of the terms associated with corporate goals or objectives. Whether goals refer to higher-level activities than objectives is arbitrary. We recommend you agree one is higher than the other and leave it at that.

Organizations, units, and individuals typically have many goals. Each goal addresses a specific aspect of how the organization plans to achieve its overall purpose. However, constituents assign different importance to the different goals. Moreover, goals often conflict with one another or with the goals of other individuals or units in the organization. For example, the sales department most easily meets a goal of increasing sales if the company produces many versions of products tailored to the desires of different customers. However, this often conflicts with a production department goal of reducing cost per unit, a goal most easily met by producing long runs of a limited range of products.

Regardless of terminology, it makes sense that the organization has some overarching general rules or principles about what businesses it should be in and how it intends to win in those businesses. Ideally, it can describe these overarching principles very clearly and concisely.

Companies need short, clear statements of strategy for several reasons. First, being short and clear encourages the organization to trim the number of good things included in their strategies. Organizations often try to make everyone happy by generating broad, ambiguous strategies or strategies that include something for everyone.

Second, short clear goals are easier to communicate and remember. Walmart's emphasis on low prices every day is clear and easily remembered. In contrast, universities and business schools often have vague, general, and largely useless statements of strategy, often a variant on "training socially aware leaders for the global community in the twenty-first century."

Third, employees need some coherent ideas about what matters and how the company operates. For example, every staff member in a retailer with a high service strategy needs to understand that strategy. A single employee who does not understand this can easily ruin the experience of many customers—customers who will not come back. Likewise, a company intending to win by using a low-cost strategy needs everyone to understand this. Effective low-cost strategies start with senior managers who restrain their interest in fancy offices and high-quality travel expenses and continue all the way to the bottom where employees care about waste. Without such coherence, our high service retailer can end up with a high-cost structure but customers who do not perceive the company as delivering high service, and the low-cost strategy firm can give up the benefits of status and service but not have low enough costs to compensate. Tool #1 at the end of this chapter provides one way to come up with a coherent strategy.

To get consistent, coordinated action from 100, 1,000, or 100,000 employees, often with differing local environments and different backgrounds, you need a clear, coherent statement of strategy.

CORPORATE SOCIAL RESPONSIBILITY

Inherent in a firm's strategy, purpose, goals, objectives, etc., are judgments about the contributions the company intends to make both to the people and organizations involved in the firm (termed stakeholders), and to society in general. Substantial controversy exists over whether corporations should consider their impacts on society or should simply attempt to maximize (note that we say attempt, since organizations cannot really maximize) profits or returns to the shareholders.

Some poorly informed commentators have claimed that U.S. corporate law requires that firms maximize shareholder wealth. With one exception, this is wrong. The law requires that boards of directors and management act in the interests of the corporation and shareholders, but leaves the meaning of this statement ambiguous. As long as management or the board of directors exhibits an appropriate amount of due diligence and does not engage in self-dealing or fraud, the courts resist questioning their goals or judgment. The only time a U.S. board of directors, in theory, must act directly to maximize shareholder returns is when the company is in play to be purchased. That is, if someone has started a takeover or attempted to buy the company, the Board of Directors is supposed to maximize the returns to the shareholders.

We take the stance that organizations make ethical choices through their decisions about corporate strategy, purpose, and so on. We distinguish between two levels of concern related to these choices and decisions. The first stems from a fundamental stance that organizations should or should not do certain things; it thus relates to the ethics (not to mention the legality) of the firm's choices. For example, many of us would agree that it is unethical for a firm to sell consumers a drug the firm knows to be misrepresented and dangerous. A second level refers to a less fundamental stance; firms do things beyond the legal requirements, based on their awareness that what they do impacts those around them. For example, firms demonstrate their corporate social responsibility by curbing pollution beyond the legal requirements, donating to charity, or paying employees better than the minimum needed to obtain their labor.

Do (or should) firms consider ethics? From a "do" standpoint, most large Western firms claim some ethical standards. If you look at the websites of large Western firms, many will include some statement of social responsibility. That brings us to the "should."

There is a story of a philosopher at a party who sits next to a rich heiress. The philosopher asks the heiress if she would sleep with him for a million dollars. She says yes. The philosopher asks if she would sleep with him for $10. The heiress says, "What do you think I am, a prostitute?" The philosopher replies, "Yes, we have established that; now we are discussing price."

In the case of firms, if there is anything profitable that a corporation would not do due to ethical or moral constraints, the issue is not whether ethical and moral constraints should bind the company, but rather where to draw the lines.

Highly profitable activities exist that almost any conventional Western business organization would refuse on ethical grounds. There is clearly (illegal) money to be made in human trafficking, illicit drugs, travel to less-developed countries in search of bonded labor, etc. Many companies would refuse some legal or quasi-legal activities on ethical grounds, such as various forms of discrimination or bribery in countries where such activities are legal or widely tolerated. If there is anything you or the corporation would not do for ethical reasons, then we are discussing where to draw the line, not if there should be a line.

While some claim firms should be strictly concerned with profits, a company solely concerned with profits would engage in illegal activity whenever the activity had positive expected value. That is, the firm would balance expected benefits versus the probability of detection and punishment and the level of punishment if caught. Given relatively low probabilities of detection, and generally low punishments relative to the profits available, corporate misbehavior, even illegal behavior, often pays. Connor and Lande estimate the expected benefits to antitrust violations as 5 to 10 times the expected punishments for such violations.[2] Connor and Lande's analysis suggests managers only concerned about returns to the stockholders should generally engage in illegal price fixing. A similar calculus applies in many other areas.

In short, from both a descriptive standpoint and a normative standpoint, most large U.S. companies claim to avoid some ethically questionable profitable actions, and indeed do so to some extent. We cannot tell you where to draw the line, but we can give you some guidance on how to think about the problem.

THINKING ABOUT CORPORATE ETHICS

First, a position associated with Immanuel Kant, the German philosopher, says that moral actions conform to several conditions.[3] First, would this action have value if everyone engaged in it? Lying only has value if most do not lie, so under this criterion, lying is immoral. Likewise, forging checks would be immoral because forging checks only has value because most people do not do so. If many people forged checks, then no one would accept a check. Second, you should treat yourself and others as an end, not strictly as a means. This implies treating others with respect, and rules out coercion and deceit. Finally, rules should consider the interests of all affected stakeholders and should apply to all. This does not mean that a rule may not hurt certain groups, but in making the rule we should at least be aware of the trade-offs we make.

In some ways, such ethical rules help us conduct business effectively. A company that consistently misrepresents will have difficulty dealing with other companies, suppliers, and customers. A company that attempts to exploit whomever it can exploit (such as its suppliers) may run into serious problems in maintaining such relations. The company that blithely ignores what it does to others is quite likely to take actions that will result in serious damage to itself. However, as we noted above, some profitable illegal and unethical actions remain, so being ethical does not necessarily align fully with seeking profits.

The second basis on which we might judge whether something is ethical has been restated by various individuals including Warren Buffett[4]: would you be willing to state your position publicly? Stated another way, would you be happy to have your parents or children read in a newspaper that you took this action? If what you anticipate doing would shame or embarrass them, you should consider whether that action is ethical.

This second criterion, like all criteria, has limitations. Sometimes a person might take ethical actions but try to hide the actions due to fear of retribution. Alternatively, a person might take ethical actions but try to hide their identity (e.g., an anonymous whistleblower reporting securities violations), again due to fear of retribution.

WHERE SHOULD WE DRAW THE LINES?

Some business people have a knee-jerk reaction against *any* externally drawn lines that limit their actions, whether these take the form of government regulation or arguments about social responsibility. However, sometimes regulation is essential. First, when an action imposes costs (called externalities) on individuals who do not get to make decisions about that action, the market mechanism will not result in the production of appropriate amounts of that entity. Thus, if I can pollute without any charge and others bear much of the cost of pollution, I will not value the cost of pollution appropriately from a societal standpoint. Likewise, if my actions create benefits that accrue to others, I will not produce the socially desirable level of output because I cannot capture the full benefit of production. In these conditions, economists generally favor some form of government intervention, often in the form the form of taxation or direct regulation.

Economic regulation often stems from particularly egregious actions by one or more companies. Most political processes respond to particularly visible and horrendous behaviors. Thus, the U.S. system for regulation of chemicals grew out of a number of examples where companies exposed communities to exceedingly dangerous and harmful chemicals. The recent changes in regulation of financial institutions stemmed from the excesses prior to the recession of 2008. Organizations do precisely the same thing. For example, one individual abusing travel funds often results in onerous travel reimbursement regulations for all employees. This pattern appears in many areas of our lives; we all face legal and organizational constraints created because some small number of people behaved badly. One "shoe bomber" or two or three liquid bombs results in tens of thousands of flyers with liquid restrictions and shoe checks.

Effective free-market economies require a balance between the free market and government regulation. A free market without regulation quickly becomes a Hobbesian "war of all against all." A small number of unscrupulous and corrupt individuals often come to control such a "free market." Some observers claim that, in the move from communist to free-market economies in Eastern Europe and the U.S.S.R., some countries adopted free-market reforms without a corresponding set of regulatory controls. In contrast, in the United States, we take for granted government regulations that force public companies to reveal information to investors and to follow mechanisms designed to ensure the integrity of such information. Similarly, regulation requires specific forms of publicly visible governance for publicly held companies. In other words, effective economies require a balance between business freedom and government-imposed ground rules.

Contrary to the rhetoric of the shareholder wealth maximization advocates, a great many large American corporations, as well as large corporations in other parts of the world, explicitly state that they consider the social impacts of their actions. They claim to constrain their decisions by the morals and ethics of their leaders and by their own organizational history and reputation.

The entire business ethics debate becomes irrelevant if socially responsible behavior were to provide the best course for business. In such a case, profit maximization and corporation social responsibility would provide the same decisions.

The empirical evidence is that firms that engage in socially responsible behavior on average do as well as firms that do not. Some studies find some forms of socially responsible behavior pay off, but other studies find no significant impact on profits. Few studies find socially responsible behavior hurts firms in general. We generally do not have evidence that socially responsible behavior is a handicap. If it does not cost to be socially responsible, then why not be so?

SUMMARY

A company's strategy rests on basic ideas about what the company wants to achieve—its purpose, mission, vision, or goals. While we do not need a formal mission statement or vision statement for a company to run effectively, the managers and employees of a company must have a clear understanding of the company's strategy.

Inherent in a company's strategy are the company's ethics and values— what the company will or will not do. We can use two criteria to think about whether a company should or should not do something. The first asks whether a decision rule or behavior would have value if everyone engaged in it, requires the rule treat everyone with respect, and applies the rules to all. The second simply asks whether you would be willing to state your position publicly.

While debate exists about the value of external restrictions on corporate behavior, we believe that free markets without at least some regulations or restrictions on corporations' actions will quickly devolve into markets that are the opposite of free.

FOOD FOR THOUGHT

1. Costco and Sam's Club (run by Walmart) are direct, low-cost competitors in the same industry. However, some estimates suggest that Costco pays its workers 72 percent more than Walmart. Costco also offers more generous benefits than Walmart. How can Costco afford to do this? What offsetting benefits might Costco enjoy that allow it to pursue a low-cost strategy against a competitor with a lower wage bill?[5]
2. You find that your major supplier (based in Asia) uses child labor. However, firing this supplier would increase your costs—potentially causing you to lay off thousands of upstream workers in your home country. How could you apply Kant's and Rawls's criteria to decide what to do?

TOOL #1: SWOT

As we noted in the introduction, we cannot give you rules that will make you a champion, but can give you guidelines that will help you work things out.

Many firms use the SWOT framework, which stands for strengths, weaknesses, opportunities, and threats.

Strengths refer to things you do better than your competitors. Ideally, these things have direct relevance to the efficiency or effectiveness with which you operate your business in the markets in which you compete. If you find you have substantial strengths that do not apply in the businesses in which you compete, you should probably consider competing in other businesses.

Weaknesses refer to things you do worse than your competitors. We may hesitate to acknowledge that we do some things worse than our competitors. However, almost inherently, in getting good at one thing, you become not so good at something else.

Opportunities refer to things you could do that would have positive value. Often, opportunities come from changes in technology or changes in customer values and perceptions.

Threats are naturally the opposite of opportunities—changes or things that could hurt you.

Addressing threats and opportunities focus you on things happening outside of your organization, and encourage you to think dynamically. Even a small organization needs to think ahead about what customers will want next year or the year after and what competitors might do. Large organizations take substantial amounts of time to change direction so they may need to think even further in advance.

For all four, you should strongly encourage the organization to find objective data. Just as our beliefs about ourselves often differ from the objective facts, members of organizations develop shared beliefs about the organization and the organization's environment that differ greatly from the facts.

There is an old adage that "it's not what I don't know that kills me; it's what I know for sure that ain't so." Attributed to various people, this summarizes why you need to make a real effort to get objective evidence.

Strengths
- Solid brand name
- Large number of stores provide economies of scale

Weaknesses
- Large, impersonal company image
- Outsider

Opportunities
- Wi-Fi and other network innovations
- New countries reaching appropriate wealth levels
- Moving from coffee to a broader product line

Threats
- Changing customer tastes
- Perceptions that coffee is not healthy
- Lower cost equivalent alternatives

Figure 2.1 SWOT and Starbucks

In all of these, do not become bogged down in definitions and debate. A strength could become a weakness depending on other factors. McDonald's had incredible strength at producing a standard product at very low cost, but it became a weakness when customer tastes changed. A strength when competing in one manner or in one market may constitute a weakness in a different manner of competing or different market.

Do not make this a philosophical debate; use it to help you lay out what the world looks like, so you can think about what you should be doing.

Figure 2.1 offers a very cursory SWOT analysis of Starbucks. If you were running Starbucks, what would you worry about at night? How would you try to change the organization or the strategy?

NOTES AND BIBLIOGRAPHY

1. See, for example, Collins, J. C., and Porras, J. I. "Building Your Company's Vision," *Harvard Business Review* 74(5) (1996):65; Hamel, G., and Prahalad, C. K. "Strategic Intent," *Harvard Business Review* 83(7–8) (2005):148.
2. Connor, J. M., and Lande, R. H. "Cartels as Rational Business Strategy: Crime Pays," *Cardozo Law Review* 34 (2012):427.
3. Bowie, N. E. *Business Ethics: A Kantian Perspective* (Malden, MA: Blackwell Publishers, 1999).
4. See, for example, Berkshire Hathaway Inc., Code of Business Conduct and Ethics, http://www.berkshirehathaway.com/govern/ethics.pdf.
5. Hint: See Cascio, C. "Retailing: The High Cost of Low Wages," *Harvard Business Review* 84(12) (2006):23.

CHAPTER 3

Environment

You cannot think about good strategy until you have figured out how things work in your industry and what your competition looks like. We now turn to these issues.

We begin with the macro-environment: situational factors that tend to influence a large number of firms within and across a variety of industries.

MACRO-ENVIRONMENT

Any business is embedded in its environment. Pestle is an acronym to help you remember one classification of the major dimensions of that environment:

- Political
- Economic
- Sociocultural
- Technological
- Legal
- Environmental.

For each of these dimensions, the strategist needs to understand the current situation, trends in the situation, and the impact of the current and anticipated situations on the organization and competition so that the organization can take advantage of or protect itself from changes in these dimensions. Let us consider each in turn.

Remember, the objective here is to help illuminate your understanding of the relevant environment. On any of these, one can parse the terminology and generate confusion. For example, you could debate whether environmental law appears under legal or environmental, but do not waste your time debating what heading to write something under. In addition, while in many cases, we talk about foresight or prediction, as we noted in our first chapter, managers and other decision makers face cognitive limitations. Hence, simply using any of the acronyms, frameworks, or tools we discuss in this chapter (or anywhere in this text) will not result in an "optimal" decision. The biggest benefit of these tools is that you will at least consider the main factors that influence your firm and industry before making any strategic decisions.

POLITICAL

A wide variety of government policy issues influence most businesses. The ones that matter most for a given company clearly depend on the company and its industry. Many defense contractors live (and die) on government defense spending. Almost every organization or business deals with a wide variety of government regulations covering things such as transportation, employment, social welfare policies, tax policies, etc.

Many businesses see changes in government regulation as largely negative. However, as the saying goes, "It's an ill wind that blows nobody any good." Thus, while a regulatory change may hurt many companies, the change will usually benefit some companies. For example, changes in government regulations regarding employment may make it harder for one company to deal with the workforce at the same time as it levels the playing field for firms that already used such practices, in addition to creating jobs for human relations consultants and others. Changes in environmental regulations may hurt profitability in some companies even as they create opportunities for companies that plan to offer products that satisfy the new environmental regulations. For instance, the United States has regulations attempting to force car companies to improve the mileage of their automobile fleets. On the one hand, some companies see this as a problem because the current fleets do not meet the standards. On the other hand, some will gain substantial advantage by meeting the needs created by these regulatory changes. Thus, Toyota began making the Prius under conditions of low oil prices and weaker regulations on gas mileage and car emissions. However, future increases in gas prices and environmental regulation appeared likely. When these two things happened, Toyota's move into hybrids with the Prius increased in value dramatically.

Internationally, you need to think about a wide range of policies that vary dramatically across countries. The question is not whether a particular policy is good or bad, but rather, whether the policy helps or hurts a particular company. The benefits and losses will depend on the specifics of each company, its relations to the government, the changes that may occur in the government policy, and the firm's proactivity.

ECONOMIC

While we will discuss the microstructure of economics within an industry later, a wide variety of macroeconomic factors influence companies directly. Anyone who worked through the recession of 2008 should recognize the importance of understanding macroeconomics and thinking about how macroeconomics influences firm strategy.

However, macroeconomics includes more than the business cycle. It includes factors like the trend in gross national product. For example, in the years around 2014, the European Union expected growth in the 1–2 percent range, whereas the United States expected growth in the 3–4 percent range. China expected a reduction in growth rate to 7 percent. Growth creates demand for an incredible variety of products from housing (and everything that goes into housing) to nonessentials to business capital investment.

Depending on your situation, you should also be worried about interest rates, inflation or deflation, unemployment, disposable income, and other macroeconomic factors.

Interest rates influence both the cost and demand sides of many companies. Many companies depend on debt that has floating interest rates so changes in interest rates directly influence the income statement. Interest rates also influence expenditures on capital equipment as well as consumer durable purchases such as cars and houses.

Inflation reduces the value of money, lessening what money will buy. While the United States has experienced only modest inflation in recent years, it saw almost 15 percent inflation in the 1980s. Other countries have seen much higher inflation rates. Increases in inflation benefit borrowers with fixed rate loans and hurt the lenders. In the 1980s, the U.S. savings and loan industry suffered numerous bankruptcies because savings and loans had loaned money on mortgages at fixed rates and funded those loans with deposits from borrowers at variable rates. As interest rates rose and bank regulation weakened, savings and loans found that they had loaned money at 3 percent and were funding those loans with money that cost 6 percent and up. This led to many bankruptcies.

Unemployment likewise has numerous implications. Low unemployment encourages consumer confidence and hence all sorts of discretionary purchases, but may also increase wage rates. Local rather than national unemployment matters for some firms. When major businesses shut down, they may create high levels of unemployment in some cities. In turn, we see a tidal wave of economic change in those regions—lowered tax revenue, outmigration, dropping house prices, etc.

You should think about these factors in both current and prospective terms. In 2007, organizations that saw the coming recession could protect themselves from the subsequent recession. Those who did not often invested in new plant and equipment funded with debt; this led to high interest payments related to excess capacity when demand collapsed. Additionally, many companies invested in financial instruments that later became almost worthless. At the individual level, those who thought about it correctly may have avoided purchasing a house at the peak of the housing price cycle and may have moved their capital from stocks into other investments before the collapse of the capital of the stock market. In many cases, firms (and individuals) only see the issues after they have transpired. By this time, it is often too late to respond effectively.

SOCIOCULTURAL

Again, depending on your business, a wide variety of social and cultural factors may influence your company.

Consider demographics. In the United States, the baby boomers born after World War II are rapidly reaching or have reached retirement age. This implies substantial increases in demand for a range of services associated with the elderly. It also changes demand for housing as the elderly need or want less space, and it changes the supply of labor as we have fewer employed individuals relative to the number of retired. Japan and many countries in Europe face even more extreme aging of their populations. Rapidly aging populations pose serious challenges for many countries. At the other extreme, high birth rates have produced large and growing young populations along with chronic unemployment in other countries.

Changes in social and cultural factors also influence firms. The dramatic increase in employment among women changed a wide variety of industries involved in clothing, daycare, food, transportation, and housing. Increases or decreases in ethnic populations often translate directly into changes in demand for group-specific products and services.

Culture heavily influences consumer tastes. One only needs to look at the differences in what individuals around the world find desirable to eat to recognize that many of our tastes reflect cultural factors rather than some underlying requirement. Changes in the social environment can change these consumer tastes. For example, the increase in "healthy eating" in the United States pressured a variety of restaurants to change their menus. Some industries like fashion depend heavily on short-term variation in consumer preferences. As with political changes, a firm can see such changes either as a threat or as an opportunity depending on the firm's situation and the options management perceives relative to the changes.

TECHNOLOGICAL

Technological change has influenced almost all businesses. Even the most traditional companies have had to move to modern financial services mechanisms for paying for transactions and technical applications in areas like inventory management. Customer loyalty cards and scanners at the checkout provide retailers with incredible data on their customers and enable the management of inventories and products in previously inconceivable ways. These changes occurred in industries we would normally see as low-tech.

While technology may seem hard to predict, it is often quite predictable within given forms of technology or technological regimes. For example, Moore's law that the power of computers doubles every 18 months has reasonably predicted changes in computing power for over a half century. If you simply graph the log of processor speed versus time (taking logs makes exponential factors like constant growth rates linear), you see an extremely predictable trend in performance. Similar trends appear in many technologies, including batteries, mobile phones, etc.

However, the foregoing applies largely within technological regimes. Forty years ago, mobile phones existed, but the incredible changes associated with mobile phones and smart phones were largely unpredicted. While we can predict the advancements in batteries within a technology, when we move from chemical to super capacitors or nanotechnology for storing electricity, we will see a breakpoint. In electronics, the change from vacuum tubes to transistors constituted a similar breakpoint. While the efficiency of internal combustion engines is quite predictable, economically competitive fuel cells and electric cars offer a new technological regime.

Reaction to changes in technological regimes can come quite quickly. Consider the trade-off between traditional hard drives and solid-state hard drives. Solid-state has clear advantages but currently and historically higher costs. If solid-state storage becomes as cheap as or cheaper than conventional disk drives, we might see a wholesale switching to the new technology. The rise (and fall) of demand for thumb drives has occurred in a few years.

LEGAL

Businesses in all countries operate under a wide variety of legal structures. Legal requirements and constraints influence a wide variety of business activities.

ENVIRONMENTAL

Finally, trends associated with increased concern for the natural environment, and at the extreme, global warming, present both threats and opportunities to businesses.

On the opportunities side, businesses that appropriately present themselves as offering better environmental outcomes may gain advantage in a variety of ways. For example, Los Angeles recently switched the companies it uses to collect waste, as well as the way it collects solid waste, in an effort to reduce environmental impact. A wide variety of products claim they are better for the environment; in the United States, this is sometimes reflected in Energy Star ratings.

Firms often find that actions they take to meet environmental regulations end up saving them money. If the firm tries to reduce its pollution simply by fixing it at the end of the pipe, adding more equipment and technology to clean the effluent stream, reducing pollution has substantial costs. However, firms that reengineer or redesign their systems often find that they also reduce their total costs at the same time as reducing pollution. Pollution reflects discarded resources; systems that can avoid such waste can save firms money. These reductions come from a variety of factors including simply using their inputs more efficiently, but some also find that they can develop markets for their effluent outputs.

KEY ASPECTS OF ENVIRONMENTAL ANALYSIS

As always, you need to identify the key factors and the key forms of change. As you can see from the list above, you could spend weeks discussing almost any of these issues. Books have been written about most of them. In addition, these factors interact. Legal requirements may interact with government and with environmental issues in complex ways. Technology interacts with environment and legal regulation. Pragmatically, this means you need to consider what matters most for your industry and for your company now and in the near future.

INDUSTRY ANALYSIS

The other major approach to environmental analysis is Porter's five forces, also called an industry analysis.[1] You can think of the previous pestle analysis as setting the stage, while industry analysis looks at the factors that determine the profitability of an industry.

Industrial organization economics examines the impact of market or industry structures, particularly the number of firms, on competition, innovation, and firm performance. It forms the basis for much of antitrust policy. As you probably learned in microeconomics, in highly competitive markets where everyone produces similar products, sells to an undifferentiated set of customers, and has similar productivity, firms should all earn roughly the same low return on investment. Porter turned this on its head and asked, "How can firms assess the competitiveness of markets and so find (or create) less competitive markets?"

Firms use the five forces analysis to try to find less competitive markets or parts of markets. Note that this analysis is at the market or industry level, not the firm level. It speaks primarily to how the average profitability of firms in this market rather than the profitability of a given firm. Once you understand the market, then you can think further about the firm.

Students often err in thinking the five forces model works at the firm rather than market level.

Let us begin by defining an industry or market. An industry refers to firms producing the same primary products or services and competing largely for the same customers. Generally, this means that changes in the price, availability, or quality of one product influences demand for the others in the market.

People often disagree on how to define their industry. If I analyze McDonald's, for example, do I want to consider the industry as fast food or hamburger chains? When I think of Six Flags amusement parks, do I want to consider the industry theme parks or entertainment? The important thing is to be consistent. Depending on how you define the industry, you will end up with categorizing different things as either rivals, substitutes, potential entrants, or suppliers. Thus, if I define the industry as all of fast food, then hamburger and taco chains are rivals, but if I define the industry as hamburger chains, then taco chains are substitutes. How one arrays the factors will differ depending on how you set up the definitions, but the conclusions should be similar. For example, the existence of rivals should tend to reduce profits just as the existence of close substitutes does.

In addition, industry definitions should be broad enough to include major rivals or potential rivals to the firm of interest, but not so broad as to include an overly wide array of firms. For example, if you classify a company that makes aluminum soda cans as belonging to the container industry, you would have to include manufacturers of shipping containers and cardboard boxes in the five forces analysis in addition to other metal soda can manufacturers.

Industries can emerge, merge, converge, or disappear over time. The mobile phone industry barely existed 40 years ago. For most of its history, mobile phones were clearly phones, but recently the distinction between the mobile phone industry and parts of the computer industry have blurred as mobile phones now have more features of computers built into them and tablet computers have more features associated with mobile phones built into them. These changes can both eliminate and create new markets and segments. While five forces analyses often emphasize current situations, you should also worry about the dynamics of industry change.

Researchers often define industries using aggregate, standard classifications of industries like the Standard Industrial Classification (SIC code) or North American Industry Classification System. They carefully examine the structure and competitiveness of industries using these classifications. However, real competition often occurs at a much lower level. Many businesses only compete within limited geographic regions, so the question is not national or even state markets, but rather the market in that very limited region. If you have the only gas station in a small town that is 60 miles away from the next town, you probably should think almost like a monopolist. Others may have such specialized products that they compete in a very different market than businesses that fall in the same SIC code. A company that rewinds electric motors for trains may be in a very different market than other companies that service other kinds of electric motors. A service company that handles extreme low temperature refrigeration for researchers operates in a different market than those who repair home refrigerators.

Let us now turn to each of the five forces as shown in Figure 3.1. Note that three of the forces in the center of the figure, threat of new entrants, intensity of rivalry, and threat of substitutes, deal with current and future competition for the firm. The remaining two forces—bargaining power of buyers and bargaining powers of suppliers—are mirror images of each other and deal with the negotiating power of the firm with respect to important constituents.

We begin with the three competition-related forces.

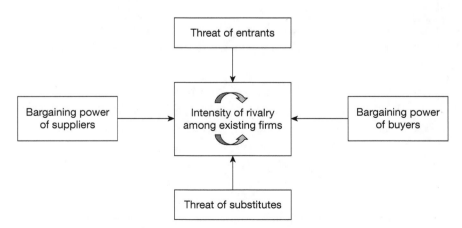

Figure 3.1 Porter's Five Forces for Analyzing an Industry

THREAT OF NEW ENTRANTS

If other companies believe that firms in your industry make substantial profits, then you should expect other companies want to join you. Similarly, if other companies believe that firms in your industry will make substantial profits—think, for example, of all the internet firms that have an attractive app but no way yet to monetize that app—then you should expect they will want to join you. Note that the threat of new entrants only matters for profitable or otherwise desirable industries. Few firms rush to join an industry where most firms have very low profits or prospects.

If we have a profitable industry and others know it, then others will want to enter. If sufficient numbers enter, they will drive down profits, so we ask: what will prevent entry? Various factors will do this.

Economies of Scale

In some industries, firms cannot enter at a small scale and compete effectively. The benefits from large-scale operation, termed economies of scale, mean that cost per unit declines with units per period.

Consider, for example, the automobile industry. Over the last 40 years, many small car companies have gone bankrupt or have had their brands purchased by larger companies. At the same time, a variety of entrants have tried to get into the market and usually failed.

The economies of scale in automobiles come from a variety of factors and apply across a variety of functions. In manufacturing, large-scale, highly specialized factories have greater efficiency than smaller factories. Large scale often justifies more carefully tailored equipment, specialized training, etc. In purchasing, economies of scale exist where purchasers of large quantities of inputs can command better prices. For example, General Motors or Ford pay suppliers less than a small company would pay for the same product.

Distribution can also have economies of scale. You need some minimum number of dealers so consumers know they can get their car serviced wherever they want to travel. Each distributor outlet will be more efficient if it sells many cars rather than very few. The creation of a large, efficient dealer network can form a substantial barrier to entry.

Economies of scale also exist in sales and marketing. The cost of producing an advertisement is a fixed one-time charge. The company that can use that advertisement more can write off that cost across more showings, resulting in a lower cost per unit. Thus, a company that only sells in part of the country would not be able to use the advertisement as much as a national firm could. Furthermore, large purchasers of advertising time get much better deals than small purchasers and have access to more efficient portions of the advertising market. A company that only operates in New York City has difficulty using television because the price of advertisements on New York TV stations reflects the many station viewers on Long Island, in Connecticut, and in New Jersey. The company would have to pay to have the ads seen by many people who cannot buy the company's product. The company that has full national coverage does not have this problem.

Research and development often appears a fixed cost. New technology costs a given amount to develop and prototype regardless of whether the company puts it in one car or one million cars, so the cost per unit again declines substantially with scale.

A related concept to economies of scale is minimum efficient scale. Minimum efficient scale says that below some particular output per time, production is not economic. For example, largely due to mechanization, the minimum efficient scale in agriculture has increased in many countries. The ability of farmers to handle large regions of homogeneous kinds of activities, whether crops, milking cows, raising poultry, or whatever, has meant that large firms have become more efficient than small farms. Consequently, we have seen substantial reductions in the number of small farms.

Learning or Experience Curves

Think about the first time you play a videogame. You are seldom good at it in the beginning. As you play the game, you quickly get better. Indeed, the feeling of accomplishment that comes with this rapid improvement forms part of the attraction of videogames. However, as you play more and more, the rate of improvement slows. This is a learning curve. Almost any human activity, whether producing hamburgers, performing surgery, manufacturing widgets, or whatever, involves learning curves. Figure 3.2 presents a learning curve.

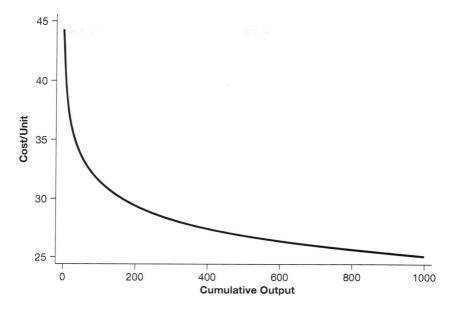

Figure 3.2 A Learning Curve

The learning curve essentially says price per unit declines with total number of units produced, and the rate of decrease lessens with total number of units produced. That is, as cumulative production, or the total number of units produced, increases, price per unit decreases. As Figure 3.2 indicates, learning curves are steeper at low values of a cumulative production (indicating a rapid decline in price/unit initially), and flatten out at higher values, just like your skill at a videogame.

Learning curves can create barriers to entry because current firms have moved down the learning curve while a new entrant starts at an earlier point on the curve and so has much higher costs than current firms. That is, new entrants must start and move down their own learning curve before they can compete with current firms on price. Figure 3.3 illustrates the learning curves for two firms. The firm with the solid line started first. The dotted line firm started second. As you can see, for a substantial range of output, the solid line firm can price and make profits at a price below the dotted line firm's costs. This makes it hard for the dotted line firm to enter.

Note that the firm with the dotted line did not have to start quite as high on the cost per unit basis as the firm with the solid line. This reflects that some

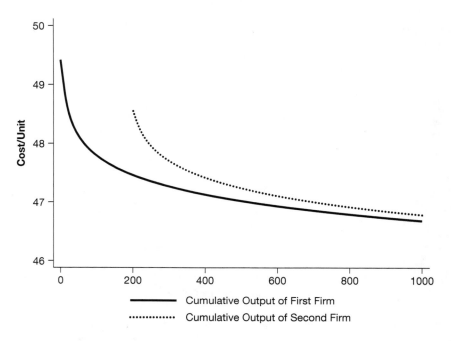

Figure 3.3 Learning Curves for Two Firms

information and technology often diffuses across companies, but the solid line firm still has a substantial advantage. As you can see, the new entrant, the dotted line, has higher costs through a long range of cumulative output, becoming competitive only at high levels of cumulative output.

Capital Requirements

In some industries, and at some times, the capital required to start up, often closely associated with economies of scale, forms a substantial barrier.

Whether this really happens in a particular industry needs to be assessed on a case-by-case basis. If you have a very profitable industry in which large corporations believe they can make substantial profits, capital requirements do not prevent large multinational companies from entering. Integrated steel mills and oil refineries cost a lot, but large companies, often with government subsidies, routinely create them. However, in markets where such companies cannot or do not want to participate, capital requirements may be a barrier.

Note that this large company situation differs dramatically from the situation in entrepreneurial companies. Most entrepreneurial companies face continuing funding problems; capital requirements can form a very strong entry barrier for such firms.

Access to Supply or Distribution Channels

In some industries, firms sometimes lock up either the best suppliers or the best distribution channels and consequently make entry by others exceedingly difficult.

For example, one of the world's biggest chocolate makers, Ferrero, is also the world's biggest hazelnut buyer. It purchased the world's largest hazelnut processer, The Oltan Group, to lock up access to a key raw material, making it harder for a new entrant to enter the market.

As another example, consider car dealerships. The agreement of a dealer to sell a particular brand of car often includes a commitment that the supplier of the car (the manufacturer) will not sell through a competing dealer in the same neighborhood. Consequently, this ability to lock up supply restricts entry at the dealer level.

Barriers can also exist on the distribution side. Suppose you invent a new, exciting, small consumer product. The big distributors like Walmart or Target have little interest in dealing with very small companies, yet these large retailers command a substantial portion of the sales and distribution market. In the U.S. soft drinks industry, Coke and Pepsi have exclusive deals with the biggest, most efficient bottlers across the country. A startup trying to sell a soft drink that directly competes with a Coke or Pepsi product cannot use these bottlers. When it comes to competition for the grocery shelves, Coke and Pepsi have much more access than any startup, resulting in more and better shelf space. In the United States, local telephone service forms the distribution channel through which users purchase long-distance services. Historically, local monopolies in telephone service could dictate consumers use their long-distance services. Independent long-distance companies largely came after changes in U.S. federal regulation forced local phone companies to offer customers a choice of long-distance carriers, essentially creating a competitive long-distance market. Without access to the local network, these long-distance carriers could not reach potential users.

Customer or Supplier Loyalty

In many markets, consumers have strong brand loyalties. Whether it is dish soap, laundry soap, beer, clothes, cars, or soft drinks, individuals often have exceedingly strong preferences for specific products.

Often, these loyalties are emotional. Even a competitor with a better product may not overcome such loyalty. Perhaps the best example of this is Coca-Cola's introduction of New Coke. Market research had clearly found that Coke drinkers preferred the taste of New Coke to the old Coke in blind taste tests. A company like Coca-Cola does not launch such a radical change in its product line without immense market research. However, Coca-Cola consumers rejected New Coke because they wanted their Coke. Eventually, Coca-Cola dropped New Coke completely.

Such loyalty only occurs with highly differentiated products. People do not become emotionally attached or highly committed to a product that they see as undifferentiated from other products.

Switching Costs

In addition to overcoming an emotional attachment or a strong preference for a product, as a new entrant, you may have to address the costs to the buyer of switching to your product. Some of these costs are monetary; others relate to the time and effort a buyer has to put in before he or she can use your product. We discuss this in more detail in the section on buyer power.

Expected Retaliation

A potential entrant also has to consider how the companies currently in that market will react. Will they ignore you, or will they fight back?

Retaliation can take many forms. For example, an airline that dominates a specific route might resist other airlines entering by lowering prices on flights competing directly with an entrant. Alternatively, incumbent firms may offer benefits like frequent flyer or frequent buyer programs that have more value with the larger incumbent firm than a new entrant. Incumbents may mimic the features and products of new entrants to reduce the benefits from switching to the new entrant.

Legislation or Government Action

In many markets, government activity severely limits or controls entry. Often, these regulations exist in natural monopolies where serving the market with one company is much more efficient than serving the market with multiple companies. Thus, for example, landline telephone, cable TV, electricity, water, and natural gas services appear as natural market monopolies because it is highly inefficient for two companies to produce duplicate infrastructure to serve the same residents. Companies often refuse to invest in wiring or running gas lines without a monopoly guarantee. Regulation then prevents other firms from entering the market.

However, the degree to which government actions form barriers are not always this clean and definite. Many government regulations make it more difficult to enter particular industries even though the legislators may not have intended to control entry per se. For example, licensing requirements to practice in activities ranging from plumbing to auto repair to medicine may restrict entry and competition. Many cities limit the number of licenses they offer to operate taxicabs, consequently keeping the number down and increasing average revenue per cab. While often supposedly created to maintain quality, these regulations also serve to limit entry and raise profits for incumbents.

Similar effects occur at the corporate level. Requirements for sophisticated wastewater treatment created difficulties for smaller companies in many industries. A smaller scale operator could not efficiently develop the necessary technology and facilities to handle such requirements. Small drug companies usually cannot afford the costly drug approval process in the United States; they often sell the company or its patents to a larger firm that can afford the approval process.

COMPETITIVE RIVALRY

Competitive rivalry means how hard the companies in the industry compete with one another. Price competition in an industry with high rivalry often hurts everyone in the industry.

In concentrated markets, economic theory does not offer a simple model of price. Indeed, economic theory has several competing models of price setting in oligopolies.

In almost all markets, the average cost of goods is higher than the marginal cost contrary to what they may have told you in microeconomics. All you have to do is look at an income statement to recognize that variable costs are only a portion of total cost. Consequently, it often appears to firms that reductions in price that are above marginal cost will increase profits. However, retaliation by competitors who likewise price above marginal cost can result in the entire industry moving to pricing below average cost.

This happened after U.S. airline deregulation. While the marginal cost of the passenger seat is very low—it costs almost nothing to put one more passenger on a plane—the average cost is quite high. Consequently, airlines dropped prices to increase the number of passengers while keeping price above marginal cost. However, competitors mimicked such price changes until the majority of the industry lost money. Indeed, the entire industry lost $51 billion between 2001 and 2011. Eventually, airlines adapted their pricing rules and their flight structures to reduce competition and the airlines became profitable again.

The level of rivalry depends partially on economics but also partially on social factors. Probably the most important factor is how many competitors exist in the market. Having fewer competitors increases the chance each one will know the others. Consequently, firms will behave better toward one another. Fewer competitors also make it more obvious that a firm's actions trigger specific reactions from its competitors.

The historical and social background of the competitors also matters. A common industry and social history reduces the likelihood competitors will engage in aggressive rivalry. Similarity of backgrounds helps the organizations learn how to coexist. Sometimes, this coexistence breaks down when another competitor enters with a fundamentally different background or with fundamentally different technologies.

Other factors that determine rivalry relate both to the firms involved (their size, cost structure, and type of product or service sold) and to the market growth rate. Competitors of equal size tend to compete harder than if one is large and the others are small. Historically, in the U.S. steel industry, the largest company, U.S. Steel, set prices that the others followed.

High fixed costs also encourage rivalry. As with airlines, high fixed costs pressure managers in manufacturing industries to generate sales to cover the fixed costs of plants. With low fixed costs, a firm can more easily adjust its cost structure to output and consequently not feel as much pressure to increase sales. In downturns, consulting firms readily lay off employees to match capacity to demand, but firms with large fixed costs do not have that option.

Lack of product differentiation increases rivalry. With undifferentiated products, price often becomes the primary determinant of customer decisions, increasing rivalry.

Rivalry increases as the market growth slows or becomes negative. With a growing market, every firm can have growing revenues and profits without taking those directly from a competitor. Given that managerial incentives usually depend on targets that require sales and profit increases, growth reduces the pressure for managers to compete very hard. Once growth ends, a firm can only increase sales by taking them from another. Rivalry is particularly high in declining industries.

Finally, in some industries, exit barriers become an issue. If we have a declining industry, or even one with stable sales, the question arises whether the current companies can gracefully exit the business. For example, consulting firms readily drop areas of consulting that become unprofitable. Many geared up for the year 2000 scare, but simply geared down afterwards. In contrast, consider your position if you are a steel mill manager or steel company executive, and the demand for steel declines. With declining demand, the mill has almost no value; no one wants old mills to make steel that no one will buy. You may have few outside job prospects as executive employment in steel declines with the industry. Consequently, management may stay in the business as long possible, even if it reduces shareholder value. A high cost to exit the industry will increase rivalry (and reduce profits) in a declining industry.

THREAT OF SUBSTITUTES

Substitutes can lower industry profitability in two ways. First, customers may actually switch to the substitutes, lowering industry revenue and profitability. Second, the threat that customers could switch can depress prices or increase product/service quality and consequently, reduce profits.

Let's look at a few examples. Firms can make many things (drink cans, various mechanical items, etc.) from steel or aluminum. Often, aluminum has advantages over steel—aluminum is lighter and does not rust. A firm selling steel must therefore price to make sure it remains a desirable alternative to aluminum. The presence of aluminum as a substitute depresses the price of steel. Similar issues occur for uses where steel or aluminum competes with plastics. Alternatively, consider the cost of transportation. Firms can ship many products by truck or train. The need to stay competitive means that the pricing for one must consider the price of the other. Bus companies must keep passenger fares sufficiently far below the price of air travel that enough people view the price savings as justifying the difference in travel time and comfort. In communication, the rise of email has dramatically reduced the demand for postal services.

A change in one product may change the need for another product even though the product is not a direct substitute. For example, improved vehicle durability diminishes demand for a variety of services. Likewise, as some products become sufficiently cheap, people may switch from repair to replacement.

Finally, generic connections exist among different categories. Most people will buy food and put gas in their cars before they buy vacations or upgrade their houses. Consequently, dramatic increases in food or gas prices may reduce the consumption of vacations or house remodeling. Many people face limitations on time or money available for entertainment or nonwork activities, so one form of entertainment or nonwork activity may substitute for another.

We now turn to the negotiating power of the firm with respect to two key constituents: its buyers and its suppliers.

BUYER POWER

You get a sale when the price exceeds the cost of the item to the seller and the value of the item to the buyer exceeds the price. In other words, the transaction creates value. In any sale, the price determines the allocation of the value of the transaction between the buyer and seller. Naturally, buyers want lower prices and higher quality, and will tend to demand them when they have higher power. Several things can increase buyer power.

Having fewer buyers results in more power for each buyer. If you sell auto parts to automobile companies for original equipment purposes, you have a very few buyers. However, if you sell the same or very similar parts to mechanics or do-it-yourselfers, you have massively more buyers. Obviously, the automobile company gets a better deal than the do-it-yourselfer.

High switching costs reduce buyer power. A buyer who cannot readily switch between sellers has little power. Thus, once you buy a particular brand of printer for your computer, you often have only one supplier for the printer cartridges. Indeed, the printer industry takes advantage of this by almost giving away printers but charging royally for printer cartridges. People accustomed to a given computer operating system have invested in learning that operating system and so do not want to switch to other systems. They will pay high prices to maintain the operating system on their new computers. People accustomed to a given piece of software often have high switching costs to switch to another package; they have little power. Equipment designed to burn one fuel often cannot change to other fuels.

Switching costs also depend on buyers' perceptions of the product. If buyers believe a product or service offers unique features not offered by others in the market, they will not look for alternatives and will pay higher prices. Across the entire spectrum of consumer goods, brand-loyal consumers willingly pay extra to stay with their brand rather than switch to similar products.

The portion of the buyer's cost that the component reflects influences the price sensitivity of industrial buyers, and consequently, how hard they bargain. For example, the concentrate used in a single serving of your fast food soda is only a very small portion of the cost of actually producing and delivering the soda to the user, and the price of the soda greatly exceeds the cost. Consequently, we expect fast food organizations not to be terribly sensitive to the price of concentrate. In contrast, labor forms a substantial portion of the cost of operating a conventional restaurant, so we would expect such restaurants to be very concerned about wage rates. At the extreme, increasing the price excessively might make the customer unable to make money using the component—a firm seldom benefits from driving its customers into bankruptcy.

In addition to what portion of the buyer's cost the component reflects, buyer price sensitivity depends on how critical the product is to the buyer. In buying a house, you bargain less when you need housing immediately than when you have alternative options for residence. While traveling to a new country, people need local currency and often use the first ATM they see (ignoring transactions fees) rather than look for a specific ATM that charges lower fees.

Finally, buyers have more power when they can threaten to backward integrate and essentially cut out the focal industry. For example, the companies that use substantial quantities of tin cans can either make those cans internally or buy them. The threat of internal manufacture pressures the suppliers to both meet customer service demands and keep prices low. Major corporations often contract out for a wide variety of activities that they could operate internally, like photocopying services, messenger services, office cleaning, etc. Firms that can realistically threaten to do something internally have substantial bargaining power over both quality and price.

SUPPLIER POWER

Supplier power essentially mirrors buyer power. So, the suppliers are powerful when the supplier's industry has few companies, when the focal industry has many companies, when the suppliers sell unique, critical products, when individuals in the focal industry have difficulty switching products or suppliers (or becoming their own supplier through backward integration), and when the supplier can threaten forward integration.

KEY POINTS

The industry analysis primarily addresses the expected profitability of the industry, setting the stage for firms to select industries in which they will compete, and for firm strategies that find and exploit profitable parts of an industry.

Even in very difficult industries, firms may find some highly profitable niches. Generally, such firms have found ways to protect themselves from the competitive forces, often by appealing to specific product/customer niches. For example, even though the retail food industry is highly competitive, retailers who appeal to specific customer groups (e.g., Whole Foods in organic) may prosper. While the automobile industry is exceedingly competitive, Rolls-Royce in the super luxury market has few competitors. Likewise, for some years, Prius in hybrids and Tesla in luxury electric cars had few competitors. The continued profitability of these niches depends on whether other companies decide to service them. The size of the niche often strongly influences whether the larger competitors find a niche worthwhile. For example, it appears that few, if any, of the big companies have an interest in matching Rolls-Royce's super luxury status, but many of the larger car companies have moved to challenge Prius in hybrids and Tesla in electric cars. We will discuss firm strategies and their effects on the five forces in more detail in the next chapter.

When you do a five forces analysis, just listing things does little good. You need to derive the implications of those forces for the industry. You also need to consider the connections among the five forces. In the end, this lets you answer how profitable the average firm should be and why.

Essentially, the processes of production and sales generate a certain amount of value between the beginning and the end of your value chain. The inputs from your suppliers have a certain value that is generally much lower than the value when final customers buy the product. Industry analysis tries to determine which group of firms keeps most of the value generated by this set of businesses.

For example, consider PCs. For the companies that assemble PCs, are there any very powerful suppliers? The answer here is obviously yes—Intel, with its brand name associated with processors, and Microsoft, with its operating system, both have substantial power. How hard is it to enter the industry assembling PCs? Pretty easy; you can assemble a quite functional PC at a reasonable cost in your home. How powerful are the customers? Once customers began to see PCs as commodities, not seeing substantial differences among PC manufacturers, then even though many different, independent buyers purchase PCs, Wintel buyers can easily switch among PC assemblers to the assembler that provides the best performance/price ratio. Are there substitutes? Historically, not particularly, but as the computing power of mobile phones increases, they become a viable substitute to a PC for many activities. Finally, would we expect rivalry here? Many PC assemblers produce largely undifferentiated products, face price-sensitive customers, and come from a variety of backgrounds. Thus, we would expect them not to cooperate. In short, the average return to assembling PCs is relatively low and Microsoft and Intel, with their domination of their product categories, receive the largest share of the profits from the Wintel computer market.

VALUE NET ANALYSIS

Value net analysis, based on game theoretic considerations, offers an alternative tool to analyze an industry.[2]

The value net analysis identifies four players in a company's value net: customers, suppliers, substitutors, and complementors (see Figure 3.4). As in the five forces framework, customers and suppliers are people or business who buy from and sell to your company, respectively. Substitutors are competitors, either existing or potential, from whom customers could buy their products or to whom suppliers could sell their products. Complementors are firms that supply complementary products (e.g., ski boots to go along with skis) to customers, or to whom suppliers could sell complementary products.

The basic insight of the value net analysis is that it suggests a possibility of a win–win strategy among the players in an industry in addition to the win–lose strategy that is implicit in Porter's five forces analysis. Stated differently, the value net identifies the possibility of both cooperation and

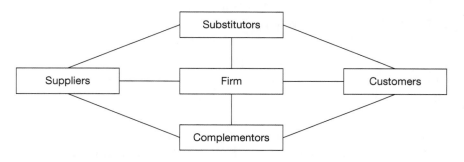

Figure 3.4 A Company's Value Net

competition among the competing firms. For example, suppliers, firms, and customers come together to create value; however, they may compete as to who captures how much of the value that is created. Likewise, firms may cooperate with substitutors (e.g., car companies jointly lobbying the government for lower fuel emissions standards) while competing against each other for customers. Companies may cooperate with complementors, however, they may also create competition among complementors to ensure more value for their customers.

While not offering as detailed an analysis as the five forces framework, a value net can nonetheless add to a five forces analysis by forcing managers to think of potential collaborations among the players in an industry. In turn, this may alter assessments of industry attractiveness.

STRATEGIC GROUPS

An analysis of strategic groups looks at rivalry within a subsection of an industry. Think of it as offering a more fine-grained look at part of an industry than the full industry picture offered by a five forces analysis.

Strategic groups are groups of firms that compete more directly with one another than with other firms within the same industry. These firms may follow similar strategies, compete for similar customers, or offer similar products. For example, in the restaurant industry, restaurants physically close together and catering to similar tastes compete more directly than restaurants further away or appealing to different tastes. At the extreme, two Chinese take-out restaurants next door to each other or two hamburger chains next door to each other compete very directly, whereas they do not compete very much with an upscale sit-down restaurant even if that restaurant is geographically close to the Chinese or hamburger selling restaurants.

We identify strategic groups by taking various dimensions related to competition in the industry and then plotting the firms of interest on those dimensions. The dimensions will differ depending on the industry. For example, in restaurants, plotting firms by location and format may give the most insight (see Figure 3.5).

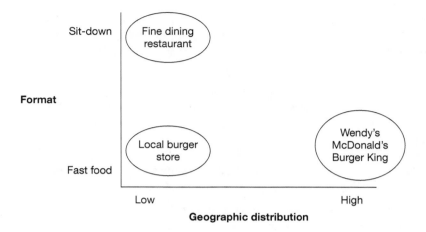

Figure 3.5 Strategic Group Map for the Restaurant Industry

In beer, for example, we might differentiate between craft and mass-market brews. Within craft beer, we might further differentiate by type of beer. Often, different groups compete on different bases. Some groups in the soft drink and beer industries compete by advertising, while other others compete on price. Likewise, in women's clothing, many compete with narrow product lines that cater to the preferences of specific groups of customers (at the extreme, the boutique stores), while others aim for a more mass market, often with a concern for price (Walmart and Target).

A strategic group plot offers a visual representation of the competitive structure of the industry. It helps you understand which firms your firm should primarily worry about. Firms in your firm's strategic group probably matter the most to your firm. The size and characteristics of firms within the group may influence rivalry through the factors in the five forces analysis.

However, you cannot completely ignore firms outside your strategic group. Firms may migrate between groups, depending on how easy it is to enter another strategic group. Your firm may want to move to a different strategic group within the industry, or alternatively, face a threat of entry from other firms in the industry that find your strategic group attractive. If we differentiate between the luxury car group and the luxury electric car group, a luxury electric car maker should worry about migration into the electric car category.

Your identification of firms that do or do not belong in your strategic group depends on how you perceive your environment—and hence, faces all the cognitive and information processing limitations we discussed in Chapter 1. A study of knitwear manufacturers, for example, finds that a group of manufacturers in Scotland saw Scottish knitwear as a separate group and so ignored potential competition from other high-quality knitwear. Group identification may benefit firms in the group by allowing managers to economize on information processing related to the external environment, while also coordinating activities and stabilizing competition.[3] At the same time, this kind of identification may mean firms fail to identify competitive threats from outside the group. Arguably, for example, car manufacturers focused on their traditional rivals namely, other car manufacturers, may have paid insufficient attention to electric cars or the threat posed by firms that enable a "sharing economy."

A five forces or strategic groups or any other kind of competitive analysis helps you understand the landscape that includes your current and potential competitors. Whether (or the extent to which) you decide to respond to an action by a firm in your industry—whether within your strategic group or not—depends on your perceptions of the threat posed to your competitive position by that action. Again, these perceptions are influenced by cognitive and information processing limitations. A study on competitive aggressiveness, for example, finds that both the time horizons that executives consider when contemplating past and future events and the rate at which new opportunities emerge and disappear in an industry shape a firm's propensity to challenge rivals directly and intensely in order to maintain or improve market position and firm performance.[4]

KEY SUCCESS FACTORS

Finally, your environmental analysis should identify key success factors (KSFs)—the things that differentiate winners from losers in the industry.[5]

Any business or organization offers too many things to watch. When one of the authors served on a credit union board, the president brought in a so-called strategic plan with 50 top priorities. If you have 50 top priorities, you have no priorities.

As you go through these analyses, try to identify a small number of things that differentiate winners from losers. Knowing these primary drivers of performance (termed key success factors), you can design the organization and management activities toward those factors. Often, improving performance on KSFs may require lower performance in other dimensions.

Take, for example, 3M. Being innovative means 3M spends a lot of money on R&D, product design, failed products, overhead, etc. To obtain the advantages of product innovation means 3M cannot effectively compete in cost-sensitive markets unless it has a technology-generated cost advantage.

At the other extreme, Emerson Electric historically bought businesses that had good solid products and solid brands and then reduced the cost of production. To do so, it developed a very complex planning and budgeting system with a heavily quantitative approach to control. Along with other factors, the planning system included rules of thumb, for example, that your margins can never go down. Consequently, Emerson Electric corporate strategy worked best in businesses where the KSFs involved product quality and cost, but worked poorly in industries that required continuous innovation.

In addition to focusing your attention on a smaller, more manageable set of variables, the idea of key success factors recognizes that you cannot be the best at everything. Just as in your personal life, for a company excel in one dimension usually requires low performance in another. Companies and people must carefully choose what they want to be good at recognizing the trade-offs involved.

SUMMARY

In this chapter, we looked at five different tools we could use to analyze an industry. The first, the pestle analysis, looks at macro-forces (political, economic, sociocultural, technological, legal, and environmental) that influence firms and industries in general. The second, the five forces analysis, offers a snapshot of an industry; it looks at three competition-related forces (the threat of new entrants, intensity of rivalry, and the threat of substitutes), and two forces that relate to the bargaining power of your firm with respect to buyers and suppliers. This analysis helps you predict the profit potential of your industry. The third, the value net analysis, suggests the possibility of collaboration in addition to competition among the players in an industry. The fourth, strategic groups analysis, offers a finer grained look at an industry; it focuses on firms that resemble your firm in terms of strategy, markets, or products, and offers insights on the specific competition that you will face. The fifth analysis, key success factors, identifies factors that differentiate between winners and losers in the industry.

All of these tools work to provide you with an awareness of the things in your industry that could potentially influence your firm's profitability. There is no one right way to do these analyses; as you may have noted, similar things impact many of the five forces, or may be classified in more than one category of pestle. The tools' benefits come from providing you with a systematic way to look at an industry. Obviously, the quality of your analysis depends on the type of assumptions you make, and the purposes for which you will use your analysis.

Once you have done an environmental analysis, you can identify key success factors—the small number of things that really differentiate winners from losers in the industry. Designing your organization and management around these key success factors will allow your organization to improve its performance in critical areas.

FOOD FOR THOUGHT

1. In the first chapter, we talked about belief structures and the models we hold of the world. How much do such belief structures influence our analysis of an industry? What are the implications of this for firm performance?
2. Many undergraduate students typically believe that an attractive industry is one with low barriers to entry—it is after all, by definition, easy to enter such an industry. Would you agree? If you were setting up a new business, would you prefer to be in an industry with low or high barriers to entry?
3. A student in our MBA class is a personal trainer and wants to start a chain of personal training shops. What would you tell him?

NOTES AND BIBLIOGRAPHY

1. Porter, M. E. "How Competitive Forces Shape Strategy," *Harvard Business Review* (March–April 1979):137–145; Porter, M. E. "The Five Competitive Forces That Shape Strategy," *Harvard Business Review* 86(1) (2008):78.
2. Brandenburger, A. M., and Nalebuff, B. J. "The Right Game: Use Game Theory to Shape Strategy," *Harvard Business Review* (July–August 1995):57–71.
3. Porac, J. F., Thomas, H., and Baden-Fuller, C. "Competitive Groups as Cognitive Communities: The Case of Scottish Knitwear Manufacturers," *Journal of Management Studies* 26(4) (1989):397–416.
4. Nadkarni, S., Chen, T., and Chen, J. "The Clock Is Ticking! Executive Temporal Depth, Industry Velocity, and Competitive Aggressiveness," *Strategic Management Journal* 37 (2016):1132–1153.
5. Leidecker, J. K., and Bruno, A. V. "Identifying and Using Critical Success Factors," *Long Range Planning* 17(1) (1984):23–32; Rockart, J. F. "Chief Executives Define Their Own Data Needs," *Harvard Business Review* 57(2) (1979):81–93.

CHAPTER 4

Generic Strategies and How to Implement Them

Any given market offers a limited number of basic ways to compete. Strategy academics talk about two fundamental ways—differentiation and low cost—and two permutations of these (focus or niche, and value) that also merit discussion.

As noted at the beginning of this book, you need to design the organization around your strategy. An organization that has a coherent idea of what it wants to accomplish succeeds more often than one that does not. Consequently, the organization needs clear guidelines about how it will compete with other firms.

Let's start with a few simple examples. In soft drinks, you can compete with a low-cost strategy, in which case you produce and sell a generic or store brand with little or no marketing. Alternatively, you can compete by differentiation, in which case you spend substantial funds on advertising and (maybe) product development. Thus, in the soft drinks industry, we have undifferentiated, low-cost competitors like store brands and branded, differentiated products such as Coke and Pepsi. The prescription drug industry includes some drug companies that develop new drugs and others that emphasize low-cost production of unpatented drugs. The companies that develop drugs spend heavily on research and development, along with large expenditures on marketing to convince physicians to prescribe the new drugs. The generic drug manufacturers spend very little on product development or marketing; if they spend money at all on research, it goes to process improvement. In both the soft drinks and the prescription pharmaceutical industry, the market can support the two sets of companies—low cost and differentiation—because they compete in fundamentally different ways, often for different customers who want different things from the products.

The value–price–cost framework in Figure 4.1 offers one way to map firm strategies.[1] Each of the four strategies—low cost, differentiation, niche, and value—falls somewhere along the framework. Differentiators target the upper end or the value part of the framework—they charge a high price for their product compared to other products in the marketplace, but customers willingly pay this premium because of the additional value (in terms of, e.g., product quality and customer service) customers believe

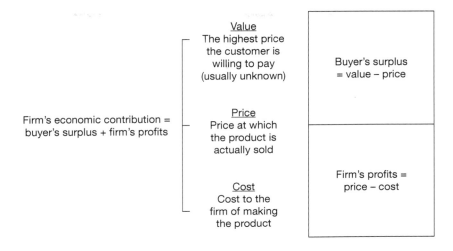

Figure 4.1 The Value–Price–Cost Framework

they receive from consuming the product or service. For example, customers who believe that branded drugs work better than generics will often pay more for brands. Alternatively, consumers may like to show their friends that they own the latest iPhone, enjoy superior service when they fly first class, etc.

Cost leaders, in contrast, target the lower end of the framework. They manufacture functional products with little additional value added in terms of brand name, product quality, or service. Consumers buy these products because cost leaders' lower costs let them offer customers lower prices than competitors' products. Consumers who buy generic soft drinks or generic drugs, for example, appreciate the lower price of the generics more than the cost to obtain whatever additional benefits the branded alternatives offer.

Value strategies combine cost leadership and differentiation strategy to provide a good price for customers who want a given value level. The mass-market retailer Target, for example, offers customers more chic clothing, better customer service, and so on than does its arch-rival, Walmart, which focuses almost exclusively on offering customers low prices. Niche strategies can follow any one of the strategies we have discussed—low cost, differentiation, or value—but target a specific segment of the market instead of the whole market. Weight Watchers, for example, started out focusing almost exclusively on trying to help women—not overweight men—lose weight.

Irrespective of which strategy you pick, you must make some fundamental decisions about how your firm creates value, where value refers to the amount buyers will pay for your firm's products or services. Obviously, the greater this value relative to your firm's costs, the more profitable is your firm.

VALUE CHAIN

Between the cost of the inputs and the value of the outputs, the firm adds value. In manufacturing, this might mean taking steel and making a table. In services, this might mean taking skilled technicians and providing a service that have greater value than the technician's salaries.

A value chain analysis views the firm as a sequence of value-creating activities or subsystems.[2] Primary activities directly contribute to the creation and sale of a product. In the case of manufacturing firms, these would include activities such as inbound logistics, operations, outbound logistics, marketing and sales, and service. Support activities either add value themselves, or add value in combination with other primary or support activities. For our manufacturing firm, these activities would encompass things like human resource management, procurement, technology, and so on. Figure 4.2 shows a generic value chain for a manufacturing firm.

Looking at each of the activities in your firm's value chain would give you an idea about your firm's bases of competitive advantage—what your firm

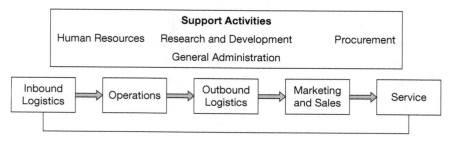

Figure 4.2 Generic Value Chain for a Manufacturing Firm

does better or more efficiently than others in the industry. The bundle of decisions you make about all of these activities determines your actual strategy; the more consistent these decisions are with one another, the greater the likelihood that you will implement your firm's strategy effectively.[3] We return to analysis based on the value chain in Tool #2 at the end of this chapter.

Let us now look at the four strategies in a little more detail.

COST LEADERSHIP

If some group of customers or the entire market either does not perceive substantial differences among products or cannot (or does not care to) choose based on such differences, then customers will choose on price. This means that a firm that can offer the product at a low price has a solid position. We see many examples of low-cost strategies—discount airlines, unbranded gasoline retailers, makers of cheap clothes or toys, and producers of all varieties of commodities.

However, to win by selling at a low price, you need low costs. With costs lower than your competitors' costs, you can make a profit at any price the competitors will set. How do you achieve low costs? We talked about two of the most important ways in our previous chapter as creating barriers for new entrants: learning curves and economies of scale.

LEARNING OR EXPERIENCE CURVES AND LOW COSTS

A learning curve means that the more of something you have produced, the lower the cost. For example, think of fixing something in your house or assembling a piece of furniture from IKEA. The first time you do it is often extremely difficult. You may not have the appropriate tools. You may have trouble finding or understanding the instructions. You may damage the thing you are trying to fix, and have to purchase another. The second time, if it is not too much later, usually goes much better. This process continues in what is termed a learning curve. However, the benefits of additional experience decline quickly—you are unlikely to be much better the 30th time than the 25th time.

Strategically, this means that firms who get into an industry early and get experience can have an enduring cost advantage. As we see in Figure 3.2 in Chapter 3, while a new entrant to an industry usually does not have to start the learning curve quite as high up as the first mover, the second entry faces a substantial cost disadvantage at the time of entry. The first firm can price at a point below the cost of the second firm, but well above its own production cost. The second entrant has an enduring cost disadvantage, although one that, assuming the second entrant can stay in the market, declines over time.

Learning curves, like most things in business, are not ironclad, God-given rules. However, in most organizations with normal efforts to control cost, cost generally follows this kind of curve as your experience in producing a particular product increases.

ECONOMIES OF SCALE AND LOW COSTS

Economies of scale mean that cost per unit declines with units per time. That is, the more you produce per day or hour, the cheaper it becomes.

The reduction in costs that accompany economies of scale stem from various factors:

- Greater scale provides more opportunity for specialization and improved skills. In a small startup, one manager may handle both production and marketing, whereas in a larger firm, specialists handle different kinds of marketing, and a variety of specialists will deal with different portions of production. Specialization usually results in greater efficiency and lower costs.
- Larger scale can reduce the cost of experimentation, risk taking, and intellectual development of the business. For example, if you operate one grocery store, the cost of experimenting may seem very large relative to the likely benefits. However, if you can learn from one store and apply that learning to 50 stores, then the cost/benefit of experimentation becomes much better.
- Larger scale often offers market power, or at least more favorable treatment by suppliers, again reducing costs. Obviously, the home baker who buys a few pounds of flour a month pays dramatically higher prices than the small bakery that buys a few thousand pounds

of flour; both will pay higher prices than the industrial bakery that buys many tons of flour per month.

- Larger scale often allows more efficient resource utilization and the use of more efficient technologies. A small medical practice needs a certain minimum sized waiting room and staff; larger practices can operate with lower waiting space/patient and staff/treated patient. High volume technologies often operate more efficiently than low-volume technologies. A small bakery will have more human involvement resulting in higher personnel costs/unit than a large bakery that can efficiently use automated technologies.

- Some activities or equipment may simply not be divisible and so end up costing small producers more per unit than larger producers. For example, many information technology applications cost a certain amount to install but the cost only increases modestly if you want the technology to handle greater volume. The information technology to handle a bank's ATMs or to track grocery store inventory and sales has substantial installation costs, but adding another ATM or store has only modest incremental cost. Thus, a bank with a few ATMs or a small grocery store adding a sophisticated inventory/sales system faces much higher per unit cost than larger competitors do. Often, smaller competitors simply cannot afford cost-saving technologies larger competitors find valuable.

As we mentioned in the previous chapter, the relation between cost and scale results in what economists term minimum efficient scale. At least in some markets, firms may need some minimum size to compete competitively. This minimum efficient scale will vary dramatically across industries. Thus, the minimum efficient scale for haircutting may require three or four workers, whereas the minimum efficient scale for producing automobiles may require the tens of thousands of workers. Scale economies can occur in any portion of the business including production, advertising, and distribution.

As with anything else, managerial beliefs about these factors often constrain firms without managers recognizing it. For example, managers who believe that a small scale is not viable will not search for technologies that make that scale viable.

Furthermore, larger scale often comes with managerial issues that can result in firms not achieving all the potential benefits from scale. For example, small-scale operations often have an owner-manager with a global view of the organization, and an extremely strong motivation to keep the organization efficient. Larger scale often requires middle managers and others who have only partial views of the organization and much weaker incentives for efficiency. Interdepartmental friction and lack of coordination can consume some of the potential benefits from larger scale.

To summarize, two important ways firms can reduce costs are by moving down the learning curve and by obtaining economies of scale. Both require significant amounts of production, in turn favoring firms with higher market share. Historically, a lot of research has addressed the influence of market share on firm performance. However, researchers have difficulty differentiating empirically between whether (i) the best firms have high profits and high market share due to their efficient or effective management, or (ii) firms with high market share gain some advantages that in turn lead to superior performance. We would expect the market share offers great benefits in industries with scale economies, since the firm with the largest market share generally can operate at the highest scale. Learning curves have less tie to market share, but do suggest the need for sustained and high cumulative production.

In addition to learning curves and economies of scale, firms use a variety of other approaches to achieve low cost.

MINIMUM VIABLE PRODUCTS

Firms often have difficulty identifying the set of features essential to a product and often offer features that many customers do not want. Instead of a long and expensive product development process, the minimum viable product approach recommends rushing a product to market with what management sees as the minimum necessary. Once sales begin, the firm learns quickly what additional features customers value. We discuss this approach in more detail in Chapter 10 of this book.

DESIGN FOR MANUFACTURE

Historically, engineers often designed a product and then essentially threw it over the wall to the production department that had to figure out how to make it. Any firm, and particularly a firm hoping to achieve low-cost, should carefully consider manufacturing issues during the design process. Often, modest changes in designs can dramatically change production, maintenance, and inventory costs.

PROCESS INNOVATION

A firm trying to achieve low-cost position should consider investing in process engineering to reduce production costs. Holding scale constant, the highest and lowest cost producers in most businesses have dramatically different efficiencies. Operations management courses offer many tools to improve processes—we will not attempt to repeat them here. While substantial improvements in production cost may come from off-the-shelf solutions, efficiently using those solutions often requires some in-house understanding. For example, while many companies need to contract for much of their IT development and installation, the company with no in-house understanding of information technology will get less for its IT dollar than a company with some in-house understanding.

OUTSOURCING (ESPECIALLY OVERSEAS)

Over the last 60 years, we have seen fads about doing more within the company and doing more outside of the company. While we will discuss this extensively in the corporate strategy section later, it has a particular place when we talk about low-cost strategies.

Whether you start your own plant in lower cost regions or outsource to companies in lower-cost regions, the benefits of producing in lower-cost regions have resulted in a massive move of manufacturing from the United States and Western Europe to lower-cost countries, often in Eastern Europe or Asia.

Overseas outsourcing or running your own plant overseas offers several benefits. Perhaps foremost, lower wages result in substantial cost savings, particularly for labor-intensive products. In some cases, overseas production can result in weaker constraints on employee safety, environmental pollution, etc. Furthermore, countries often offer incentives to get companies to produce there. In many cases, there is a positive feedback loop; as more companies move overseas, overseas locations like China develop a better ecosystem of suppliers than other countries. Some firms that want to produce at low cost face pressures to move overseas if only because these countries have a wider network of suppliers located close to their plants (and therefore, more options in terms of suppliers) than the company's home country. For the most part, if you take a low-cost strategy, and you produce a transportable product or service, you probably want to make it in a low-cost region. Note, however, that in doing so, you may incur additional transportation and coordination costs that may reduce some of the cost advantages you gain from outsourcing or manufacturing overseas. Similar but perhaps less extreme considerations also can occur when moving production between U.S. states or other jurisdictions.

AUTOMATION

Automation can reduce cost in both manufacturing and service industries. Many manufacturing companies use automation (e.g., industrial robots) to reduce the need for employees, lowering labor costs and often improving reliability. In other cases, the firm's customers use technology to self-serve, that is, provide themselves with the services the firm's employees provided previously. Whenever you scan your groceries, automatically check out of a hotel, or print and scan your own boarding passes, you help a firm lower costs by reducing employment.

EFFICIENCY IN CUSTOMER MANAGEMENT

Customers involve different amounts of effort on the part of the company. As in so many things in life, the 80:20 rule probably holds—80 percent of the profits often come from 20 percent of the customers. Frequently, some of the remaining 80 percent of the customers cost more to service than they pay for the service.

Particularly if the products involve some degree of tailoring to customer needs, a low-cost strategy may require aggressive control over which customers you serve and the extent to which you customize for them. Ideally, the decision should rest on a careful understanding of the relative profitability of selling to different customers within the context of overall capacity utilization, economies of scale, and so forth. For example, mobile service providers and insurance companies have reputations for weeding out unprofitable customers. Sometimes, large customers can command such low prices that the biggest customers are not the most profitable, that is, customer size does not necessarily align with profitability.

CONTROL, CONTROL, CONTROL

An effective low-cost strategy requires lean operations from one end of the company to the other. This usually requires extremely careful performance measurement systems tied to effective motivation and change processes. You need quantitative feedback to understand your cost and quality performance. You need effective motivation and change processes to do something about it.

This does not necessarily mean a heavy-handed approach. For example, some mini mills in the steel industry achieve exceedingly high performance by highly motivated teams of workers who, because they receive bonuses based on team output, strongly encourage their team members to perform well.

Management needs to take a hard look at the cost of many things that appear desirable. For example, a low-cost strategy often requires low (or no) spending on new product R&D. The R&D costs necessary to innovate in a company like 3M mean that 3M is not a low-cost producer unless it has a technological advantage. A low-cost strategy benefits from a management team that does not go overboard on management compensation and executive perquisites.

DANGERS OF A LOW-COST STRATEGY

Perhaps the biggest danger of a low-cost strategy is imitation. We see this in various situations. For example, if cost depends largely on production technology and all firms can buy the same production technology, firms may have similar cost structures. Price sensitive customers may make a low-cost strategy essential, but the strategy will not provide high profits. In such industries, we sometimes see firms moving from a focus on their primary activities to attempting to differentiate and make profits on what had historically been secondary activities. For example, firms in many highly competitive industries such as grain trading and computer assembly have tried to move into consulting where the service's intangible characteristics make it difficult for customers to compare prices.

A low-cost strategy can also lose to competitors that offer low-cost products with better or more features. For example, simply offering the lowest price on a bottle of painkillers may not work if your competitors offer painkillers at similar prices but can convince customers their products are safer and more efficacious.

Finally, if you have achieved low cost by gaining economies of scale through large-scale investments in plants or equipment, you may be extremely vulnerable to an industry slowdown; the sheer scale of your investments may lock you into operating your plants or equipment at a loss. For example, in 2011, the container shipping company Maersk Line ordered 20 supersize ships. The large size of these ships, combined with advances in technology that allowed these ships to operate with lower fuel and labor costs, allowed Maersk to cut costs relative to its rivals. However, due to the large scale of their investments, both Maersk (and its rivals who also ordered supersize ships to be cost-competitive with Maersk) had to continue to operate these ships even as they absorbed lower shipping prices following a slowdown in global shipping. This damaged financial performance; the shipping industry as a whole lost money in 2016, with Maersk Line alone reporting a loss of $376 million in 2016 compared with a profit of $1.3 billion a year earlier.

DIFFERENTIATION

Differentiated providers exist in soft drinks, hard liquor, cars, or almost any product we buy. Differentiation can depend on both tangible—observable differences in the actual product or service, etc.—and intangible differences. Differentiation depends on customer beliefs, whether or not those align with reality.

Most of us have strong preferences for specific brands in some products. These preferences span the entire economy from industrial equipment to consumer consumables and services. In most domains, many buyers perceive substantial differences among brands.

Differentiation can take any form so long as it influences customer perceptions of value. Note the emphasis on perception. While for some products, differentiation depends on truly different performance characteristics, for many products, differentiation depends on perception that has little factual basis. The old saying is you sell the sizzle, not the steak. Thus, car ads on TV emphasize images designed to make buyers want to be like the people who drive the cars in the ad; very few offer any substantive data about vehicle performance. Alternatively, you can have real product performance differences that customers do not perceive; here, real performance differences do not provide market differentiation.

Even where individuals believe that they can tell the difference between products, they often cannot. Repeated studies on the ability to taste demonstrate that the average consumer (and even the experts) cannot differentiate well among many food products. Repeated studies with expert wine tasters and others demonstrate they cannot distinguish among wines reliably. Indeed, wine experts given the same wine twice in a series of tastings gave dramatically different scores to the same wine.[4] If this is the performance of the experts, you can imagine how well the average consumer differentiates among wines based on taste. However, customer perceptions or beliefs drive buying regardless of the facts.

We mentioned the story of Coca-Cola introducing New Coke in the previous chapter as an example of customer loyalty deterring new entrants within an industry. The failed introduction of New Coke, however, also illustrates the importance of customer's perceptions in a differentiation strategy. Coke customers believed that they could tell the difference between the old and new versions of Coke, and that the old version tasted better. This was despite the fact that in blind taste tests, people clearly preferred the new product to the old version.

The importance of perception means the firm must strive for consistency in all the dimensions that touch on the customer relation, often termed product integrity. When people buy a high-end luxury car, they expect a substantially different customer experience than if they buy a low priced subcompact. That experience influences customer purchase decisions. Rationally, the pleasantness of the few hours one spends in a dealership should have little importance relative to the many hours and dollars one invests in a new car. However, sales experts recognize the customer experience depends significantly on the layout, furnishings, presentation, etc. of the dealership.

Differentiation (creating a perception in the customer that your product offers more value than other products) does not inherently require market segmentation (i.e., targeting particular subgroups of customers). For example, Coke and Pepsi are highly differentiated but not segmented in any way whatsoever—they appeal to the general public. In contrast, strategies in some highly segmented markets allow differentiation where customers in different segments have very different interests or values. For example, restaurants segment based on a wide variety of factors including the kind of cuisine, location, price, facilities, etc.; different sets of these factors appeal to different segments of the consuming population. Note that segmentation alone does not necessarily lead to differentiation; one can have segmentation that facilitates a low-cost strategy by allowing production to standardize the product to meet the needs of one specific set of customers.

VALUE CHAIN AND DIFFERENTIATION

Ideally, a firm taking a differentiation approach examines all of its activities seeking additional ways to differentiate the product. This may range from better raw materials through more sophisticated processing all the way to better packaging and after-sale customer service.[5]

An effective differentiation strategy requires understanding the consumer. While this may come from extensive experience with the consumer group, in larger companies, it usually reflects sophisticated market research. In general, a differentiator invests more in marketing, new product development, and customer relations than the company taking a low-cost strategy.

DANGERS OF A DIFFERENTIATION STRATEGY

In taking a differentiation approach, the company has to be careful that the perceived benefits of differentiation to the customer outweigh the costs of differentiation. Sometimes, the customer who prefers your differentiated brand will not pay a sufficiently high premium to justify the cost of producing it. Though this may be most obvious at the top end of the market where, for many products, very few customers are willing to pay the price for an ultra-differentiated product, it can also occur throughout the price range where the cost of differentiation simply exceeds what customers will pay for that specific set of attributes.

Easily imitated differentiation will only provide temporary advantage. For example, many food manufacturers have followed the trend toward healthy eating and tried to differentiate their products by highlighting their avoidance of ingredients such as high fructose corn syrup or trans fats. As these practices become widespread, they may become the new normal and fail to give the companies a continuing differentiation advantage.

Alternatively, some companies overextend their differentiation strategy by having a very large product line. Additional products may simply increase costs and make the buyer's decision harder. For example, Steve Jobs is said to have cut back on the Apple computer line when he found he could not tell his relatives which model they should buy. Alternatively, extension of the product line can dilute customers' perceptions of differentiation for the company's products as a whole. For example, luxury fashion companies that extend their brand to more standard priced products risk customers no longer seeing the brand as exclusive.

FOCUS OR NICHE

Almost by default, smaller companies must adopt a niche or focus strategy where they target a given set of customers or offer a narrow range of products or services to achieve either low cost or differentiation.

You can think of much of strategic management as modeled by war on the plains between big armies. Here, generals have reasonably good information about the other army's movements. In such cases, a winning strategy often requires directly beating the competition. Thus, if we look at compact cars, for one automobile company to win, it must directly beat, at least in the customer's perception, the competitors' car brands.

However, some strategies look more like hiding in the mountains. Niche or focus competitors resemble people seeking a mountain valley where they will not have much competition and can live happily. Particularly if the valleys do not interest the big competitors, they often will offer a nice home for smaller competitors trying to satisfy the needs of particular groups.

For example, the marketplace contains both big and niche retailers. In clothes, Walmart knows what Target carries and Target knows what Walmart carries—the battle of the big armies. On the other hand, very few stores sell clothes or equipment geared directly to women who play roller derby or other less popular sports. A big sporting goods chain may have some relevant products, but certainly does not cater to many less popular sports. Few competitors may bother entering such small markets. Firms with a focus strategy try to achieve differentiation or low cost by serving the needs of a specific group of customers not well served by larger or broader product line competitors.

In any big city, you will find a variety of niche retailers tailoring products to a particular group or achieving lower cost because they address a particular group. Different clothing stores carefully target different portions of the clothes buying public, achieving differentiation within that target market. Specialty food stores target different customer groups with products the big stores do not carry.

However, focus and niche do not necessarily mean small. In automobile services, oil change chains achieve low-cost because they design their facilities for efficient changing of oil, have relatively low inventory of parts and material, and use less skilled labor carefully trained to perform a relatively small set of duties extremely efficiently. Similar low-cost niches exist in muffler shops, hair cutting chains, kidney dialysis chains, and a variety of areas. Starbucks traditionally has had an extremely focused differentiation strategy with an emphasis on a narrow set of products and store designs.

A company offering a focused low-cost strategy or a focused differentiation strategy achieves low cost or differentiation by mechanisms similar to those used by larger companies. This would mean, for example, emphasizing efficiency, automation, and control for focused low cost, and better products and/or customer service for focused differentiation, tailored to the specific requirements of its group of customers.

DANGERS OF A FOCUS STRATEGY

A focus strategy can collapse if a large competitor finds the niche attractive enough or big enough to move in. Starbucks may worry that a chain that offers a broader food line may effectively imitate the Starbucks coffee line and ambience. Chains like Whole Foods that emphasize organic foods face increasing competition from larger retailers adding organic lines for their products. Jeep and Land Rover dominated the SUV market for decades before most of the large car companies started producing competing models.

The niche market targeted by a focus strategy may disappear; over time, the needs of consumers in the niche may become aligned with those of the broader market or simply disappear. For example, historically, only a few specialty stores sold large size clothing. As the average size of the population increases, conventional clothing stores will carry larger sizes, cutting into the specialist market. As interest in hobbies like photography with film and stamp collecting decline, so do the firms that focused on these niches.

VALUE

While we present it as a separate category, any strategy will trade-off perceived performance against price. However, the importance of intermediate levels of differentiation and cost merits specific attention.

Consider auto companies. Some emphasize low cost; cars like the Tata Nano, for example, offer few frills, very limited options, etc. Others emphasize differentiation with high performance or luxury accoutrements. However, most consumers choose cars with intermediate price/ differentiation pairings. Consequently, we have an extremely crowded distribution of automobiles offering different levels of performance (defined along different dimensions—speed, comfort, carrying capacity, etc.) at different prices.

Similar patterns appear in many industries. For example, in general retailing, we have a continuum of retailers offering clothes with different price-perceived quality matchings, ranging from retailers that compete strictly on price to others that compete almost completely on differentiation. Likewise, liquor stores offer a continuum of price-perceived quality matchings in liquor, beer, and wine. Restaurants likewise provide a wide range of price-perceived quality alternatives. Note, while we refer to perceived quality, perceived quality is not a unitary thing; different groups often perceive quality quite differently.

Consequently, a viable strategy exists where you provide an appropriate intermediate level of quality or differentiation at an intermediate price. The winner in such competitions will offer more perceived quality at a lower price than competitors offering similar quality or price, or will offer higher perceived quality at the same price as competitors offer lower perceived quality. In other words, for any price level, you have to offer a product that customers perceive as good as or better than your competition. Naturally, if you want high profits, you have to offer a product that has a better price—perceived performance point than the competition.

Firms need to understand what drives customer perceptions of quality and to differentiate between the firm's managers understanding of quality and customers' perception of quality. Managers live their product categories and often see quality differently than customers. For example, in class, we have had employees of major car companies express exasperation that customers see Subarus as better than their products when they do not believe a real difference exists. Company managers also often have different preferences than many consumers—managers often are aficionados for their products (car people work for car companies, food people work for restaurants), and their preferences often differ from the average consumer. Such managers may have difficulty understanding car buyers who just want transportation or restaurant customers who just want food. We had a Toyota employee describe the first-generation Prius as a piece of junk, to which the instructor noted his 10-year-old first-generation Prius never caused any trouble.

DANGERS OF A VALUE STRATEGY

A value strategy faces two basic dangers. First, the customer of interest must perceive the value. Branded gasoline may have useful additives that generic gasoline does not, but the customer must find the additives sufficiently attractive and believable to pay the higher price. For a fast food restaurant offering high-quality hamburgers and fries, customers must enjoy the high-quality burgers and fries sufficiently more that they will pay more for these products than they would for lower quality burgers and fries at cheaper places.

Second, companies must guard against feature creep. Often, the dimensions professionals in the field perceive as valuable differ from those the average customer perceives as valuable. Professionals often use features that the average consumer ignores. Marketing departments often hear most from their most sophisticated customers, customers who want features only the sophisticated user wants. Companies must carefully prevent the professionals from adding things that experts like but the average consumer does not value.

Consider the keyboard on your computer. It almost certainly has keys that you have never used. Likewise, your word processor has many features few users even bother to explore. Each additional feature adds to development costs, increases the complexity of the product and the likelihood of problems, and adds to production and service costs. Computer-oriented people design and build software and keyboards—they will use features most customers ignore.

Alternatively, consider university textbooks. Textbooks often start out relatively small but grow. For example, the first edition of Kennedy's *A Guide to Econometrics* was a nice little book of 175 pages. The fifth edition had grown to 623 pages. The first edition of Robert Grant's strategy text was under 400 pages; by the eighth edition, it had grown to 842 pages. New ideas occur to the author, or others ask about things the text did not have. Over time, the text evolves from a tight description of the issues to a broad coverage that includes a variety of ancillary discussions not directly of interest to the beginner. While the expert may appreciate the more complex later editions of these texts, they have lost the conciseness that originally appealed.

Photocopiers offer another example. Most individuals use a photocopier to print from a computer or to run a simple photocopy. Advanced users undoubtedly press the companies for additional sophisticated features. In many brands, the addition of multiple features has resulted in users having trouble knowing what buttons to push to make a photocopy.

The value strategy is perhaps the most difficult strategy to implement successfully, simply because it requires being both efficient and innovative. It needs companies manage their value chains to reduce costs while also coming up with features that make products distinctive. Given this scenario, firms often stumble—instead of being both efficient and innovative they may end up neither.

These problems have no simple solutions; the general approach requires continued efforts to understand exactly what drives customer preferences and adapt or even lead those preferences.

CUSTOMER RETENTION

Irrespective of firm strategy, your company needs to retain customers, that is, ensure that they do not defect to the competition. Obtaining new customers requires convincing someone to take a specific action, while retaining customers often requires that they do not act. Obtaining new customers usually costs more than retaining customers. Many businesses from airlines to grocery stores, for example, use a variety of loyalty cards or programs explicitly designed to retain customers. Having customers locked into using your products or services becomes especially valuable to you when your customers perceive your product or service as less sophisticated or valuable than your competitors. Why might customers not switch to a superior product or service when one is available?

There are several reasons. It takes time and effort to search for the new product—in many domains, including banking, television cable services, mobile phone services, home insurance, etc., customers do not continuously compare the price and quality of service offered by their provider to that offered by the competition. Therefore, once a firm lands a customer, it only needs to provide a service good enough to prevent search by the consumer.

Many products and services involve learning curves. You have all invested many hours learning to use specific software programs, a specific design of keyboard, etc. Reducing customers' ability to switch often prolongs the benefits of your strategy. Consider, for example, the Windows and Mac operating systems. Many Windows users do not switch to a Mac (and vice versa) simply because of the time and effort it would take to make the transition.

In addition, many products and services involve network effects. While we discuss these in more detail in Chapter 6, we briefly note here that customers continue to use many products or services that they are not particularly thrilled with, simply because their friends and families use the same product or service.

In sum, if an existing product or service does a good enough job at a reasonable price, customers need a compelling reason—either a perception of substantial superiority or a price sufficiently lower than the existing price—to switch to a new one. How firms do this, while simultaneously preventing imitation by their competitors, depends on their capabilities. We turn to this in the next chapter.

SUMMARY

Companies can implement one of four basic strategies—cost leadership, differentiation, focus, and value. These strategies fall at different points of the value–price–cost framework, with differentiation emphasizing the value part of the framework, and cost leadership emphasizing the cost part of the framework. Implementing these strategies means targeting different activities along the value chains of companies. Each of these strategies has advantages and drawbacks. While some strategies fit some conditions better than other strategies, or appear more attractive than others, the ultimate success of any strategy depends on the effectiveness of its implementation.

FOOD FOR THOUGHT

1. The successful implementation of a strategy often means that the strategy changes the strength of the five forces—the company faces a reduced bargaining power of buyers, say, or a reduced threat of substitutes. How might a successful implementation of a cost leadership or differentiation strategy change the strength of the five forces facing the firm?
2. Do you think the top managers of a company following a cost leadership strategy have different belief structures than top managers of a company following a differentiation strategy? Which company do you think will be better at responding to a changing environment?

3. Uber uses surge pricing to charge for rides; prices go up when demand is high, and down when demand is low. Is surge pricing consistent with either a cost leadership or a differentiation strategy?

TOOL #2: VALUE CHAIN ANALYSIS

While almost all organizations routinely look within each activity for ways to cut costs, value chain analysis adds two important dimensions to such search: value addition and cross-function or activity potentials.

Instead of simply asking how can we reduce cost, value chain analysis asks: how can we reduce costs or increase value to the customer? Clearly, the decision depends on both the cost incurred and the value added. If you cannot add value, then reducing costs is good, but if you can add sufficient value, you might accept higher costs.

Such research should go beyond the normal domains we examine for value. That is, we normally think about value in terms of product design and perhaps distribution. The value chain analysis broadens our thinking. For each component of organizational activity, it asks: how can it add more value or reduce cost? For example, it might be that buying a different quality of raw materials adds more value than it costs. Alternatively, adopting a different set of HR practices might create value by changing the productivities or propensities of employees with different skill levels to take certain actions. The value chain analysis emphasizes that since all of the activities in an organization are essential to producing the value incorporated in the product or service produced, all of those activities have the potential to improve that value.

The analysis should look with particular care at the potential for value creation or cost reduction between activities. Frictions and problems often appear at the interfaces between activities. The tie between sales and production, for example, very often reflects the two groups having substantially different goals and incentive structures. However, similar frictions or simply an inability to look carefully at the potential of the connection can occur in almost any interunit relation. Firm cost accounting and management authority domains encourage a search for improvements within a given cost accounting entity and under a given manager's authority. Firms often overlook the potential to add more value or to reduce costs that lie on the interfaces between activities. Gaining the benefits of such interactivity improvements often faces substantial incentive and coordination problems. Indeed, an action that improves the connection between two units may generate a total increase in corporate value while reducing reported performance of one of the two units. In this case, we may need a side payment such that both units have a reason to participate in the improvements.

The search for improvements (higher value or lower cost) should include the relations between suppliers and the firm and between firm and customers. Again, because these do not naturally align with cost accounting structures, management may overlook them. As with interunit relations, prices or other payments may need to adjust to reflect the gain in value or reduction in cost. Generally, both sides must see some benefit from the cooperation.

Let us offer a couple of examples what this might look like. A chocolate manufacturer may find that its customer needs to make the chocolate liquid to work with it. The manufacturer can save the cost of solidifying the chocolate and save the customer the cost of liquefying it by maintaining the product as a liquid. Alternatively, sophisticated companies in retailing have invested immense amounts in improving the interfaces between their operations and their suppliers; Walmart, in particular, has a reputation for this.

Within a multidivisional firm, centralizing some activities (e.g., order processing or inventory management) may reduce costs for the firm as whole. Centralization may also increase value to the customer; instead of having to contact multiple divisions, the customer may simply have to place one order for all of a company's products with a single point person. However, these gains may come at the expense of reduced autonomy for individual divisions. Particularly in organizations with cultures that emphasize divisional independence, centralization may require some form of compensation to the divisions for a loss of control over activities they previously carried out independently.

NOTES AND BIBLIOGRAPHY

1. For a discussion, see The National Archives, http://webarchive.nationalarchives. gov.uk/20120823131012/; see also www.businesslink.gov.uk/bdotg/action/ detail?type=RESOURCES&itemId=1073790697. (accessed April 4, 2017). For a discussion of value-based pricing, see Macdivitt, H., and Wilkinson, M. *Value-Based Pricing: Drive Sales and Boost Your Bottom Line by Creating, Communicating, and Capturing Customer Value* (McGraw Hill Companies, New York: 2011).
2. Porter, M. E. *Competitive Advantage: Creating and Sustaining Superior Performance* (New York: The Free Press, 1998).
3. See also Normann, R., and Ramirez, R. "From Value Chain to Value Constellation: Designing Interactive Strategy," *Harvard Business Review* 71(4) (1993):65–77.
4. See www.theguardian.com/lifeandstyle/2013/jun/23/wine-tasting-junk-science-analysis
5. Levitt, T. "Marketing Success through Differentiation—Of Anything," *Harvard Business Review* 58(1) (1980):83–91.

CHAPTER 5

Firm Capabilities

The previous chapter discussed fundamental ways a firm could choose to compete. We now consider firm capabilities—what a firm does well or badly. As with goals, a lot of jargon applies to such capabilities, jargon made more difficult because writers often use terms in unconventional ways. Here we will try to cut through to the core ideas.

If we all have the same abilities and compete in the same market with the same approach, then competition should lower profits. So, one of the primary ways to win is by being better at least at some things than the competition. Winning at a low-cost strategy, for example, requires actually creating a lower-cost structure than the competitors. This, in turn, implies being better than the competition at things like efficient production, logistics, or procurement. Differentiation likewise means you produce cost-effectively something others find difficult to produce; effective differentiation may require a firm be better than the competition at a relevant capability like production, customer service, innovation, or marketing.

Doing something better than your competition right now, however, is not enough; enduring high performance requires you keep doing those things better than the competition. If you do something well that leads to high profits, you should expect others to mimic your approach, driving down performance. For example, the first to introduce a different kind of restaurant format or a new bank service may profit, but those profits will decline if others can mimic the innovation.

However, a temporary advantage in one domain may lead to more enduring advantages in another. For example, other companies may eventually mimic your innovation, but before they do, you might gain sufficiently high economies of scale or brand recognition to have enduring high performance. Consider, for example, Starbucks. Other firms can readily mimic a Starbucks outlet. However, Starbucks can maintain its success because its large scale lets it purchase coffee and other inputs more cheaply than the competitors and its reputation or brand brings in customers and lets it engage in product line extensions such as selling its own brand of coffee in grocery stores.

The importance of specific capabilities differs. Some capabilities form preconditions for surviving in an industry. Others form the core of a firm's strategy and its attempts at maintaining customer retention and preventing duplication. We discuss two categories of capabilities: threshold or hygiene and core.

THRESHOLD OR HYGIENE AND CORE CAPABILITIES

We term abilities you need to compete, but which do not differentiate performance much, as "threshold" or "hygiene capabilities." If you wish to run a restaurant, you must meet the health department standards. No one has a successful restaurant simply because it meets health department standards, but not meeting standards can close down a restaurant. Likewise, any bricks and mortar bank has to have a certain set of teller functions such as taking deposits and providing change, but the provision of such functions does not differentiate much among competitors. We call such functions or capabilities threshold or hygiene abilities.

A separate set of competencies differentiates performance within the population of firms in an industry. These are termed core capabilities or core competencies.[1] Obviously, these specific competencies vary dramatically by industry, although efficiency and reliability are generally important.

To create core capabilities—things an organization does well that differentiate it from competitors—the organization often has to organize around a specific set of activities. This organization around such activities provides what is called a dominant logic.[2] Core capabilities stemming from a dominant logic allow the organization to diversify into similar areas or industries that use the same basic processes. However, the organization usually has difficulty diversifying successfully into industries that require fundamentally different core capabilities or dominant logics.

Consider hospitals. If you wish to build a hospital that can effectively make money, or at least break even serving patients who can only afford minimum prices, or have their medical bills paid by an organization such as Medicare that enforces low prices, then you must make a variety of design choices. You would want to have a relatively inexpensive capital plant.

You would not want to subsidize medical research. You would focus on a subset of patient problems, referring patients with more complicated problems to other hospitals. Through a constellation of specific policies, you may achieve highly efficient processing capabilities.

Contrast this with a hospital that attempts to succeed as an elite provider. Such a provider would invest in much fancier facilities. This hospital would try to hire a different set of physicians, those that can handle the exceptions or the difficult cases. Such a hospital would also want to avoid low-margin activities while attempting to emphasize those that pay higher margins. Such hospitals may use their reputation to build centers for cutting-edge research and innovation that in turn attract patients.

The underlying dominant logic in either set of hospitals is not better or worse, but different. The hospital that attempts to win by developing an elite brand name generally cannot be a low-cost producer. Likewise, low-cost hospitals seldom are major research facilities.

Similar problems crop up in all kinds of businesses. If a firm's dominant logic depends on taking out operational costs, then the firm usually has difficulty with product innovation. If the dominant logic is to innovate, R&D and new product expenditures mean the firm will normally not be able to compete on low cost (unless the innovation per se lowers cost). The dominant logics that work for heavy manufacturing do not work well for most service functions, and vice versa.

Firms have difficulty changing their dominant logics. The dominant logic strongly influences top managers' mental maps—their experience with the core business drives how they see the world. The dominant logic is built into an extremely wide spectrum of firm processes and other factors ranging from the individuals the firm recruits, to how it promotes, the information systems it creates, its make-or-buy decisions, its decisions about geographic location, etc. As such, the dominant logic is embedded within the firm.

When the environment changes, firm core capabilities may become core rigidities; the organization needs to change, but the very things that made it successful in the past now stop it from changing. This explains why, for instance, companies in crisis often tend to look for outsider CEOs to turn the company around; the new CEO (and the other top executives the new CEO hires) will bring a different mindset to the company, one that perhaps better suits the firm's new reality. Whether this actually works, however, depends on both the appropriateness of the new dominant logic for the firm's changed environment and the extent to which the new management can change the firm's existing dominant logic embedded in the firm's processes and systems.

Consider, for example, the contrasting cases of Kodak and Campbell. Kodak invented the digital camera, but did not promote the technology for fear that it would destroy its core film business. When the digital camera market took off, Kodak tried to diversify into digital cameras as well as other businesses such as computer hardware, even bringing in CEOs from completely different industries (George Fisher from Motorola and Antonio Pérez from Hewlett-Packard) to do so. Ultimately, however, Kodak's diversification efforts failed, and the company had to declare bankruptcy. Campbell Soup, in contrast, brought in Douglas Conant from Nabisco to help revive the company; within 8 years, the company had moved from being the bottom performer among the world's major food companies to outperforming both the S&P Food Group and the S&P500.

Part of the reason why Kodak failed where Campbell succeeded lay in the relative abilities of the CEOs of the two companies to change the dominant logic at their respective companies. In an interview with the *New York Times*, Fisher noted that when he took the top job at Kodak, the company "regarded digital photography as the enemy, the evil juggernaut that would kill the chemical-based film and paper business that fueled Kodak's sales and profits for decades."[3] Fisher's apparent inability to move Kodak away from this mindset contrasts with the changes Conant brought about in the way Campbell's managers and employees approached their jobs. In an interview with Fast Company, Conant noted that leaders have to "Declare yourself. People aren't mind readers. They can't know what you're thinking unless you tell them. Explicitly. By declaring yourself, you might say something like, 'Okay, we're going to make it safe to challenge the status quo. We're going to make it safe to offer opinions that run counter to current thinking. We're going to have a culture that places real value on fresh ideas.'"[4]

Where do threshold and core capabilities come from? All corporate capabilities derive from tangible and intangible resources such as physical, financial, intellectual, and human resources, firm reputation, and organizational processes. We discuss each in turn.

PHYSICAL RESOURCES

While physical resources often offer obvious benefits—the plant to produce something, a prime location for retail, etc.—understanding the benefits is not so simple.

First, you need to worry about opportunity cost. That is, what is the value of this resource if used in some other way, including the value the resource would bring if sold on the open market? By ignoring opportunity costs, managers can imagine their strategies are successful, when in fact they are simply returns to an undervalued resource.

Suppose, for example, you have a wonderful location—you own a great spot right downtown, with lots of foot traffic. For years, you have been running a restaurant in this location and net $500,000 a year from this restaurant. You have fully depreciated the capital in the business. You think you are making good money. How could this be wrong?

Suppose the property alone would rent for $50,000 a month. How does this change your analysis?

While from an accounting standpoint, you make half million dollars a year in profits, from an opportunity cost standpoint, you lose money. You could make more income simply by renting the property out; all your work and effort in running this restaurant loses you $100,000 a year! In other words, if you price the opportunity cost of the property correctly, you lose money running the restaurant.

You need to consider the opportunity cost of resources, and particularly, physical resources. If an organization has particularly valuable, marketable resources, it needs to analyze the opportunity cost of using those resources in its own production system. A facility you purchased many years ago and have fully depreciated (thus presenting no cost on your income statement) appears free from an accounting standpoint. However, if that facility has a substantial market value, then you should recognize that market value as an opportunity cost when you evaluate a strategy.

Note that opportunity costs do not appear only in physical resources. For example, suppose you have a salesperson who can generate, on average, $1,000 an hour in revenue. Every hour you have that salesperson do something else—filling out forms, attending meetings, or whatever—costs you $1,000 in revenue. However, many organizations treat the time of employees as essentially free; they ignore the opportunity cost of the employee time. Sometime, when you are sitting in a particularly useless meeting, you may find it amusing (or depressing) to calculate the cost per hour to the company to have employees sitting in that meeting.

FINANCIAL RESOURCES

Oddly, while many young firms have great difficulty obtaining financial resources, traditional theorizing in strategic management questions the importance of financial resources. Much of this questioning derives from pseudo-efficient market arguments. If the suppliers of capital are rational in an economic sense, then money will flow appropriately to those who have proposals or businesses that have high expected returns.

However, in the real world, markets are not that efficient, particularly for highly uncertain activities like startups. Outsiders (and insiders) have great difficulty predicting the returns for any new business. Alternatively, in established businesses, investors cannot invest in a particular new project without investing in the entire enterprise.

Even in the largest of companies, financial resources provide strategic advantages. Financial resources give the firm options and power. A firm with financial resources might buy out potential competitors or retain customers by extending generous credit terms. Thus, recent work by Kim and Bettis finds a positive association between firm holdings in cash and future performance.[5] However, as one might expect, the benefits to holding cash decline at exceedingly high levels of cash. From a strategy perspective, exceedingly high levels of cash raise questions about the firm's future—is the firm holding cash because it lacks attractive opportunities for investment?

Maintaining financial slack (resources beyond those needed to operate day to day) provides the firm with flexibility and buffers the firm from short-term problems. For good reasons, firms often choose to have high levels of liquid assets.

INTELLECTUAL CAPITAL

Intellectual capital refers to a wide variety of information-related things that provide benefits to the firm. Intellectual capital includes patents, know-how, complex business systems, data on customers, etc.

The firm can sell some, but not all, forms of intellectual capital. However, even for the marketable forms of intellectual capital, valuation is often problematic. How do I rigorously evaluate what information is worth until I know that information? However, if I know the information, I do not need to pay for it.

We do see frequent transactions involving some forms of intellectual capital. Firms routinely pay to use technologies protected by patents or copyrights. The valuation of many technological start-ups often reflects the start-up's intellectual capital rather than some tangible income stream.

However, patents only have value to the extent that the patent holder is willing and able to sue to enforce the patent. Patents are not self-enforcing. Consequently, to achieve the value of a patent, a firm needs the financial resources and time to defend the patent in court. Large companies sometimes use costly litigation and delays to prevent smaller firms from enforcing their patents.

Patenting practices (and the value of patents) vary dramatically across industries. In some industries, firms patent anything they can. In others, they avoid patenting because patenting requires revelation of the innovation and may help competitors engineer around the patent. Larger companies often benefit from both the patent's potential for direct value creation and its ability to block competitor entry into a market. Google's acquisition of Motorola, for example, gave Google Motorola's large patent portfolio, which helped Google defend its Android operating system.

While small firms often have difficulty defending their patents, some small companies (sometimes termed patent trolls) may benefit significantly from their ownership of patents. For example, a company called Shipping & Transit LLC filed over a hundred patent lawsuits in federal court (largely against small companies) in 2016. Among other things, Shipping & Transit owns patents related to tracking systems that enable customers to track the status of e-commerce packages. By demanding licensing fees small enough to discourage firms from pursuing a legal battle, the company and its predecessor (named ArrivalStar) collected more than $15 million in license fees from over 200 parties (including large logistics firms like UPS and FedEx) between 2009 and 2013.[6]

HUMAN RESOURCES

Much of the value created by many companies comes from the firm's human resources. However, valuing and describing these human resources can be exceedingly difficult.

While a competitive market often exists for some types of human resources, wage rates often do not align with the individual's value to the company. At the extreme (i.e., ignoring many nonfinancial factors), a company only has to pay an employee slightly more than the employee could get for working elsewhere. An individual might have immense value due to knowledge about within-company factors such as custom-designed software, but that may not translate into wages if other firms cannot use that knowledge. Alternatively, a truly exceptional programmer may be several times as productive as an average programmer, but the individual often has trouble commanding the salary commensurate with actual productivity.

Pay can deviate from productivity anywhere markets have difficulty assessing differences in individual productivity. In such cases, pay differentials between low and high performers often do not align with differences in actual performance.

The value of a given individual's knowledge depends on the context within which that individual operates. The most brilliant computer programmer in the world has no value in a business without computers. Thus, the value of human capital often depends on a very complicated interaction among a variety of factors that operated over time to create the current organization. The current organization depends on hiring, training, and reward systems that have operated over many years to create and mold the profile of and interactions among the current workforce.

The difficulty in mimicking or replicating a complete system that generates human capital can make capabilities based on human capital among the most enduring advantages an organization can have. While a firm can hire someone to generate a procedure or recipe to mimic many 3M or Google products, no simple recipe exists for creating a 3M or Google innovation culture.

Indeed, many organizations have human systems that work, but the organization may not know exactly why they work or what components matter most. A firm's HR system involves a great many different things (recruiting, new hire training, selection, mentoring, etc.); identifying which ones matter most is exceedingly difficult.

Organization-based capabilities can be exceedingly durable because the competition has trouble mimicking them. However, they can also be incredibly fragile; actions that make employees want to leave can dramatically reduce the value of such skills. Management of many high-tech companies will tell you that their most important resources leave at the end of the day and have to choose to come back the next morning.

REPUTATION

Reputation offers another form of intangible resource, which is closely related to the firm's brands. Reputation applies more often to the firm as a whole than to brands and particular lines of products or services, but the two are often inextricably connected. An event that demonstrates serious problems in one brand held by a large corporation can damage that brand, and, through the firm's overall reputation, the value of the corporation's other brands.

Some have attempted to estimate the value of brands, terming this brand equity. As one might expect, such estimates depend on extremely strong and often questionable assumptions like equating goodwill or all the difference between accounting value and market value to brand equity.

Goodwill merits explanation. When firms acquire other firms, the acquiring company generally records the excess of the purchase price over the book value of assets acquired on the balance sheet as goodwill. The value of most purchased companies largely depends on expectations about the income or cash flows it will generate, not the actual value of the underlying physical assets. While part of goodwill may reflect the value of reputation or brand, it can also reflect a wide variety of other factors like the corporation's ability to innovate or produce cheaply.

While the importance of brands has been recognized for many years, research on the importance of reputation began 20 years or so ago. Reputation can help or hurt the firm in a wide variety of ways. Reputation influences the firm's ability to recruit employees and senior managers. Reputation influences the corporation's interactions with its suppliers, financial services providers, regulators, and other important outside bodies. Finally, reputation can influence the customer's perceptions of the organization and, consequently, the organization's products.

However, we should not overstate the importance of reputation. Research on reputation often suffers from a problem in that high performance positively influences reputation so it may be that high performance has caused reputation rather than that reputation has caused performance.

Furthermore, a corporate reputation has several dimensions. A firm could have a first-rate reputation in some areas and a poor reputation in others. Different observers may emphasize different facets of the firm in judging reputation. For example, companies can have a negative reputation for social responsibility activities, but quite positive reputations for the quality of products, etc. ExxonMobil has a negative reputation with environmentalists who object to the company's stance on global warming, but a positive reputation as a highly efficient operator within the industry. A firm in industries like tobacco might have an excellent reputation within the industry and with its customers and suppliers, but a poor reputation with observers who object to the product category.

While reputation may be difficult to imitate completely, other firms can approximate it by investing in brand quality, undertaking actions that demonstrate corporate social responsibility, etc. Indeed, some large firms pay for advertisements designed to boost corporate reputation rather than to promote specific products, and almost all large firms have departments concerned with the firm's public image.

Firm and market characteristics should guide investments in reputation. Building a reputation for specific things such as product quality, reliability, sustainability, or customer service often provides greater benefits than attempting to promote a general corporate reputation. Corporate actions have clearer ties to an area- or domain-specific reputation than to a general corporate reputation. Actions to reduce pollution or improve external evaluations of product quality have clear ties to reputations regarding pollution and product quality, but actions to improve general repute are hard to connect to reputation. Firms with a differentiation strategy should value reputation more than those with cost leadership strategies. People who want the cheapest gas think less about the reputation of the producer than people who want a differentiated gas product. Reputation can serve to increase customer loyalty, but its ability to do so will probably be higher for products or services essential to the customer and products where consumers cannot form product judgments empirically. For example, one might judge restaurants based on experience, while relying on the reputation of the firm for a stent that will go into one's heart. Reputation may also have great benefits where customers have difficultly guiding their purchases by their own experiences due to infrequent purchases or difficulty tying the purchase to the outcome. Thus, we see law firms investing heavily in offices and décor, along with donating funds to charities and business gatherings to improve reputation.

Industries subject to heavy government regulation or needing government intervention are an exception to these guidelines. General reputation can significantly influence political action and may influence regulators.

Finally, you can destroy a reputation more easily than build one. Whether for individuals or organizations, a positive reputation usually requires repeated positive actions, but one major negative action can destroy it.

ORGANIZATIONAL PROCESSES

Perhaps the most important determinant of organizational capabilities lies in the organization itself. Firms differ dramatically in how they organize, how they motivate individuals, and the thousand and one different factors that determine the output of an organization. We discussed some of this earlier, under human resources.

We will talk more about organizations and organizational processes when we talk about diversification and strategy implementation. Whether it is innovation, individual effort, relations with customers or suppliers, etc., the quality of the firm's decision and firm outcomes all depend heavily on the organization.

Much of the intellectual capital of a firm exists in the organization's structures and processes. This information or knowledge is not simply held by individuals; the organization can maintain the knowledge embedded in these capabilities through the use of routines and standard operating procedures despite employee turnover.

In recent years, a substantial amount of effort has gone into attempting to manage knowledge in large organizations through knowledge management systems. Part of this reflects a perception that organizations repeatedly attempt to solve the same problem. That is, a similar problem appears in multiple areas of an organization and the organization repeatedly spends time and money solving almost identical problems. Knowledge management systems attempt to inventory what people have solved or know and provide that inventory to others.

For example, in software organizations, some have attempted to implement knowledge management systems that make it easy for individuals to tap into the coding done by others to solve these general problems. However, the effectiveness of these systems is unclear, and almost certainly varies depending on the substance of the knowledge inventory and the details of the system. Such systems often have difficulty getting people to enter information into the system because they receive relatively little immediate benefit from doing so. Users of the system may not use the system if they do not find useful information the first few times they search it.

As we discuss toward the end of this book, the structure, systems, and processes of an organization not only provide its capabilities, they determine how well an organization actually uses those capabilities. The structure and processes of an organization may thus provide an enduring source of competitive advantage, especially when, as we discuss later in this chapter, we take into account the extraordinary difficulty of duplicating a rival's structure, systems, and processes.

ASSESSING CAPABILITIES

As is clear from the discussion above, assessing an organization's capabilities, or assessing the value of these capabilities for the organization is quite challenging. We can give a few suggestions.

First, with the exception of opportunity cost considerations, firms do not need to identify precisely the value of specific capabilities. We gain little from saying "human resources is worth $X to the company." Instead, work to understand how capabilities influence firm's performance.

Second, try hard to have real evidence. Organizations develop stories about their abilities. You can see this in individuals. Just ask your classmates where they would place their ability as drivers on the distribution of drivers; most likely, 90 percent or more claim to be above average. Organizations with positively motivated individuals likewise tend to overestimate their organization's abilities. People who feel good about an entity generally rate that entity high on a variety of factors that may have little to do with the reason they feel good about the entity.

While some tools attempt to compensate for specific biases in individual decision making, we have not seen evidence that these actually work for the kinds of complex problems that organizations face. Consequently, the best strategy is to look for real data. If you claim your customers love you, then do honest surveys eliciting customer opinions of you and your competitors and question your claim if customers buy from the competition. You cannot claim to be good at production if your cost per unit is above your competitors, but your quality is not. If you claim you are good at order processing, you need to back this up with concrete data on speed and cost of order processing. We will discuss at least one way to go about this as we talk about benchmarking later in this chapter.

Note that corporate aggregate performance in itself does not indicate you are good at any specific activity. A profitable firm will do some things exceptionally well even though it may do others very badly. High performance in some of the organization's activities could easily cover for low performance in others. At the extreme, some firms may succeed simply because they had the good luck to hit one big home run. This does not mean that they have good organizations or that they do things well.

Third, try to focus on the important issues rather than making this into a massive exercise. You can spend years trying to define and measure all the capabilities of a firm. Why bother? Instead, focus on the few abilities that most influence firm performance. This comes back to key success factors—what factors determine who wins and who loses in this industry?

MATCHING ABILITIES AND STRATEGY

Given evidence about your capabilities, you next need to ask if your strategy takes advantage of what you do well and mitigates the problems from what you do poorly.[7]

People tend to talk about what they do well and ignore what they do not do well. Just as it is important that your strategy exploits what you do well, it must not depend on what you do not do well. Ikea, for example, excels at product development and presentation, but not in advising customers. Indeed, one of the authors once visited an Ikea store that had posted a sign explicitly discouraging customers from approaching employees, with the rationale that this would result in higher costs for everyone. Ikea should probably avoid businesses, products, or services where customers need employee advice.

Almost automatically, as we have mentioned before, doing some things well means doing others poorly. Good strategy means you consciously choose to do some things well, recognizing that this will result in doing some things poorly. The best technical analysts may not be people you want in sales. A waiter who does a good job in a diner would not thrive in a four-star restaurant, and vice versa. While exceptions exist to every rule, on average, very few organizations or individuals can excel in all dimensions of an activity.

SUSTAINING RETURNS FROM ABILITIES

We mentioned in the previous chapter that if a strategy pays off, we should expect others to attempt to copy it. While we can use patents or similar tools to protect our position, the success of any strategy depends on how well we implement it—which, in turn, depends on our company's capabilities and how easily others can copy them. Economically oriented strategy texts emphasize this to the point that they say valuable resources or capabilities must be impossible to copy.

We take a more modest approach. Capabilities differ dramatically in how easy they are to copy. If a firm's advantage comes from using a new piece of equipment bought from an equipment supplier, other companies can copy that advantage simply by buying similar equipment. However, copying many other firms' capabilities is by no means trivial. Even within organizations (where one might expect copying to be extremely easy), companies often have immense difficulty transferring capabilities from one division to another division.[8] Note that, in such transfers, organizations often have exceedingly good information about processes in the divisions where the capability works well, as well as a relatively unfettered ability to apply that information to other divisions.

Now consider the situation where you want to copy something another company does well. First, you actually have to know it does it well. For example, imagine your competitor has success attracting and retaining customers. However, a customer's reaction to an organization depends not just on a single product, but rather on the interaction of the product with the entire set of activities that face the customer—quality of sales people, quality of service, location of stores, etc. How can you know which specific factor or factors generate your competitor's success with customers?

Second, you have to figure out how your rivals do what they do. While for relatively simple things, one might hire a former employee or two and obtain information on your competition, for complex behaviors driven by organizational processes, even the managers operating the processes may not know precisely what matters.

We give you an extreme example. Basic training in many military organizations can turn an individual into a highly disciplined soldier in three months. Such basic training often includes somewhat abusive supervision, sleep deprivation, indoctrination or teaching of traditions, and a wide variety of substantive skills such as shooting, marching, etc. Military services have done this for centuries. However, the services may still not be sure which parts of the basic training process matter most in determining this transformation.

For-profit organizations often follow a similar if much less rigorous pattern where new hires take some time before they become fully functioning and effective organizational members. Exactly what creates this may not be fully obvious even to the employing organization. Perhaps more dangerously, managers may believe they know what matters, but such a belief could be wrong. Making a new hire an effective employee probably depends on training and selection, but also on on-the-job experiences that depend on how current employees treat new hires. We may know that after X years employees have become fully effective operators in a given activity, but not know exactly how that transformation occurred.

Consequently, abilities vary dramatically from those that transfer relatively quickly and easily to some that may not be transferable at all. If a fast food restaurant thinks it has created a new ability by learning how to produce salads, others can copy that relatively easily. Likewise, banks adding new financial products reap exceedingly short-lived benefits because competitors can easily duplicate such products. A combination of legal requirements in customer facing activities and regulatory requirements make it relatively simple to copy another bank's or insurance company's products. On the other hand, competitors may have great difficulty duplicating the customer experience of another bank.

Copying is harder if the ability depends on complex interactions within or across organizations. Thus, a fast food company may be able to copy the menu of McDonald's quite readily but may not necessarily be able to copy their HR or supply chain management processes.

In addition, all organizations are history dependent. The characteristics of founding CEOs and CFOs influence firm behavior long after those CEOs and CFOs have left. Many skills take years for an organization to develop. Think about learning mathematics. You cannot jump into calculus until you have taken and understood algebra. You probably cannot understand algebra until you have understood arithmetic. Thus, the jump to calculus requires a long sequence of learning. Likewise, in many organizational activities, we can only do the new because we already have the old. Often referred to as absorptive capacity, this is one of the reasons why firms invest in R&D rather than simply purchasing the information from outside; doing your own R&D makes it easier for you to recognize (and possibly imitate) your rivals' innovations.[9]

However, all of this reflects a bias in strategy writing in that it focuses on the positive benefits of capabilities. Unless one defines capabilities tautologically, then we should expect that many abilities actually have negative value. By tautological, we mean that if you define a capability as something that creates profits, then one cannot find capabilities that do not create profits—the definition generates the relation between resource and profit rather than any causal relation. When we recommend organizations identify and develop some of their capabilities, we must believe that developing those capabilities positively influences (i.e., partially causes) subsequent performance.

Most organizations have wide distributions of capabilities. In executing any given strategy, some of those capabilities may help, some may be neutral, and some may hurt. Most firms probably do not fully understand the pluses and minuses of all their capabilities. For example, Emerson Electric's ability to reduce the cost of operations goes along with an inability to do substantial product innovation. 3M's ability to generate new innovative products goes along with an inability to produce low-cost standardized products in which it does not have a technological advantage.

To bring it to a personal level again, most of us probably have some habits we know are good for our health or our careers, while we also have some habits we know are bad for our health or careers. Furthermore, we are probably unaware of some of our habits that will influence our health or career. The same goes for organizations.

PRACTICAL ADVICE

Given the difficulties associated with identifying capabilities and their impact on the organization, how can you assess your organization's capabilities? As we noted earlier, try to find real evidence of capabilities and evidence of their ties to performance.

Some firms use benchmarking—comparing your organization's performance on a few key indicators to your competitors' performance on those same indicators—to assess capabilities. Benchmarking helps provide a reality check on what you identify as the strengths and weaknesses of your company—it tells you what good really means in a given dimension. It also may suggest better ways to operate specific activities. Many consulting organizations offer benchmarking services.

Alternatively, you might use either the balanced scorecard approach or one of its many variants.[10] The balanced scorecard essentially works backward from organizational performance. You start by defining the outcome you want to reach. For example, you may want to increase return on assets.

Then, you ask what things influence that outcome—level of revenues, level of costs, etc. For each of these things, you work further back to ask what factors influence them: what influences revenue, for example? By working back to identify intermediate factors, you can make these intermediate factors into measureable, meaningful goals. Making these intermediate factors into measureable objectives helps allocate organizational attention and effort across the range of things important to firm performance. Firms that only emphasize financial performance risk encouraging managers to take actions that boost short-term performance, but hurt long-term performance. Any firm can improve its net income this year by cutting employee training and R&D, but such moves, at the extreme, hurt subsequent performance.

In essence, the balanced scorecard makes explicit the causal links between strategy and actions. It thus allows managers to test the validity of their assumptions about the organization and identify potential leverage points—what the organization can do differently to achieve its goals.

Bryson, Ackermann, Eden, and Finn present an alternative tool to clarify such causal links (see Tool #3 at the end of this chapter).[11] In their book, *Visible Thinking*, they recommend managers develop explicit diagrams that reflect how they believe the business factors interact. This makes causal assumptions clear and offers the potential for empirical estimation of some important connections. For example, what is the response of sales to increased marketing expenditures or hiring more sales people? Such causal diagrams also help focus managerial discussions on specific areas of disagreement.

SUMMARY

Firm capabilities, or what firms do well, underlie the extent to which a firm can implement its chosen strategy using its dominant logic. Capabilities include both threshold or hygiene capabilities (those that are essential for a firm to compete) and core capabilities (those that allow a firm to win); a variety of tangible and intangible resources underlie both these types of capabilities. Capabilities differ both how easily others can copy them and how much value they create for the firm. Identifying the real capabilities of a firm can lead to successful strategy implementation.

FOOD FOR THOUGHT

R epeated studies show that a number of commonly used management practices, for example, providing employees with feedback, keeping track of inventory, TQM, etc. improve firm performance. However, many firms do not implement these beneficial practices. Why do you think this is the case? Would you expect to see any patterns of adoption or nonadoption of practices across the globe?

TOOL #3: DEVELOPING A CAUSAL MAP

I n their book, *Visible Thinking*, Bryson, Ackermann, Eden, and Finn suggest causal mapping as a tool for solving complex problems. Bryson et al. describe the basic steps of this process as follows.

Situation: Imagine that your company wants to explore a new business stream. How would you do this?[12]

DEVELOPING A CAUSAL MAP

Step 1: Beginning the map

Begin the process by identifying participants. Ask participants to brainstorm ideas related to the issue or problem. Also ask participants to identify six to eight action statements beginning with a verb.

Note that participants may begin with negative positions (identifying things that may hold back the organization) before moving on positive actions or ideas.

Once participants have developed statements, ask participants to transfer each statement to a numbered "oval" and to post these ovals to a wall. Then, ask participants to group similar statements together in clusters.

At this point, at a very simplified level, you may have something like Figure 5.1.

Step 2: Identify a hierarchy of concepts that move the map from assertions and actions to overarching strategies and then to goals or negative goals. To achieve this, begin the process of linking, that is, developing chains

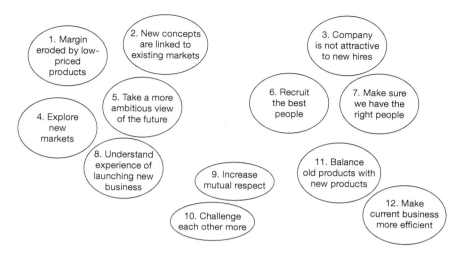

Figure 5.1 Step 1

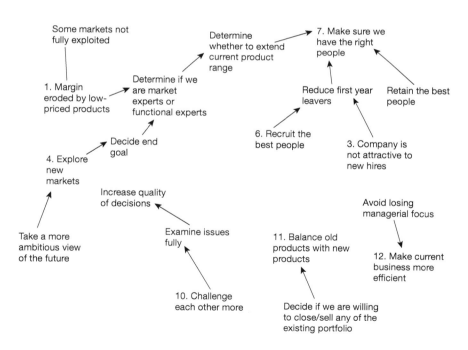

Figure 5.2 Step 2

of argumentation within each cluster. Linking makes the big picture more apparent. For example, your causal map may now look like Figure 5.2.

Step 3: Used the linked map to identify strategies and goals. At this point, the statements should become more inclusive, general, and abstract.

Your causal map may end up looking like Figure 5.3.

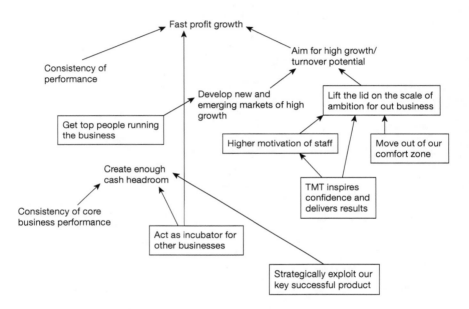

Figure 5.3 Step 3

Step 4: Finish the map by making commitments to action. Have participants attach priorities to goals, strategies, and actions.

Finally, follow up by providing a tangible product, along with an explanation of next steps and details of agreed actions and people responsible for completing those actions.

NOTES AND BIBLIOGRAPHY

1. Prahalad, C. K., and Hamel, G. "The Core Competence of the Corporation," *Harvard Business Review* 68(3) (1990):79–91.
2. Prahalad, C. K., and Bettis, R. A. "The Dominant Logic—A New Linkage between Diversity and Performance," *Strategic Management Journal* 7(6) (1986):485–501.
3. Deutsch, C. H. "Chief Says Kodak Is Pointed in the Right Direction," *New York Times* (December 25, 1999). http:// nytimes.com/1999/12/25/business/chief-says-kodak-is-pointed-in-the-right-direction.html
4. Duncan, R. D. "How Campbell Soup's Former CEO Turned the Company Around," *Fast Company*, 4 Minute Read (2014), www.fastcompany.com/3035830/how-campbells-soups-former-ceo-turned-the-company-around (accessed March 14, 2017).
5. Kim, C., and Bettis, R. A. "Cash is Surprisingly Valuable as a Strategic Asset," *Strategic Management Journal* 35(13) (2014):2053–2063.
6. Simon, R., and Chao, L. "The No. 1 Filer of Patent Suits," *Wall Street Journal* (October 28, 2016): A1.
7. Porter, M. E. "What is Strategy?" *Harvard Business Review* (November–December 1996):61–78.
8. Szulanski, G., and Winter, S. "Getting It Right the Second Time," *Harvard Business Review* 80(1) (2002):62–69.
9. Cohen, W. M., and Levinthal, D. A. "Absorptive Capacity: A New Perspective on Learning and Innovation," *Administrative Science Quarterly* 35(1) (1990):128–152.
10. Kaplan, R. S., and Norton, D. P. "The Balanced Scorecard—Measures That Drive Performance," *Harvard Business Review* 70(1) (1992):71–79.
11. Bryson, J. M., Ackermann, F., Eden, C., and Finn, C. B. *Visible Thinking* (Hoboken, NJ: John Wiley & Sons, 2004).
12. The figures presented here are a simplified version of some of the figures in *Visible Thinking*.

CHAPTER 6

Industry Life Cycles

You have probably learned about the product life cycle in marketing. Industries also have life cycles. Let us begin with an example.

The personal computer industry began with a few firms making equipment that hobbyists could use to make very primitive computers. Soon, many companies entered the industry; these companies made fully operating computers, often with proprietary operating systems. Eventually, IBM entered the fray with the MS-DOS operating system. This evolved into what we now know as Windows, and quickly became the most common operating system. It became a standard: a set of technical specifications by which we can have different products interact together. The number of competing operating systems and substantively different technology standards rapidly collapsed while sales volume of computers (and the associated operating system, Windows) took off. Through this growth period, new users bought personal computers repeatedly and consistently. Eventually, the technological and service differentiation the customer perceived early in the industry declined as customers began to perceive the products of different personal computer suppliers as interchangeable—almost commodities. Finally, the industry had fewer new users to sell to, so sales growth flattened. Simultaneously, new industries like smart phones with computing power took off. Many would argue that eventually, few people will buy the workhorse of the personal computer industry—total sales of desktop computers will decline. Thus, we have an industry life cycle for the desktop computer industry from birth to potential decline.

Nothing guarantees that an industry will follow this full cycle. Sometimes, technological innovation can keep renewing the industry as new technologies force customers to switch their equipment, resulting in a continuing growth in demand. For example, TV manufacturers continue to develop new technologies resulting in many consumers discarding their current TVs. However, demand cannot continue to grow exponentially forever.

Observers often describe industry life cycles in four stages: birth or introduction, growth, maturity, and decline. Figure 6.1 illustrates these stages. Let's talk about each in turn.

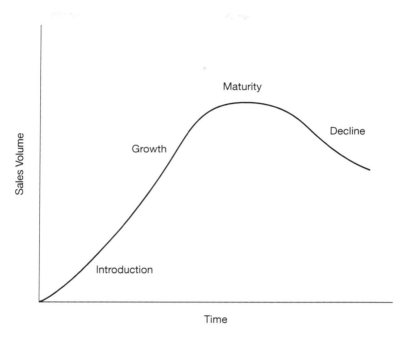

Figure 6.1 Stages in the Industry Life Cycle

INDUSTRY BIRTH/INTRODUCTION

While by definition only one company can be first into an industry, very often, many firms enter a fledgling industry almost simultaneously. Early in the life cycle of automobiles, hundreds of companies developed competing automobile products using a variety of technological solutions.

In the early years of an industry, many of the features we take for granted later in the industry life cycle (i.e., things that we will consider standard) have not have been defined. At the dawn of the automobile industry, for example, firms produced cars with propulsion systems based on electricity, steam, diesel, and gasoline. The early years of the videotape industry saw a competition between two very different technologies to record programs—namely, beta and VHS. Currently, in the self-driving car industry, manufacturers offer a variety of technologies and features; eventually, some features will become standard, and others will disappear.

This early heterogeneity reflects several things. First, no one knows exactly how the different technologies will develop. Different technologies will develop at different rates and in different ways.

Second, no one knows what combination of features and performance will appeal most to customers. Indeed, customers themselves have difficulty imagining what they want from a new product. Early in the life cycle of mobile phones, customers could have told you they wanted high tone quality and an ability to call from anywhere, but few would have dreamed they would need or want the computing power and flexibility of the modern smart phone. Mobile phone companies largely saw the demand as restricted to business users paying high fees for the service.

Early in the development of a technology, many industries struggle to convince customers to try the product. While some products like the Sony Walkman or the MP3 player may solve a problem that many people perceived relatively quickly and thus achieve general usage rapidly, often, consumers do not see the need for particular products. App stores have many apps that solve problems customers did not want solved. In addition, different age groups and different cultures have different proclivities to try new things. Most of you have probably heard a parent or grandparent saying that they had always done without a particular product, and hence, do not need it.

Usually, the finally successful product differs substantially from the product the innovator anticipated. Early experience in trying to sell and support a product results in feedback on customer preferences. Customer preferences evolve. Customers imagine uses for products or new features for products that the inventors never considered. Perhaps most famously, early observers saw the digital computer as strictly a tool for computation-intensive science and so claimed the entire global market for high-power computing machinery was about 10 computers. As computers hit the market, people found new uses for them. The originators of the Internet never dreamed how embedded it would become in our lives.

For a technology to reach full potential, we need an industry standard—a dominant design—to emerge. Technological standards not only cover almost any case where different product categories must interact, they also enable the development of a wide set of product support capabilities. Think of all the support services our cars need—standard grades of oil and gasoline available from thousands of stations, service centers, and mechanics ready to repair the cars, parts suppliers, car insurance, laws governing driving, driver training, etc. All of these need to be in place for the car to have its full value and require convergence on a narrow set of automobile designs.

Dominant designs surround us; often, they are so dominant that we cannot even perceive what alternatives might look like. Thus, we all know what a filter coffee maker should look like. Apartment houses share strong design commonalities as do most types of buildings. Dominant designs not only help consumers they also direct the future development of a technology.

Dominant designs are not necessarily inherently better than alternative designs. Think about electric outlets. While countries use many different designs for electric sockets, they all do the job. Nevertheless, countries need a standard design to make equipment compatible. The dominant design for a restaurant meal also varies around the world, where some countries charge for bread or drinking water and others do not, some provide a wide variety of salads before the meal without charge and others do not, some expect tipping while others do not, etc. Having a dominant design makes the exchange between the supplier and buyer of the product much easier.

Sometimes, in the beginning of an industry, companies do not know exactly how the industry will make money—what we call the business model. For example, for many years, software companies sold copies of their software to new users. By continually changing the products, the companies could repeatedly sell to the same consumers. Now, however, companies tend to treat software as a service. Instead of buying the software, we often lease it. Interestingly, the reverse is true for computer hardware; at the beginning of the computer industry, IBM leased rather than sold computers. Internet startups fell somewhere between the two models: before the crash of 2001, many Internet startups had websites individuals liked to visit, but did not know how to generate income from such websites—would users pay a monthly fee, a fixed fee per usage, no fee but tolerate advertising, etc.? Indeed, how to generate revenue remains a continuing challenge for internet start-ups.

Let us introduce one final important concept here—network effects, sometimes called positive externalities. In many industries, the value of the product to one person depends partially on whether other people use it. Most of us use one of two computer operating systems and one of a very small set of application programs. We do this partially because using the same programs as others increases the value of the products. Using the same operating system as our friends or the same operating system throughout a company lets us ask for help when we run into trouble, share programs, documents, and related material, and so forth. The number of users influences how many developers will write for an operating system, and having more software makes the operating system more valuable to users. Social networking offers the extreme example of network externalities; there is no point in belonging to a social network without other members. Much of the value of LinkedIn or Facebook derives from the many other people using them.

Network externalities appear in many places. In eBay, the more buyers who use the site, the more the sellers want to be on that site, and so on in a positive feedback cycle. The value you get as a buyer from eBay increases with the number of other users since this drives the number of sellers offering a wider variety of products at competitive prices. For new car technologies, such as fuel cells or full electric propulsion, more users will increase the availability of service, fuel, and electric connections.

Industries spend different lengths of time in the initial or birth stage. MP3 players took off quickly with technological standards, similar products, and the supporting industries necessary to make them work well. In contrast, people did not recognize the potential of high-speed computing for many years. The duration of the initial stage depends on a wide variety of factors, both technological and business related. Apple's adoption of the MP3 format and IBM's adoption of the MS-DOS format created standards that let the industries move from initial to growth stages quickly.

Often, the number of current users significantly influences how many new users we get. People hear about the buzz surrounding new products from their friends or from a variety of media or other social sources of information. That is, the number of current users approximates how many people will hear about the product from their friends or know about it. Thus, we might see continued 20 or 25 percent growth rates for a given category of product because current users inform other potential users about the product, thus driving growth. This results in many new products growing at a constant rate for several years. A constant growth rate results in exponential growth of total demand.

GROWTH

O nce we have one or a small number of dominant designs and consumer acceptance, a variety of things change.

The emergence of a dominant design means that the rate of technological innovation declines. That is, innovation remains, but now it is along a defined trajectory rather than across a wide range of potential technologies. Technologies that did not become dominant languish and often disappear. Standardization of products makes mass production more efficient and increases the likelihood that we will see process innovation as firms compete to produce standard or well-defined products more cheaply. This kind of competition generally improves quality and lowers costs.

Many companies struggle to make this transition. The managers and organizations that innovated effectively and handled the uncertainty of industry genesis often have difficultly producing a smaller set of products cheaply or at satisfying customer needs in other ways. Frequently, the managers that started the company exit (often forced by investors); growth firms need different managerial skills than startup firms. Greater clarity on the business model, technology, and size of the market may draw large competitors into the industry, and some of the original firms usually exit.

In the early growth stage of the industry, firms typically race to gain economies of scale, to advance the technology to deter entry by new competitors, or to develop customer allegiance. This race often begins at the end of the birth stage, but often continues through the early part of the growth stage.

Organizationally, the surviving firms often find the growth stage exceedingly comfortable. In an industry growing at 10 percent year, a company can grow at 10 percent just by maintaining its market share. Firms often reward managers for growth even if that growth just matches industry growth. Sometimes, industry growth lulls some firms into a false sense of achievement; firms can have growing sales and profits even while the firm loses market share.

MATURITY

Nothing can grow at 20 percent a year forever; every industry eventually becomes mature. At some point, the industry runs out of new customers to sell to and sales growth slows to a replacement rate. At the same time, customers become better informed and more knowledgeable. As you might expect from a five forces analysis, this better information and increased knowledge increases price pressure on the industry.

Price pressure also occurs because most organizations use revenue and profit targets for managers that increase each year. Whereas during the growth stage, every company could meet increased yearly targets simply by maintaining market share, this does not work in maturity. Without market growth, meeting targets for increased sales and profits means a firm must take sales and customers from its competitors. Competition often becomes extremely intense.

Industries frequently enter maturity with overcapacity, worsening the situation. If many companies invest in new capacity assuming continued industry growth, when growth slows in maturity, the industry can find itself with substantial overcapacity. Such overcapacity results in downward price pressure.

Managers may not know, in advance, when the industry reaches maturity. Real sales often do not follow a textbook revenue curve like Figure 6.1. On top of that curve, substantial variation comes from various macro-economic and other factors. Firms may have difficulty differentiating between short-term revenue variation and industry maturity. Given that continued industry growth makes managers' lives easier, managers have a bias toward assuming continued growth.

Various factors change during maturity. First, as customers put more price pressure on producers, firms increase the cost reduction moves we discussed in terms of low-cost strategies earlier in the book, such as developing economies of scale, cost cutting, and lowering overhead.

Second, firms often find that they have more products than the market really wants. As mentioned previously, when Steve Jobs found he could not tell a relative which Apple computer to buy because he could not differentiate among his company's products, he dramatically reduced the number of products offered.

Often, the skills or techniques associated with the industry diffuse and become quite well-known by industry maturity. Although early in the product life cycle, firms may have had substantial proprietary knowhow and equipment, over time, patents run out or competitors learn to engineer around patents. Employee movements help transfer knowledge and skills across the industry, evening out skill differences across firms.

Sometimes, knowledgeable consumers and diffusion of technology change a highly differentiated product into a commodity. We discussed this in terms of the PC where IBM in the early years had a very powerful brand and a highly differentiated product. Over time, differences between manufacturers disappeared. Likewise, while early automobiles differed dramatically, over time, the range of performance narrowed as all manufacturers achieved relatively similar reliability and durability. While after World War II oil companies effectively differentiated their products through branding so that they could command a substantially higher price than nonbrand alternatives, consumers now see less difference among gasoline brands, making it harder for brands to charge much higher prices.

While fundamental technological innovation slows in mature industries and process innovation increases, some product innovation or business model innovation often continues. For example, we may see firms reaching out to customer groups that traditionally did not buy the company's products. We may see them trying to bundle their products in new and different ways. For example, in the mature restaurant industry, we see a variety of theme restaurants. In the 1990s in the retail books trade, bookstores tried to transform themselves from selling books into destinations where consumers could enjoy coffee and a nice environment as well as purchase books.

Often, both commodity and differentiated products continue to exist in mature industries. For example, while soft drinks and toothpaste are both mature industries in the United States, low cost and differentiated competitors remain.

While maturing industries generally move toward a narrower product range, sometimes we see the continued development of new and different segments, particularly those that have traditionally been more profitable than others. Social changes sometimes drive the development of these segments. For example, the trend toward healthier eating has resulted in an increased demand for organic foods in the mature food products industry.

In maturity, such segmentation may become more important because crowded traditional product categories or segments no longer generate good returns. Firms often try to move into the more profitable segments; Walmart and other large grocery stores, for example, followed Whole Foods by offering more natural or organic products. Alternatively, some firms continue to try to subdivide the market to add more segments trying to maintain profitability. Whether this work depends on how much customer needs (or perceived needs) vary. While the market for razors in the United States is clearly mature, if not declining, razor and razor blade companies continue to try to subdivide the market to find products of particular interest to subgroups while continuing to innovate within a given tradition.

Sometimes such differentiation occurs in the real product, but often it occurs in ancillary activities. For example, U.S. airlines face largely price sensitive customers who perceive customer experience either as not that important or as not that different across airlines. Here, airlines try to differentiate by providing frequent flyers benefits like early boarding, free trips, upgraded seating, etc.

Such changes—whether related to innovation or differentiation—often do not succeed. For example, frequent flyer programs, while having clear costs, often provide benefits to many travelers without changing their airline preference. Management in mature industries generally has developed a firm idea of how competition works in the industry. Often, management has difficultly imagining more than cosmetic changes.

Even in mature industries, leading firms often maintain high profits. Some may have strong brands resulting in continued customer loyalty. Others may have exceptional abilities for low-cost production. However, inherently, most firms cannot follow these strategies.

DECLINE

At some point, most industries decline. Having run out of the new customers who might want the product, demand falls to the replacement level. Sometimes, new technologies or new fashion overcome the industry's products.

The problems that started in the mature industry get worse. It becomes harder to differentiate and harder to find ways to innovate. Often, the average age of equipment and employees rises. Reductions in demand mean firms no longer hire new people to fill new jobs; many must lay off current employees. The most desirable employees either do not come to the industry or leave it.

With reductions in total demand, overcapacity becomes a major problem. However, companies often have difficulty eliminating excess capacity because assets tailored to this industry may have little value in other industries. At the extreme, such assets can have negative value. For example, many old steel plants and chemical-related facilities have negative value because the previous companies have so polluted the ground that fixing the pollution would cost more than the value of the property.

Think also of the problem of the manager in such an industry. With declining demand, the manager's skills become less valuable. Few companies in the industry want to hire. Management has a strong incentive to keep the business running as long as it has cash left to operate. As long as the company operates, management keeps its jobs. Consequently, such companies sometimes stay in business beyond where it makes economic sense.

By staying in business, such firms make things harder for everybody else. To stay in business, a firm needs sufficient cash to operate—a much lower level of profitability than generating a reasonable return on capital. If a company only wants to cover its cash costs, it can price at a level that allows it to do that—which means no one else earn a reasonable return on capital. In financial institutions, for example, banks or lending institutions with a high probability of bankruptcy have already lost all their investors' money. They have little left to lose. Consequently, they often take risky actions and offer loans at rates that no one else would reasonably offer. This lowers profitability for all the other firms in the industry.

Some firms adapt to this by shutting down some of their own capacity or by purchasing competitors and shutting them down. A free rider problem occurs here; if firm A removes excess capacity from the industry, the benefits from the improved industry structure accrue not only to firm A, but also to all the remaining firms in the industry. Firms may avoid spending money to reduce industry overcapacity when the spending will benefit their competitors as well.

Consider, for example, the global steel industry. While this industry is not in a decline stage, it is currently (as of 2016) facing overcapacity. Chinese steel mills, in particular, contribute heavily to the overcapacity problem; China has more surplus capacity in steel than the entire steel production of Japan, America, and Germany combined. While China's ruling State Council recognizes this problem and encourages consolidation among steel makers, consolidation has not reduced overcapacity substantially. While closing any single plant would benefit the global steel industry, the pain of closing the plant accrues only to a small group of people—in this case, the people who would lose their jobs as a result of closure and consolidation. Hence, Regional Communist Party officials (who actually have to implement the consolidation) prefer to keep local steel plants open with subsidies instead of shutting the plants and risking unemployment and unrest among the local populace.[1]

As with maturity, firms can have difficulty predicting demand in a declining industry. The cyclic variation from the business cycle often exceeds the variation from the underlying trend of declining demand. In addition, given all the incentive and cognitive structures we talked about before, managers may grasp for any straws of positive news while ignoring or underplaying the dangers of decline.

Succeeding in a declining industry requires a change in managers' mental models. For example, a study of U.S. railroad executives during a period of significant decline in the industry finds that managers of the more successful railroad changed their mental models while those of the unsuccessful did not. Where managers of the successful firm took 6 years to unlearn their old mental models and develop new ones (with the process of learning appearing to continue for at least 19 more years), managers of the unsuccessful firm did not appear to demonstrate a learning process at all, instead shifting abruptly from one mental model to another.[2] We return to this topic of learning in the next chapter where we consider how it influences the diffusion of a technology.

That said, several structures or strategies have worked for declining industries.[3]

LEADERSHIP

The largest or the lowest cost firm in a declining industry may sustain a reasonable profit level despite the havoc in the rest of the industry—a last man standing strategy. Even as the industry declines, pockets of demand may continue. As other firms exit the industry, the structure of the industry improves for the survivors. For example, 3M used to make a product that produced proofs for photographs for magazines. This product depended on film-based photography. Obviously, as photography became digital, the demand for the product collapsed. However, at least for some time, a residual demand existed from magazines unable to move to digital or from magazines that still preferred film photography.

After the Surgeon General's reports attacked smoking in the United States, smoking moved from a growth industry to a declining industry. However, several of the remaining companies have done very well. By investing in efficiency, and at the same time introducing new brands and products, Philip Morris remains highly profitable.

NICHE

Decline seldom influences all portions of the industry alike. Consequently, some firms may focus on small, desirable, or simply underserved niches and do quite well. For example, given very few U.S. producers of snuff (smokeless tobacco), the largest snuff producer does well. Likewise, a company that produces baby blankets for hospitals has an extremely high market share. These companies thrive despite tobacco, blankets, and bedding being stable or declining markets.

HARVEST

In some cases, a firm can use a business as a source of cash flow, that is, harvest the business. By not reinvesting in the business, a company in a declining industry can use the cash flow to invest in more profitable activities elsewhere.

DIVEST

Finally, a firm that anticipates decline and does not see a reason it would do well in decline often benefits by quitting early while the business appears valuable rather than waiting for the decline. Alternatively, as we discuss later in this book, some firms use global expansion to find local markets where the industry's products are still in the growth stage of their life cycle.

SUMMARY

Like products, industries go through different stages during their life cycle: introduction, growth, maturity, and decline. Firms face very different challenges as the industry moves from one stage to the next; these range from identifying a successful business model in the introduction stage, dealing with increased competition in the growth stage, and increasing efficiency or coming up with new innovations in the maturity stage.

FOOD FOR THOUGHT

Companies like Google (self-driving cars), Tesla (electric cars), Uber (taxis), and Airbnb (rental apartments) have come up with industry disrupting innovations. While incumbents in some of these industries have responded by trying to stop these new entrants (e.g., taxicab companies have tried to get legislation passed to restrict Uber), others (e.g., automobile companies) have ignored new entrants or tried to develop their own alternatives to the products offered by other new entrants (e.g., to electric cars). What might account for these differences in response?

NOTES AND BIBLIOGRAPHY

1. "Industry in China: The March of the Zombies," *The Economist*, February 27, 2016. www.economist.com/news/business/21693573-chinas-excess-industrial-capacity-harms-its-economy-and-riles-its-trading-partners-march. Accessed March 14, 2017.
2. Barr, P. S., Stimpert, J. L., and Huff, A. S. "Cognitive Change, Strategic Action, and Organizational Renewal," *Strategic Management Journal* 13 (1992):15–36.
3. See also Kim, W. C., and Mauborgne, R. "Blue Ocean Strategy," *Harvard Business Review* 82(10) (2004):76; Kim, W. C., and Mauborgne, R. "Blue Ocean Strategy: From Theory to Practice," *California Management Review* 47(3) (2005):105–121; Harrigan, K. R., and Porter, M. E. "End-Game Strategies for Declining Industries," *Harvard Business Review* 61(4) (1983):111–121.

CHAPTER 7

Technology and Its Impact on Industries

In the previous chapter, we talked about the different stages of the industry life cycle and the different challenges facing firms at each stage of the life cycle. However, the life cycle of an industry is not set in stone. In particular, changes in technology can disrupt an industry, throwing a mature industry back into the growth stage or accelerating its descent into decline. The development of online businesses like Amazon, for example, has led to the rapid decline of traditional bricks and mortar bookstores like Barnes and Noble as well as bricks and mortar computer stores like CompUSA and CircuitCity. In contrast, the move to digital television broadcasting has forced viewers to replace their functioning old televisions with new digital models.

To think about technology and its effects on industries, let us start with some terminology. First, the environment includes a certain amount of organizational knowledge and technical knowledge. Depending on the industry, advances in fundamental technological or scientific research feed into invention. In some industries, such as biotech, such advances have direct and substantial impacts on invention, while in others, such as publishing, the impact is more muted.

Second, we differentiate between invention and innovation. Invention means the discovery or creation of something new. Inventions include a wide variety of things from organizational processes to specific novel entities. The invention itself, though, is not generally suitable for selling as a product in the marketplace. Innovation includes the creation of something new and the transformation of that something new into a marketable form or a form that can influence something else that is marketable. For example, a chemist may invent or create a new molecule, but a firm might innovate by creating a new molecule and then converting that molecule into a demonstrably safe and effective drug that can cure a specific disease.

Sometimes people look at the time that has elapsed between filing the first patents and marketing the first commercial product based on those patents. For example, patents underlying certain kinds of jet engines appeared in the 1930s even though commercial jet engines did not become feasible until the 1950s. Many observers claim that the time between invention and innovation has declined in recent years. This goes along with the claim that the product life cycle has also become shorter. On these points, we are agnostic. We do not see how to sample appropriately to allow a rigorous estimate of the time between invention and innovation. In addition, such studies generally ignore the large fraction of inventions that never become innovations. Let us just say that at least some observers claim that the time between invention and product launch has declined. However, a businessperson cares more about the time to develop and launch a specific new product than the average time between invention and innovation.

Third, we differentiate between incremental and disruptive innovation. Incremental innovation refers to minor changes in a product for example, increasing a mobile phone's picture quality. Disruptive innovations or technologies, in contrast, fundamentally alter the product or service, for example, people reading books on e-readers rather than on paper. Given their huge impact on industries, we examine disruptive innovation in more detail below.

DISRUPTIVE INNOVATION

Disruptive innovation (relative to current technology) refers to a particular set of ideas about technological innovation. How do disruptive innovations develop?

First, extant firms in an industry generally communicate most with their most interesting and excited customers. Over time, these firms' products often become more sophisticated and more adapted to the interests of these power users rather than the average user. One only needs to look at the control panel on a modern business photocopy machine to see that the addition of new capabilities has made it harder for the casual user to make a copy. As we noted before, short textbooks grow in length until they are no longer short textbooks. People who work in automobile companies generally like cars. Consequently, they favor cars with more of what they see as desirable and attractive features over cars that fulfill simple transportation needs. Adding all of these new features allows extant companies to charge more for newer versions of their products—even though these newer versions often have features of little to no interest to the less sophisticated user.

This opens the door for disruptive innovations or technologies. At first, these new technologies often have lower performance than the old. Though often they sell at a lower price than products using older technologies, their cost structures are higher; they are not made as efficiently as products using existing technologies since they have not run down the learning curve and have not obtained economies of scale. For example, the original hybrid Prius lost Toyota substantial amounts of money for each car sold. New technologies often have bugs, resulting in higher service costs.

Often these new technologies find some buyers who find the current level of service or product features of incumbent companies excessive. They want a cheaper alternative with lower performance. Individuals who want a cheaper technology with lower performance or who specifically value the new technology itself support the new, disruptive technology.

However, the new technology improves more quickly than the older technology. Think about mobile phones. The original mobile phones were large, expensive, and had limited capabilities. Users who valued the flexibility of the mobile phone tolerated these drawbacks. However, the rate of change in mobile phone technology dwarfed the rate of change in land line technology. Likewise, with a new technology like fuel cells, we would also expect rapid changes and improvements in the technology. In contrast, we would expect that, after 100 years, gas and diesel powered engines will improve only incrementally. Consequently, these new entrants gain a foothold, get economies of scale, and move down the learning curve, at the same time as they improve their technology.

The incumbents often have difficulty meeting these challenges for several reasons. First, the incumbents listen to their current "best" customers—often the power or sophisticated users—who want the more sophisticated products as defined by the traditional technology. Second, firms make much higher profits on the more sophisticated products than on the less sophisticated products. In the United States, the U.S. car manufacturers have had difficulty becoming fully committed to small cars because their profit margins on SUVs and luxury cars have been much higher than on small vehicles. Third, the incumbents are often cognitively committed to the older technology. Anyone who was a top manager in a U.S. automobile company in the middle of the twentieth century grew up and worked most of his or her career in a world of gasoline internal combustion engines where bigger was better. After succeeding for many decades with a given set of premises, managers have difficulty giving up those premises (not to mention the organizational expertise, systems, processes, and incentives they have built around these premises) in favor of the unknown. Consequently, incumbents often do not respond effectively to entrants with disruptive new technologies, letting the entrants grow and often come to dominate the industry.

The inability of incumbents to meet challenges of entrants stem at least partially from organizational and cognitive factors, making them hard to fix. Two features are often necessary.[1] First, you need top management or some portion of the powerful individuals in top management to understand the problem and invest in trying to solve it. This includes a willingness to consider new mental models or dominant logics. Second, you often need to segregate the individuals trying to respond to the new technology—in ways that are distinct from the ongoing business—so they can make progress in adopting the new technology. For example, IBM created a separate facility far from the rest of its facilities to develop the IBM PC. We should note that this does not always work, particularly if the first component—top management commitment—is missing. For example, General Motors tried to set up a different kind of a car company with the Saturn—it had separate plants, separate dealerships, etc. However, in spite of a good response from customers, GM shut down Saturn essentially because Saturn represented a complete departure from GM's traditional model of car manufacturing.[2]

WHO WILL LEAD?

Firms differ greatly in their orientation toward substantial technological change. Part of the difference depends on whether the changes enhance or destroy the value of current capabilities.

Capability-enhancing changes do not change the fundamental bases of competition while improving performance on current capabilities. Thus, many firms work on technological changes that improve current products or even invent new products, but largely retain current technologies. For example, technological changes that make PC mechanical disk drives faster and cheaper are capability enhancing. Organizations usually embrace such changes. Indeed, technology companies usually have routines carefully designed to push technological advance in such dimensions.

In contrast, capability-destroying inventions do not improve current products; instead, moving from one fundamental technology to another often destroys the capabilities that an organization built in the previous technology. For example, cloud storage reduces the value of fast disk drives in computers, and requires a different business model than conventional disk drives. Likewise, e-commerce destroys many of the benefits that accrue from having many stores and expert, highly paid, salespeople. Improvements in medicine to treat certain diseases can lower the need for surgery but the skills to develop medicines have little overlap with the skills for surgery.

Organizations develop and adopt capability-enhancing innovations more readily than they do technologies that damage their traditional sources of advantage. Thus, our disk drive manufacturer that can adapt rapidly to changes in the composition or technical features of mechanical PC disk drives is unlikely to lead the industry into cloud-based storage.

Many recommend larger companies invest in projects of different levels of time horizon and change, often using tools such as McKinsey's Three Horizons framework.[3] Thus, larger firms may want a portfolio of research projects that include short-term improvement of current technologies, medium-term investigation of moderately different approaches, and long-term investigation of substantially different technologies. Thus, in the short term, our PC disk manufacturer might invest in improving performance of current disk products, in the medium term look at other formats for mechanical–electrical disk drives, and in the long term look at fundamentally different technologies.

However, by definition, *capability*-destroying change makes the capabilities that gave the firm its current levels of performance less valuable. Often the current producers have no particular advantage under the new technology. For example, the mechanical–electrical design and manufacturing skills critical to manufacturers of traditional disk drives become of little importance when manufacturers switch to making solid state drives.

Sometimes, technological change literally destroys incumbent firms. Almost none of the typewriter makers survived the move to PCs. An immense majority of the moderate and low-priced watch makers died when watches became electrical. A great many bricks and mortar retailers (including many of the leading computer stores) went bankrupt and continue to go bankrupt with the move to internet retailing. Even if these firms saw the change coming, many of them lacked skills to win in the new technologies.

These patterns continue. AOL dominated internet service provision when most users connected through phone modems, but did not thrive once hard-wired connections became the norm. Cable providers and telephone companies largely eclipsed AOL because their wired connections to homes gave them technological capabilities AOL could not duplicate. HP, once a technological leader, has suffered for many years. As HP became largely a PC and printer firm, the technologies for both became widely available making price critical, but HP historically has not been a low-cost producer. Both AOL and HP face a world where their traditional sources of advantage have questionable value. Traditional telephone and PC manufacturers did not succeed in establishing a durable early leadership position in smart phones. Indeed, most did not enter the smart phone market although Apple successfully entered the market very late. We will discuss the possibilities for late entrants later in this chapter, but let us note that normally their success depends on other capabilities rather than technological leadership. Many of the innovations moving to internet-based services derive from new entrants rather than traditional providers of similar services.

However, technological changes do not necessarily doom all incumbents to irrelevance. For example, after many years, a small proportion of bricks and mortar retailers succeeded in moving to the online world. Often, they have some underlying capabilities that new online entrants have difficulty replicating. For example, in the aftermarket for auto parts, the large bricks and mortar chains have substantial economies of scale in purchasing and warehousing (when you need an immense number of items available, large scale is an advantage). Thus, online auto parts dealers have had difficulty replacing the bricks and mortar firms and bricks and mortar firms may have the time they need to succeed in going online.[4]

When faced with technological change, incumbents have several options.[5] First, firms should ask if they could leverage their current advantages under the new technological regime. Thus, when biotechnology began to encroach on drug invention, large drug companies leveraged their skills in regulatory approvals and marketing. Indeed, large drug companies routinely purchase biotechnology companies after they find promising drugs, and then handle the costly and time-consuming regulatory approval and marketing stages. Some large bricks and mortar retailers have leveraged their market power in purchasing along with their brand names to move into internet sales.

Second, firms may need to view the old technology as a declining industry and apply the strategies noted in the previous chapter—sell out early, find profitable niches, and use cash flow from the old technology to find and enter new industries where their capabilities have value.

WHY IS IT HARD FOR INCUMBENTS TO ADAPT TO NEW TECHNOLOGIES?

Several things make it hard for incumbent firms to adapt to the new world. An effective organization requires an effective integration among the parts. Strategy, structure, and systems are like a three-legged stool: they must all fit together for the organization to work effectively. While one might imagine that managers come up with a strategy and then implement the strategy by making appropriate changes to the organization's structures and systems, in reality, current structure and systems influence managerial choice. Organizations' existing structures and systems strongly influence the data that managers have available, and therefore, the strategies and technological paths they see as promising. Existing structures and systems also substantially influence the difficulty and cost of implementing new strategies.

Further, as we discussed previously, some managers have trouble imagining truly different worlds. Having grown up under a given technological regime, people often have difficulty recognizing new technological regimes until these regimes have completely taken command. This observation ties to our earlier discussion of the cognitive limits of managers.[6] With a few exceptions, visionaries come from outside the industry or from the junior management or technology ranks rather than from the senior management of current large firms.

Many industries have a history where firm employees envision major technological changes that their employers reject, so the employees start their own firms. The history of Silicon Valley involves many such establishments. Likewise, many employees have left medical technology firms to found new firms using technology their previous employers did not want.

Sometimes, difficulties in moving to a new technology also tie into organizational politics. Any organization consists of people who have interests of their own separate from those of the organization. They interpret change or potential change as positive or negative to the extent that it improves or hurts their position or their interests. Indeed, it would be quite naïve for anyone not to do so. Currently powerful individuals often have a lot invested in the existing technology, organization, and customers. Such individuals may resist technological change if it damages their positions.

As you would expect, the politics vary dramatically across firms. Some technology- or innovation-oriented firms readily adopt new technologies, at least within the domain of their normal business. That is, they often have a domain within which they expect rapid technological change and often hope to drive such change. Here, the politics and systems favor such change. That does not necessarily mean they welcome technological change in other areas of the business.

In addition, previous success makes change more difficult. Successful organizations have difficulty changing fundamentally. Consequently, if you want to change a successful organization, you have to take steps to define it as unsuccessful. For example, if you wanted to make a division willing to change, you would need to set the targets for the division that it cannot reach by conducting business as usual. To reach these targets, divisions will have to take riskier actions than before, opening them to the idea of significant change. GE and many other companies use this technique under the rubric of stretch goals.

However, some firms adapt quite well to change. The adaptation often is within capability-enhancing technological changes rather than technology destroying changes.[7] A software company can readily perceive and adapt to new applications and even new hardware while its underlying skills in understanding customer needs and software design remain valuable. Nevertheless, change is harder than one might imagine. Microsoft dominated the PC operating system market for many years and succeeded in adding new applications packages over time, but its efforts to move into smart phones have not worked out so well.

Google could readily move into new kinds of software and new platforms, but may have greater difficulty moving into hardware. Whether Microsoft's and Google's moves into radically different technologies (hardware, cars, etc.) will work out remains unclear. Both firms may have a better than normal chance of succeeding in fundamentally different technologies because they both grew up in industries with rapid technological change and have extremely large resources.

HOW CAN YOU INTRODUCE NEW TECHNOLOGIES INTO ORGANIZATIONS?

Our discussion about incumbents' adaptability to new technologies has important implications for how you introduce new technologies into organizations. If you want to introduce a new technology in a large organization, you probably want to look for a low performance division or group. Such divisions know they need help and so often are more receptive to new technology and potential improvement whereas the successful divisions see less need for change. While high performing groups still seek improvement, they are less likely to make massive changes than lower performance groups. Given their past success with the existing technology, high performance divisions will feel that their best chance for future growth and profitability lies in continuing with that technology.

Firms also face limitations because they generally learn from experience, which means they know a lot about the old technology and relatively little about the new. Furthermore, the available data addresses the old technology rather than the new. Our disk drive manufacturer can accurately estimate the cost structure of modest changes in disk drives and the benefits from investing in particular innovations in mechanical disk drives. It has greater difficulty thinking about or estimating the costs and benefits of solid-state drives and even newer technologies.

Think about how companies estimate the value of a particular investment. Many firms use formal management tools like net present value. Unfortunately, these tools have an inherent conservative bent. Investments that marginally modify the current system will have much better data and much better substantiated budget requests than those trying to do something truly innovative. Cost reduction often has quicker returns than real innovation. Since management processes generally prefer good justifications over vague ones and quicker returns over delayed returns, the system usually favors incremental over substantial change.

This is not a statement about bad people—it is a statement about people behaving normally, and systems resisting change. Consequently, substantial change often requires sponsorship from the top; to be effective, such change usually requires change in multiple domains and such changes often require top management backing.

The ability of an organization to change also depends heavily on the ability of an organization to learn.[8] While organizations often learn from experience, organizations may also learn vicariously, from the experience of others. However, consider the potential traps awaiting organizations as they try to learn about new technological regimes. When learning from others, as happens during the diffusion of a technology, organizations may only gain an incomplete understanding of the new technology. Alternatively, the new technology may turn out to be a fad, in which case organizations have learned something without long-term value. When learning from experience, as we noted in our discussion of politics and change, different groups may evaluate an outcome as a success or a failure depending on whether they see the accompanying organizational change as positive or negative for themselves. In addition, organizations may learn superstitiously, with managers developing mistaken beliefs about the potential of a new technology based on their limited experience with it. In part, this arises because organizational learning often uses small sample sizes; managers do not have the luxury of repeatedly making the same changes to their routines to observe if these changes consistently lead to desired outcomes (such as the successful adoption of a new technology). In sum, while organizations must learn to adapt successfully to a new technology, the process of learning is fraught with potential missteps.

Throughout, we must remember that hindsight is 20/20. We can easily look back and say that the firm should have done something. Indeed, after almost any major system failure, you can look back and find that somebody warned management about that problem. However, somebody also probably warned management about 50 other problems that did not actually occur. We can look at the successes of Airbnb or Uber, but often forget the large number of internet-based startups that fail. While we know we need some revolutionaries, management sometimes has difficulty differentiating the geniuses with new ideas from the fools. Even the best run innovative companies generally try out many products that do not work out.

WHO KEEPS THE MONEY FROM INNOVATION?

Just as the five forces analysis dealt with who benefits most from a product or service, the value created during the manufacture of a product accrues unevenly to the participants in that value creation; the benefits of innovation are not always allocated in the manner one might imagine. The primary beneficiaries from innovation might be the suppliers, the customers, the innovator, or the innovators' competitors who follow.

We examine two major factors that determine who benefits from an innovation: the protection of the innovation or intellectual capital, and the presence of complementary resources. Let us consider how these work.

PROTECTION OF INNOVATION/INTELLECTUAL CAPITAL

Innovating firms must worry about how to protect the innovation. Innovation normally involves intellectual capital. Intellectual capital is a catch all term that refers to any nonphysical things that have value. Firms have several ways to protect intellectual capital including patents, copyrights, trademarks, and secrecy. Copyright applies to written or otherwise recorded intellectual contributions including software. For largely political reasons, in the United States, copyright has a very long duration relative to patents. Trademarks refer to the exclusive right to use specific words or symbols to distinguish goods. Trademarks may also be registered. Patents refer to the registration of intellectual property involved in processes for doing, machines, manufactured articles, the way an article appears, newly invented asexually reproduced plants, and chemical compositions.

Copyrights, trademarks, and patents fall under a legal system in which innovators file their innovation with a government agency (or with the World Intellectual Property Organization for a worldwide patent). After review, the agency decides if the innovation is real and if it is new. If the agency decides it is real and new, the filer receives a copyright, trademark, or patent. Copyrights and patents provide the producer the right to the fruits of that innovation or entity and the right to control that innovation for a set number of years. Trademarks must be periodically renewed but may extend indefinitely.

While this sounds good in theory, firms have some significant problems relying solely on copyrights or patents to protect innovations. First, the copyright or patent does not self-enforce. The firm must sue companies that infringe on the patent. A small company or one that lacks funds may have trouble suing a big company that infringes on a patent. Sometimes, large companies can outspend and out-delay most small companies.

Patent enforcement varies by country. Some companies contracting for manufacturing innovations oversees find their manufacturer produces for the patent holder and then turns around and produces equivalent products that it sells through other channels. While this violates patent law, innovators often must sue in the country where the violation occurred. Innovators who win a judgment must also have the legal ability to get the judgment enforced. Both can be difficult. A small company may lack the funds to sue another company halfway around the world. Further, the suit may be heard in courts run by fellow countrymen of the sued company, who may favor local companies. Some foreign countries see great benefits in violation of specific copyrights or patents. For example, people in the third world countries seldom see value in upholding the first world drug patents that keep drug costs high. At the worst, one can win a lawsuit only to have the sued company close shop and disappear—and then appear again under a new name.

Partly to overcome some of these problems, companies often do not patent some patentable innovations. To patent something you have to provide information about what that something does and generally how it works. This can provide competitors useful information on viable technical approaches. Some companies prefer to keep things secret. The trade-off here between secrecy and patents varies substantially across industries and across technologies. Thus, in some industries, firms try to patent a great many inventions, and in other industries, very few.

Firms often try to restrict the flow of information from their companies by requiring employees sign contracts that restrict the employee from working for competitors within a given amount of time after leaving the company. In the United States, state law governs such restrictions. However, state law also varies as to whether the firms can actually enforce the restrictions. For example, in California, firms cannot enforce restrictions on subsequent employment even though companies can ask employees to sign such contracts. However, this does not mean that the employee can take secrets and give them to another company. It just means the employee can work for someone else. To actually take secrets and provide them to a competitor constitutes theft of intellectual property.

Firms also try to protect intellectual capital by relying on lead time. If it will take the competitors a long time to copy an innovation, then a firm may achieve a scale or create a brand that makes copying exceedingly difficult. Often, this means that the competitors were not paying attention when you started. We have seen this in a variety of niche drink products such as energy drinks, athletic drinks, etc., where large drink companies ignored small innovators long enough for the innovators to establish reliable and defensible brand positions.

While this discussion talks about intellectual capital as specific things, some apply the term to the intellectual abilities of a firm. Firms use confidentiality and noncompete clauses in attempting to restrict the flow of such abilities. In the end, retaining intellectual abilities require the creation of a situation where the best and brightest find continued employment with your company preferable to their options with other companies.

Tesla has adopted a very different approach to intellectual capital. Elon Musk, the founder of Tesla, announced on the firm's blog in 2014 that "Tesla will not initiate patent lawsuits against anyone who, in good faith, wants to use our technology."[9] Tesla appears to assume this will allow the rapid development of the electric vehicle industry around standards created by Tesla, thereby benefiting the company. Whether this approach (similar to Google's decision to make its Android system open source) will benefit or hurt Tesla in the end remains unclear.

COMPLEMENTARY ACTIVITIES

Who benefits from an innovation also depends on the innovator's ability to create the set of complementary activities necessary to commercialize the innovation. To profit from a new gadget, you need financing to support the development of the product. You need to manufacture that product. You need distribution. You probably need marketing and after-market service. Sometimes, the value of the product depends heavily on the availability of complementary technologies and products. For example, the value of a digital music technology depends on the availability of digital music for that specific technology. In addition, as we discussed in the previous chapter, the value of a product may depend on network externalities—the value of the product to one person depends partially on whether other people use it.

If you have or can create these complementary activities efficiently or can buy them in an efficient market, then proceeding with the innovation becomes more attractive. However, if you cannot build this constellation of activities in a competitive way, then you should seriously consider licensing the innovation or collaborating with someone else with the activities. Often, inventors err on the side of producing the product themselves rather than licensing it to someone else.

How would this work? Suppose you invented a better personal hygiene product like liquid soap. What would happen once your company tries to sell your product?

First, you will have trouble getting it in front of the consumer. Stores like Target and Walmart sell a substantial portion of personal care products but have little interest in dealing with small companies that have only one or two marketable items, are of questionable reliability, and cannot back up their product with much advertising.

Second, a shortage of resources and marketing capabilities means that the company has difficulty achieving a substantial, defensible market position before well-funded competitors catch up. These competitors probably do not violate the innovator's patents. However, when a competitor sees how something can be done in general terms and that the customer wants it, the competitor often can engineer around patents to produce products as good as, or even better than, the innovator's product.

While the innovator struggles to find the funds for development and production, struggles to gain access to distribution channels, struggles to learn how to manufacture or market (or contract out manufacturing or marketing), large competitors already have these things. 3M and similar companies can successfully innovate repeatedly partially because they already have systems built around innovation, and have all of the complementary activities required to bring innovations to market.

In such a situation, the inventing company often gains more by licensing the invention to a large competitors than it would by trying to sell a product based on the invention. Not only does this save all the trouble of building the company, a small percentage of a large volume produced by licensing to a large competitor often generates more profits than full ownership of a smaller volume.

The availability of the necessary complementary resources at market or competitive prices varies dramatically. For example, dairies routinely produce products for multiple brand names. Consequently, a firm might launch a dairy product without having to produce it oneself. Similarly, breweries often produce beers for multiple beer companies using the other company's recipes. For many years, Samuel Adams brewed relatively little of its beer, contracting most of the production out to other companies. In other areas, contract manufacturing may not be a viable option.

Sometimes firms do overcome a lack of complementary resources. With very defensible intellectual property, complementary assets become less critical. Alternatively, if competitors cannot quickly launch me-too products, or competitors ignore your product long enough, and the innovator can achieve efficient scale, then the innovator may create a defensible position. Often firms generate scale and brand value by operating in smaller markets that large competitors do not address well, and then use that scale and brand to extend into new markets.

We now turn to some practical tools you can use to predict and respond to industry and technological changes (including changes to the industry life cycle that we discussed in the previous chapter).

FORECASTING

Large amounts of research demonstrate that most firms, most of the time, react to their past. However, ideally, they would actually spend more of their time considering the future. This requires forecasting.

While we will discuss forecasting in technology industries, forecasting must underlie almost any serious attempt at strategy formulation in any industry.

A massive literature addresses forecasting, and indeed, entire journals are devoted to the topic; let's talk about several basics.[10]

NUMERIC TECHNIQUES

Firms can use a variety of techniques to predict some important parameters. Let us consider three of the easiest.

First, within a given technological regime, technology and various other factors often develop in a way that you can easily predict from past results. Figure 7.1, for example, plots hard disk capacity over time. Figure 7.2 plots the line width of Intel processors over time. Line width is a critical parameter in products such as processors. Thinner lines let you cram more on a given chip, shortening the connections and increasing the speed.

However, neither Figure 7.1 nor Figure 7.2 looks very easy to forecast.

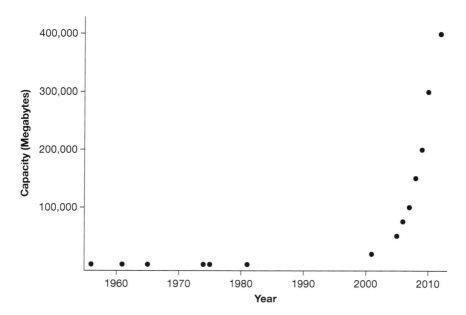

Figure 7.1 Hard Disk Capacity Over Time

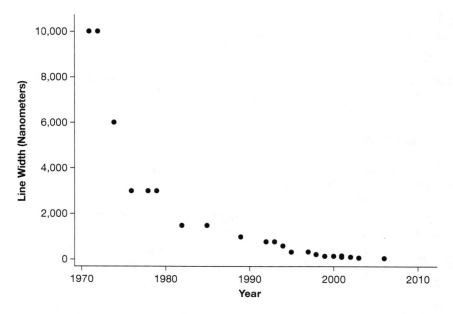

Figure 7.2 Line Width versus Year

If instead of working with the actual variable, we work with the log of that variable, odd curves often become linear. As we noted earlier, constant growth rates result in exponential growth. Thus, Figure 7.3 plots the log of the data from Figure 7.2. We can easily use simple tools like Excel's trend function to predict the future log and then take the exponential of that prediction to give us a predicted value. Often, you may want to correct for the difference between predicted and actual on the last value of the term of the series. For example, the prediction for 2008 is 0.2 above the actual value.

Prediction appears in a wide variety of contexts, including many operational issues. For example, commercial lending depends on predicting the likelihood of a borrower defaulting. In general, if you have a defined set of data and a defined outcome, you can build a simple model that will substantially assist any human decision maker. Indeed, such models often predict better than the experts do.

LIMIT ANALYSIS

In some cases, we can refine the above analysis if we know the factor of interest faces some notional limits; most processes face technological or

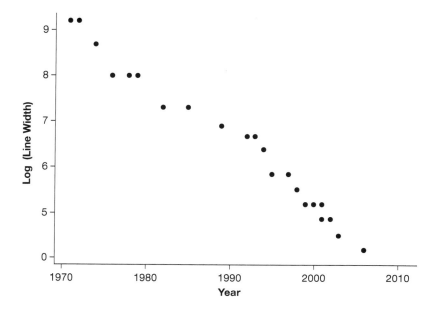

Figure 7.3 Log of Line Width

market limits. Equipment will never weight less than nothing, and sales growth cannot continue indefinitely.

TREND CORRELATION

Often, one product follows the technological developments in another product. For example, battery technology strongly influences the performance of electric vehicles. Consequently, predicting progress in batteries will help us predict the electric vehicle market.

SCENARIO ANALYSIS

While these simple techniques tend to examine one variable at a time, sometimes we want to look more broadly. For example, suppose oil rose to $120 a barrel. What would this influence?

In the short run, it would probably reduce driving and increase the purchase of fuel-efficient cars. It might reduce the consumption of other goods as individuals move funds from discretionary purchases to pay for gasoline. The financial situation of states that depend on oil revenue will change dramatically with consequent impacts on businesses in those states and any business in such a state that depends on state funding. Of course, oil price will change the economics of oil extraction and oil discovery, influencing any business that depends on such activities as well as entire communities that depend on such activities. At $120 a barrel, oil extraction in places like North Dakota grew so fast firms had difficulty finding housing for workers, but if oil drops below $30 a barrel, these communities will feel the pinch.

In the slightly longer term, higher gas prices may spur the development of new transportation technologies like fuel-efficient cars. Fuel-efficient cars will lower air pollution. In the longer term, gas prices influence housing patterns, telecommuting, regional development, etc.

How can a company deal with such complexity? Some use scenario analysis. In scenario analysis, you do not attempt to guess exactly what will happen. Instead, you try to set a set of parameters within which you think the real outcomes will fall. So, for example, a firm might explore what will happen if gasoline is at $30, $100, and $150 a barrel. Alternatively, a firm might consider the impacts of different power/weight/cost combinations in batteries. Firms sometimes consider both the future changes in the current technology and what a potential a breakthrough in a specific technology might do. Given these parameters, the analysts then think through a causal world consistent with those parameters.

Firms, industries, and international organizations all do scenario analyses. Figure 7.4 presents Shell Oil's projections of future demand under two different sets of assumptions. Scramble refers to an uncoordinated future where the market and miscellaneous reactions influence the outcome. Blueprint refers to a future where government and business coordinate their activities.

Both large and small companies can benefit from scenario analysis. Even the smallest company may need to consider what particular potential changes may do to the business.

Scenario analysis replaces planning for one anticipated future with planning in light of alternative futures. Firms using scenario analysis can assess the success of their potential strategies across various high-probability potential futures. The best strategy in a single anticipated future can have fatal

Summary quantification

Scramble	2000	2010	2020	2030	2040	2050
			EJ per year			
Oil	147	176	186	179	160	141
Gas	88	110	133	134	124	108
Coal	97	144	199	210	246	263
Nuclear	28	31	34	36	38	43
Biomass	44	48	59	92	106	131
Solar	0	0	2	26	62	94
Wind	0	2	9	18	27	36
Other Renewables	13	19	28	38	51	65
Total primary energy	**417**	**531**	**650**	**734**	**815**	**880**

Blueprints	2000	2010	2020	2030	2040	2050
			EJ per year			
Oil	147	177	191	192	187	157
Gas	88	109	139	143	135	122
Coal	97	137	172	186	202	208
Nuclear	28	30	30	34	41	50
Biomass	44	50	52	59	54	57
Solar	0	1	7	22	42	74
Wind	0	1	9	17	28	39
Other Renewables	13	18	29	40	50	62
Total primary energy	**417**	**524**	**628**	**692**	**738**	**769**

Figure 7.4 Scenarios in Shell Oil

Reprinted with permission from "Shell energy scenarios to 2050," available at www.shell.com/scenarios.

weaknesses in other futures that have just a slightly lower likelihood of occurrence.

This kind of analysis, that considers multiple potential futures, requires a slightly different form of strategic thinking. Instead of thinking about the single best strategy, when we look across scenarios, we ask how strategies will perform across the distribution of reasonable futures. Naturally, while we may want to weight the performance of a strategy in our most likely scenario more heavily, we should worry if our preferred strategy has extremely bad outcomes in other, reasonable scenarios.

Before leaving this discussion, we should note that people generally underestimate the variability in the world—they assume the future will differ less from today than it generally does. For example, if you ask people to estimate a range within which the stock market has a 90 percent chance of falling, the market will fall outside that range far more than 10 percent of the time. Likewise, when oil was at $150 a barrel, few could even dream that we would see $30 a barrel within a few years, yet we did. You probably want to consider more extreme values than you think likely.

In addition, while doing these analyses, you have to be careful to keep the number of variables and their potential values restricted. If we have three variables, each of which can take three values, we suddenly have 27 possible scenarios—far too many to manage carefully.

BASE RATE ANALYSIS

Often, we have to make predictions without good information. We need to guess how customers will react to a film, predict project times, etc. We routinely try to estimate the time and cost of projects. Generally, managers evidence systematic biases in such predictions. For example, firms, including the largest and most sophisticated construction firms in the world, routinely underestimate the cost and time large projects will take. At a personal level, we often underestimate how long tasks we do frequently (doing homework, cooking dinner, etc.) will take.

Part of the problem stems from the distribution of uncertainty. Often, we know the "normal" time something should take, and then build our estimates by adding such normal durations. However, often the time for activities has a skewed distribution; activities may seldom take shorter than "normal" times but infrequently may take much longer times. Given that a project involves a number of activities with such a distribution, most projects will have some of the realizations with longer than normal times, making the total project time longer than projected. Indeed, our normal project planning almost estimates the minimum feasible time rather than the expected value of the time required.

If you can, try to find comparable events—other big projects, market responses to similar projects, etc. These will not be identical, and people will claim the new project is different. If you begin with the mean or median of these somewhat comparable events and then justify why you should adjust the forecast up or down from that mean, you generally will make a better prediction than if you simply look at any individual project.

SUMMARY

Changes in technology, and in particular, the introduction of disruptive technologies can fundamentally alter industries. We have discussed who will lead in the introduction of the disruptive technology, and who will benefit from the technology. The dominant companies in an industry seldom introduce a disruptive technology. Dominant firms tend to cater to their most sophisticated users, constantly adding advanced features to their existing products and technologies. Instead, outsiders often introduce new technologies. At first, the new technologies have serious limitations and so appeal to customers who will take a less sophisticated product at lower price than the old technology. Companies that want to benefit from a new technology need to find a way to protect their innovation and assemble the complementary resources needed to bring the technology to market.

FOOD FOR THOUGHT

As we noted in the chapter, hindsight is 20/20. You can always look back and say that a company should have done something about the new technology. However, managers must distinguish between a technology that creates a temporary fad and a technology that genuinely transforms the industry. As a manager, how might you distinguish between the two? How can you design your organization so you are not late to market with a popular new technology?

NOTES AND BIBLIOGRAPHY

1. See also Bower, J. L., and Christensen, C. M. "Disruptive Technologies—Catching the Wave," *Harvard Business Review* 73(1) (1995):43–53; Johnson, M. W., Christensen, C. M., and Kagermann, H. "Reinventing Your Business Model," *Harvard Business Review* 86(12) (2008):50.
2. Hanna, D. "How GM Destroyed Its Saturn Success," *Forbes* (March 8, 2010). www.forbes.com/2010/03/08/saturn-gm-innovation-leadership-managing-failure.html
3. Coley, C. "Enduring Ideas: The Three Horizons of Growth," *McKinsey Quarterly* (New York: McKinsey & Co., December 2009).
4. Tripsas, M., Bhatia, A., and McGahan, A. "Driving Profitable Growth at U.S. Auto Parts," *Harvard Business School Publishing*, (2011) Case # 9–812–032.
5. See also Christensen, C. M., and Overdorf, M. "Meeting the Challenge of Disruptive Change," *Harvard Business Review* 78(2) (2000):66.
6. For more on this topic, see: Gregoire, D. A., Barr, P. S., and Shepherd, D. A. "Cognitive Processes of Opportunity Recognition: The Role of Structural Alignment," *Organization Science* 21(2) (2010):413–431; Nadkarni, S., and Barr, P. S. "Environmental Context, Managerial Cognition, and Strategic Action: An Integrated View," *Strategic Management Journal* 29(13) (2008):1395–1427.
7. Gilbert, C., and Bower, J. L. "Disruptive Change—When Trying Harder Is Part of the Problem," *Harvard Business Review* 80(5) (2002):94.
8. For a discussion, see Levitt, B., and March, J. G. "Organizational Learning," *Annual Review of Sociology* 14 (1988):319–340.
9. Watkins, W. J., Jr. "Rethinking Patent Enforcement: Tesla Did What?" *Forbes* (July 17, 2014), www.forbes.com/sites/realspin/2014/07/17/rethinking-patent-enforcement-tesla-did-what/#3cef021b7bd8 (accessed March 14, 2017).
10. See Lovallo, D., and Kahneman, D. "Delusions of Success—How Optimism Undermines Executives' Decisions," *Harvard Business Review* 81(7) (2003):56, for a discussion of behavioral factors influencing forecasting and the reference class forecasting technique.

CHAPTER 8

Vertical Integration and Diversification

So far, we have emphasized how a firm competes in a given market or what determines the profitability of a given market. We now turn to the issue of corporate strategy, which largely concerns itself with what markets we should compete in.

While one might imagine only large corporations need a corporate strategy, even the smallest company makes some corporate strategy choices. Every business must choose a level of vertical integration: what activities to do in-house and what to buy from the outside. Every business must also choose the range of products or services to offer. For example, a restaurateur must decide how much of the cooking the restaurant will do and how much preprepared materials to use, whether to hire a bookkeeper or contract out bookkeeping, whether to handle washing linens and other cloths in-house or use a laundry service, etc.—all vertical integration issues. In addition, the restaurateur must decide whether to only want to offer services in one location or whether to want to diversify geographically, what kind or kinds of food to offer, and whether to own only one kind of restaurant or whether to own multiple kinds of restaurants—geographic and product diversification issues. As another example, the owner of a building maintenance company must decide whether to handle minor renovations and maintain the plumbing and electrical systems and how far afield to offer services. Even the smallest business must make some of these corporate strategy choices.

We discuss three kinds of corporate strategy choices: vertical integration, product diversification, and geographic diversification. Vertical integration refers to the company undertaking to do something in-house that might have been purchased from a supplier or handled by its customers. Vertical integration determines the range of a company's actions both forward and backward along its value chain. Product diversification refers to the range of products or businesses the company enters. Geographic diversification refers to the geographic areas the company enters.

In all of these, we come back to an underlying question: why would this activity be better handled within our company than in other companies? Very often the analysis comes down to synergies—does combining the two entities under one corporate entity make the combination more effective than the two as separate entities?

Bringing something inside your company has substantial costs relative to purchasing it in the market. Indeed, academics often argue that managers tend to overdo vertical integration and diversification; companies often get little or no benefit (or even destroy value) through vertical integration and diversification. For example, as you read cases in your program, you will notice that many of these include a note that the company had been more diversified but then got out of several bad businesses. The case against excessive vertical integration or diversification derives from two observations.

First, most of us (and most companies) play the game we have played for years better than we would play somebody else's game. The best basketball player in the world, Michael Jordan, was a mediocre baseball player. The activities, training, and practice that made him a great basketball player meant that he was not training for baseball. Likewise, if you excel at one kind of business, you probably would not run other kinds of business equally well. Managers develop competencies in making effective day-to-day decisions in their core business; however, they seldom have an opportunity to learn how to manage a completely different business before actually committing to the diversification. A company must ask itself whether, realistically, it will run business X better than companies that have run business X for many years.

Second, we generally overestimate our abilities. For example, a substantial majority of us believe we are above average drivers. The problem is probably worse when we talk about senior management. To become a top manager, you need to have some very good management skills, but you also needed some luck along the way. This luck means top managers experienced performance somewhat better than their abilities justified. In other words, top managers generally believe they are better managers than they are. This overestimation of their abilities may lead to overconfidence in their skills at managing new businesses.

How we attribute skill often has undesirable outcomes. Often, we highly value people who take unusual stances that subsequently proved correct. However, research shows such people are generally less accurate over time than others since the consensus of forecasters is, on average, a pretty good estimate. A similar pattern probably exists for unusual business activities.[1]

Even if managers have the skills required to vertically integrate or diversify successfully, it does not mean that vertical integration or diversification will benefit the company. For example, if you buy a company at a legitimate price, but your company does not run the new company better than the previous management did and the new company does not make your company better, then you will simply receive a normal return from the new business. However, managers do not buy companies to achieve a normal return; most profitable mergers and acquisitions should make the acquirer and/or the acquired company better.[2]

Sometimes firms make above normal returns by acquiring a bargain. However, if you really find an underpriced company outside your primary business, why you would want to hold on to it? Unless the underpriced business has more value in your company than in another company (i.e., the business has higher synergies with your company than others), you could make more money selling the underpriced business to a company where such synergies exist, rather than retaining it. Some companies such as private equity firms routinely buy undervalued firms and then quickly improve performance to resell the businesses at higher values.

Alternatively, ask what corporate strategy adds to your company. Creating a diversified or vertically integrated company increases the difficulty of corporate management; we need additional oversight to cover the company's different businesses. Specifically, we need oversight to ensure that the different businesses share information and resources and collaborate on common projects. We also need to design evaluation and rewards that encourage divisions to benefit the company as a whole. In addition, we weaken the incentives for management to outperform other firms when we take an independent company and make it a division of a larger company. An owner or part-owner CEO receives a far greater return from improved business performance than a division manager of a similar business in a large corporation. Even if you retain the same people managing the business and provide them high compensation, moving people into a larger corporation generally makes more of their compensation guaranteed and less dependent on performance. The addition of the division to the corporation must therefore create value to justify these costs. We will address these issues as we talk about specific contexts.

In essence, corporate strategy concerns what businesses should be in the company. We will often talk about this as if the choice is to buy or not to buy a company in the another business. However, most of the arguments about buying another company apply to developing your own capability for doing a business in-house.

VERTICAL INTEGRATION

Vertical integration refers to a firm doing multiple stages in the value chain of a production system, sometimes called the make-or-buy decision. For example, the clothing value chain includes the original production of the material that goes into producing cloth (growing cotton, petrochemicals for synthetics, etc.), manufacturing the cloth, designing the garment, producing accessories such as buttons and zippers, producing the garment, transporting the finished garment, and retailing and distributing the garment. Often, this value chain is largely not vertically integrated (i.e., separate companies handle each stage), but portions may be vertically integrated. For example, while most clothing retailers purchase garments from garment manufacturers, some backward integrate to produce the garments. In the petrochemicals industry, some companies focus strictly on oil extraction while others extract oil from the ground and forward integrate into shipping, refining, and even retailing petroleum products.

Similarly, the value chain that produces cars starts with mining iron ore, proceeds through making all of the components, and ends with the distribution of cars at car dealerships. Companies have to decide where they draw the line around what they do and what they do not do. For example, in the United States, automobile companies differ in the proportion of their components they make versus buy—that is, they choose different levels of vertical integration. In addition, almost all automobile production companies sell through franchised dealerships. Tesla, a maker of electric cars, however, is vertically integrated both backward into manufacturing its own batteries and forward into selling directly to customers.

Further, a manufacturer can integrate an activity partially or fully. An electric car manufacturer that partially integrated into batteries would make some of the batteries it uses and buy the rest. A car manufacturer that partially integrated into distribution would own some retail outlets while also selling through independent retailers. Partial integration might seem odd: if the economics favor integration, you might expect a company to integrate fully. However, partial integration often has some substantial benefits. A company may produce enough to meet its basic needs and rely on the market to handle any variation in demand, thus avoiding the cost of such variation. Partial integration helps a company negotiate with the firms it sells or buys from; it gives the company true cost information, and allows the company to make a credible (if implicit) threat to eliminate that supplier/buyer relation.

One of the major ways to look at corporate strategy decisions is through the lens of transaction cost economics. We turn to this next.

TRANSACTION COST ECONOMICS

Transaction cost economics (TCE) essentially compares a set of costs and benefits associated with doing a particular transaction in the market to the costs and benefits of doing that transaction inside an organization. This includes the costs associated with the transaction per se and the actual production costs.

For ease of exposition, we will talk about transactions costs in context of vertical integration although the concept also applies to other areas of corporate strategy.

TCE addresses the situation where Company A needs a product produced by Company B but the most efficient production of the product depends on Company B investing in assets that have little value outside that specific transaction. Company A has an incentive to agree to a deal, but then, after B has made the investments, demand to renegotiate the deal. (The investment made by B in assets specific to the transaction are sunk costs, and therefore not relevant to determining the new pricing of the products.) Stated differently, after agreeing to a contract, the company not investing in a specific asset (Company A) may attempt to renegotiate the contract on more favorable terms, putting the firm dependent on this exchange (Company B) in a very weak negotiating position. This is termed the hold-up problem. TCE assumes managers from both A and B understand this problem and so make organizational structure choices that recognize these realities.

In analyzing these problems, managers must consider both the direct costs of the goods and the transaction costs inherent in the deal. What do we mean by transaction costs considerations? Transaction costs analyses balance the costs of doing an operation in separate companies versus in one company. These costs stem from two things: coordination costs (stemming from the need to coordinate actions between specialized agents) and motivation costs (incurred while aligning the interests of these agents with those of your firm).

Consider the following example. Your firm needs to purchase many units of a component. To get the component, the company searches the market for a supplier and contracts with that supplier. Having signed the contract, the company must monitor the supplier and provide it with the right incentives to ensure that it fulfills the contract by sending you the right amount and quality of components at the right time. Thus, purchasing the component involves both coordination costs (e.g., finding the right supplier, bargaining with the supplier) and motivation costs (e.g., getting the supplier to fulfill the contract and not take advantage of you), along with technical costs associated with producing the component.

Now assume that you vertically integrate by bringing this transaction in-house: using a hierarchy instead of a market. While this eliminates the need to find, negotiate with, and monitor a supplier, you have some new costs related to internalization. You now need to pay for internal supervision to ensure that your firm produces the component. You need to motivate the employees involved in manufacturing this material; often, however, the incentives you can provide internal employees are weaker than the incentives these employees would have if they owned independent small businesses that acted as suppliers to your company. If you brought the transaction in-house by purchasing a business, you may also need to restructure your firm to integrate this new business successfully. Bringing something inside the company also involves other costs that we will discuss later.

TCE states that companies will structure themselves to minimize the costs of transactions. Thus, firms will buy from the market if finding, negotiating with, and monitoring an external supplier costs less than providing in-house supervision, motivating employees, and restructuring. If the costs of the former exceed the latter, firms will vertically integrate, that is, bring that activity in-house.

Transaction cost economics rests on several assumptions:

- Transactions involve uncertainty. For example, your firm may need more or fewer of the item than originally anticipated. The specifications of the item might change. The price of inputs may unexpectedly rise or fall. Consequently, we cannot write perfect contracts. Almost all contracts we write can be subject to renegotiation due to unanticipated events.
- Parties will misrepresent facts when it pays them to do so. Most transactions involve information asymmetries between the buyer and the seller (i.e., the buyer and seller do not have the same information). For example, a buyer of a used car may question the seller's claims about the reliability and performance of the car. This, in turn, leads to motivation costs incurred in getting the seller to provide accurate information.
- The exchange occurs repeatedly, preferably frequently. Assuming another firm can more efficiently produce the item, it seldom pays to bring an extremely infrequent transaction in-house. For example, a firm needing a new building does not buy or develop an in-house capability in design or construction, but a firm that routinely needs new buildings (e.g., one that continually adds small stores) might do so.
- Efficient operation requires investment by one of the parties that has value in this particular transaction but much less value outside of this transaction. For example, I might want a supplier to build a plant near my factory. However, by building near my factory, the supplier puts its plant further from other potential customers. Alternatively, I might want my supplier to invest in molds or technology specifically geared to my products, but with little application outside of my products. I might want my distributors to invest in training and support systems that have little value if they quit handling my product.

We vertically integrate when the sum of transaction costs and operational costs of buying exceed the costs of in-house operation. For example, both Netflix and Amazon Video have forward integrated into offering their own original content (in addition to distributing it) rather than leasing the rights from other providers for a limited period of time. From a TCE perspective, owning content has lower transaction costs than leasing; while creating content has up-front costs, once the content is created, owning the content allows both companies to offer their products worldwide, sidestepping the need for negotiating and bidding with local content providers in each country they operate in.

Second, sometimes firms can write contracts good enough to minimize the problem. For example, firms selling industrial gases often place a plant near a customer. However, industrial gas firms have experience with this kind of transaction, and the transaction involves a sufficiently simple exchange that they can write contracts that will guarantee them a reasonable profit no matter what, as well as provide higher returns if the exchange goes well. Note that this situation involves a product that faces little technological change (removing a major source of uncertainty), and where we can clearly specify the ground rules for the exchange. With low uncertainty, we can anticipate contingencies, making contracts easier to write.

Third, if the exchange occurs very infrequently, then we have less of a hold-up problem because we do not invest in anticipation of continued exchange. I could easily have a purchase that requires a supplier make substantial investments. However, if the supplier anticipates that I will buy this product only once, the supplier will quite reasonably fully capitalize the cost of that investment in the price charged. The problem comes if the supplier anticipates making repeated sales using that investment and so prices differently.

Fourth, the hold-up problem requires specific assets. If a supplier does not have to invest anything specifically in the relation, then there is no potential for holdup. As a supplier, I would have no problem making a deal when I recognize that the deal might be short term if I do not invest anything specifically in the deal.

While stated as absolutes, these come in degrees. Note what TCE does not say. It does not say that we internalize everything that happens frequently. We might buy something every day, but if it is a standard product available in an efficient market, we probably should not make it. We might even have employees of another company producing these products or services operating physically inside our organization. Many companies contract out for services like photocopying or information technology even though the individuals provide the support work in the customer's facility.

OTHER COSTS OF VERTICAL INTEGRATION

Transaction costs analysis suggests that the vertical integration decision depends on the balance between the transactions and operational costs of in-house production on the one hand and the transactions and operational costs of purchasing from an external marketplace on the other. However, in addition to transactions costs, vertical integration involves other considerations. Setting aside (often huge) monetary costs, these additional costs derive from issues related to scale, providing incentives, business logic, competing with previous customers, the loss of specialization and flexibility, and risk.

Scale

If the scale for the efficient operation of two activities differs substantially, it may not make sense to put both in one company. If the efficient scale to produce a component is exceedingly high, and we have a small-scale operation, we may not want to take on the high-scale activity. Taking it on would require a decision that we wanted to get into that high-scale business fully, for example, by selling the high-scale product in the outside market in addition to producing enough for our own needs. However, if we do not plan to sell the high-scale product outside, the new activity would operate below efficient scale. For example, the high minimum efficient scale in oil refining means that few if any refiners only sell through their own retailers.

Issues of scale also appear in services and relate to the development of skills. Consider information technology consulting. A company may need a range of IT services. However, a company might not have the scale to justify hiring a specialist in each of those areas, which leaves it asking employees to work on things in which they are not as experienced or skilled as individuals in the consulting firms. Furthermore, because of specialization, the individuals in those consulting firms will have developed better skills than a generalist in the company that needs the IT service. This may be part of the reason companies contract out so much of their legal work—even large firms may not find it economical to develop in-depth capabilities in all of the subdomains of legal effort the firm needs.

Incentives

As we briefly noted in our discussion of TCE, market relations often offer stronger incentives than a company can offer internally.

Consider an owner who operates small company. Here, the owner–operator has exceedingly strong incentives for efficient operations and increasing profitability—the owner gets to keep the profits. However, if another company buys this small company, the person running this activity becomes a division manager or equivalent in a large organization. Division managers may get increases in pay or bonuses for high performance, but they do not keep the residual profits. Obviously, the incentives for increasing efficiency and profitability become much weaker. Often when a small company owner becomes a division manager, the guaranteed portion of the compensation increases and the incentive portion decreases.

Even if the supplier is one large organization selling to another large organization, internalizing supply can weaken incentives. When one organization buys from another, managers often have little or no social feeling about the exchange. Companies often switch to whichever supplier offers the best deal. This puts pressure on the supplier to offer the best deal. Once the company moves the supplier into the organization, the organization has sunk costs associated with this activity. Managers may become reluctant (or even not have the option) to switch from the internal supplier to an outside supplier. The internal division faces less pressure to produce efficiently than an outside company does.

Business Logic

As we have mentioned, organizations tend to handle a given set of activities well. Inherently, that means companies will not handle very different activities as well as companies specifically designed to handle those activities. For example, if our real capability is in an old-line manufacturing business activity, we are unlikely to be particularly skilled at managing experts in information technology or law.

As an extreme example, the *Saturday Evening Post* was the largest-circulation magazine in the United States at some points in the early 1900s. The organization eventually vertically integrated all the way from distribution of the magazine to the creation of content, physical production of the paper, and owning its own paper mill and timber forest. Quite obviously, the management skills for running an editorial office producing content are unsuited for managing a timber-producing forest or paper mill.

Competing with Previous Customers

If a business in one industry that sells into or buys from another industry decides to move partially into that industry, it changes from a supplier or customer to a competitor. Vertically integrating may alienate customers or suppliers.

Loss of Specialization

The management of the company that only makes widgets gets up in the morning thinking widgets and goes to bed at night dreaming about them. Bringing this company into a larger corporation that largely sees widgets as simply a single component may lose that focus.

Loss of Flexibility or Increased Risk

Once we bring something into the corporation, we give up the substantial flexibility that we had when buying it in a market. For example, companies that assemble commoditized products such as PCs and low-end servers benefit from having multiple vendors that they can switch between, depending on price and other considerations.[3] If a supplier comes up with a better technology, they can switch rapidly to that new technology. Contrast this with a company that vertically integrated into producing a component; this firm cannot change technologies easily, and is less likely to stay at the cutting edge of a technology in what the company sees as a secondary activity.

Loss of flexibility or increased risk also occurs in terms of adaptation to volume changes. The more you vertically integrate, the more vulnerable you are to variation in final sales. When sales boom, vertical integration seems like a good idea. However, when sales decline, the firm cannot use all of its plant capacity. Laying off workers and leaving the plant idle are expensive. In contrast, if a firm buys the part in a competitive market, it can simply purchase less. Consequently, if sales go down, a completely vertically integrated company hurts more than a less vertically integrated company. Many firms use partial or tapered vertical integration to mitigate this problem using outside purchases to accommodate volume changes.

ALTERNATIVE REASONS FOR VERTICAL INTEGRATION

Observers have offered several other possible explanations for vertical integration.[4] As always, these depend on the specifics of the situation.

First, if one stage of the value chain is not competitive, firms in that stage have the potential to exploit firms in other stages of the value chain. This is the classic insight of the five forces analysis. Faced with a supplier or customer with high market power, a company may vertically integrate to reduce that market power. At the extreme, the company might attempt to develop its own market power at another stage of value chain.

This may explain some of the vertical integration in media industries. Historically, one set of companies produced movies, another distributed them, and a third ran branded television stations. However, increased concentration in the firms making connections to the final viewer (cable companies and satellite TV companies) gave power to these connecting firms. Cable is what we might call a natural monopoly (it makes no sense to run two sets of cable to the same house); hence, cable companies have the ability to demand better terms from the suppliers of content. This fits with content providers like Disney vertically integrating into running their own television networks, and companies like the News Corporation doing it all—producing content through companies like Fox Searchlight, distributing content through their own cable and satellite companies, and owning television stations.

Integrating in the other direction, Sony management may have attributed the eclipsing of its beta videotape technology by VHS to content holders that produced more content on the VHS format than the beta format. Sony backward integrated into owning a movie studio.

Second, and closely related to the monopoly power explanation, vertical integration may confer greater control over a firm's value chain. Even if a supplier is not a monopolist or does not have significant bargaining power over its customer, uncertainties related to a firm's external environment can drive vertical integration. Companies running cruise ships have bought islands in the Caribbean to guarantee their passengers an empty and unspoiled place to visit. However, companies must very carefully consider whether other mechanisms like alliances or long-term contracts offer sufficient control, and therefore, a viable alternative to vertical integration.

Third, vertical integration may lead to a better, cleaner customer experience. Customers may prefer to buy multiple, well-integrated products from a single company rather than deal with different suppliers. For example, Apple's dominance in technology and software resulted in fewer bugs in the operation of Macs than Windows based computer systems using hardware and ancillary software produced by a wide variety of independent companies.

Fourth, especially for companies offering highly innovative products, other stages of the value chain may simply not exist. For example, Apple originally had to sell direct to customers because computer stores did not exist at the time.

Fifth, vertical integration may lead to increased speed to market, a valuable feature when customers look for cutting edge products. For example, Zara, a vertically integrated Spanish clothing manufacturer, employs designers, manufactures garments, and owns and operates stores. Zara has a significantly shortened product cycle than other clothing retailers—a few weeks instead of several months—enabling it to adapt to changes in customer preference faster than the competition.

Finally, vertical integration may have important regulatory or tax implications. One stage of the value chain may be regulated, restricting profits in that stage, whereas other stages may be unregulated, allowing companies to exert their market power and improve profitability.

QUESTIONABLE REASONS FOR VERTICAL INTEGRATION

In addition to these explanations for vertical integration, companies vertically integrate for less compelling reasons. These include colocation, risk reduction, and exploitation of market power.

Colocation

Just because a company and its supplier need to be close together geographically does not mean the company should vertically integrate. From the provision of industrial gases through IT consulting to store-within-store retailing, we see colocation of independent businesses.

Risk reduction

Some managers may imagine that one stage of the value chain is riskier than another stage, and so want to move into the less risky stage. However, firms must balance this risk reduction, if it exists, against the increased risk from taking on a new business—and the potential of not running the new unit at full capacity due to lower demand than expected. Managers sometimes believe owning a supplier gives them better control. However, if the uncertainty is exogenous (e.g., based on the price of energy), it will exist whether the activity is inside or outside the company.

Exploiting Market Power

Companies with market power at one stage of the value chain sometimes want to use it to increase profits at another stage. In general, this does not make a lot of sense. If a company has market power at a given stage, it normally can expropriate the profits at that stage. For example, Intel and Microsoft have market power in CPUs and operating systems. They can obtain much of the profits available in the value chain without producing PCs. In general, you should not vertically integrate into a competitive market.

ALTERNATIVES TO VERTICAL INTEGRATION

Just because a firm does do not want to buy something in the spot market does not necessarily mean it has to vertically integrate. There are alternatives.

Companies routinely use long-term contracts. Whether these do or do not mitigate the TCE hold-up problem depends on the factors we've noted above—the willingness of one side to exploit the other, the extent of uncertainty (which determines the quality of the contract), etc. However, companies often invest in assets for a specific relation based on long-term contracts.

Alternatively, firms often form partnerships. Many successful companies create partnerships with their suppliers. The legal structure under which this occurs varies substantially. When the relations between companies may continue for many years, both may have a strong incentive to make them work.[5] Big companies often lend technical expertise to their suppliers, usually where the big company is so important to the supplier that the supplier will not risk selling to a competitor. For example, Toyota frequently provides technical expertise to its suppliers, but a Toyota supplier needs Toyota's good will.

Sometimes, companies run a risk that their partner may exploit them.[6] For example, Borden, a U.S.-based manufacturer, entered into a partnership with Meiji Milk Products, a Japanese firm, to sell ice cream in Japan; Borden would manufacture the ice cream while Meiji would distribute it. However, Borden broke the alliance alleging that Meiji slowed its promotion of Borden's products while launching its own brands to compete with Borden brands. To avoid similar problems, you should seek a partner who needs the partnership as much as you do. In addition, you would want a partner you can trust, communicate easily with, and with whom you can resolve conflicts easily, for example, through joint problem solving.

Franchising offers another solution to vertical integration issues. Franchising is a contract between a franchisor who normally owns the concept or production system, and a franchisee who normally invests to produce or market the franchisor's product, often in a given area. Franchises are particularly common in retailing; many fast food and chain restaurants are franchises. Franchising retains some of the advantages of strong incentives at the operational level. A local franchise owner may also understand the local environment better than the franchisor would. However, the franchisee may free ride on the franchise reputation. For example, if I had a fast food chain outlet on the highway, I would not expect much repeat business; people would come into my outlet based on their expectations about the chain. If I lower my quality and damage the reputation of the chain, I would not bear the full cost of the chain's lowered reputation. Indeed, if I get few repeat customers, I may bear very, very little of this cost. Consequently, almost all franchise systems invest in monitoring and control efforts to maintain customer quality and standardization.

OTHER IDEAS AND TERMS

Particularly in recent years, we have seen the development of what some call the virtual corporation. Such a business may have almost no physical assets or physical locations. It operates largely by coordinating and integrating the efforts of a variety of independent individuals or corporations. Let us offer a couple of examples.

Many "consulting firms" have almost no employees. Rather, they maintain a network of consultants that they draw on as needed for projects. The company largely handles sales and coordination. Thomson Reuters operates a business that connects independent experts to lawyers needing expert witnesses.

Some internet sales organizations are essentially a server running a website. When a customer purchases the product, the company has another retailer or the producer send the product to the customer. Often, this is much cheaper than running a bricks and mortar store in any specific location.

However, some worry that as companies that have historically done much of their business in-house start to contract out, they will get to a point where it is not clear what the corporation adds. This is sometimes called the hollow corporation.

Some of these developments derive from advances in information technology. Information technology often changes the transactions costs. It facilitates arms-length transactions, as we have seen with internet retailing. But it also facilitates on-going intercompany ties. For example, Walmart's computers integrate seamlessly with the computers of its suppliers.

DIVERSIFICATION

We now turn to the issue of diversification. The central problem in diversification is what businesses should a company be in? Porter has argued that companies should consider three tests regarding diversification:[7]

1. Is the industry attractive or does it have the potential to be made attractive?

2. Is the cost of entry less than the expected future profits?
3. Is there some form of synergy? Does the new unit gain competitive advantage by joining the company or vice versa?

Note these tests are hard to evaluate. To some extent, the second criterion, whether the cost of entry is less than expected profits, is almost the same as asking whether the new business will be profitable, which is the question we wanted to answer to begin with.

They are also not necessarily consistent. While Porter starts with industry attractiveness, this may not be important. Porter's analysis assumes that unattractive industries mean low profits, but what those profits mean depends entirely on the cost of entry; with low enough cost of entry, even the modest returns on sales in an unattractive industry could translate into reasonable return on investment.

The appropriate motivations for diversification fall into two broad categories: risk and synergy.

RISK

Different academic disciplines take different views on whether diversification has risk benefits. Finance scholars generally say firms should not diversify to reduce risk. They argue that the stockholder can efficiently diversify by changing the portfolio of stocks the stockholder holds. Consequently, the stockholder will not benefit from the company changing its risk profile. However, this is within a finance theory that emphasizes the importance of systematic risk, has generally downplayed issues associated with unsystematic risk, and assumes that cash flows do not change.

Suppose that by diversifying we reduce the variability in a company's profits. This may have two major benefits. First, it greatly benefits top management. After all, managers face an increased risk of dismissal when corporate profits go down. If they just maintain or slowly grow profits, they have an exceedingly high probability of keeping their jobs. Second, and more positively for a firm's other stakeholders, a reduction in variability in income may influence the company's attractiveness to suppliers. The suppliers of debt worry about variability in income—they want an exceedingly high probability that the company will have money to make its debt payments year after year. Workers and suppliers of intermediate products or components to the company may prefer a company with stable output and stable employment to a company with highly variable employment or output. Consequently, reducing the variability of the income stream may offer business benefits. The finance analysis we mentioned above does not come to this conclusion because it generally takes the income stream (expected dividends or expected cash flows) as predetermined, and worries about pricing the stock.

SYNERGY

By far the most important reason for diversification is synergy. Synergy suggests that putting two businesses together results in increased profits. Stated differently, synergy means that when we combine two businesses, it creates additional value over above the value created when the two business units operate independently.

Synergy puts the focus on the firm: how competent will your firm be at the new business it has entered into?

The concept of synergy has several important implications for pricing major acquisition targets. First, you do not want to bid the target's value to you. Instead, you want to pay just more than the value to the second highest bidder. If you bid what the company is worth to you, you hand over the additional value you would expect from synergy to the current owners of the company. To win the bid, your bid only needs to exceed that of the second highest bidder.

Second, you should not pay for potential synergies that only appear from the target combining with your firm. The price of the target should not reflect how you are going to improve the operations of the target unless others are bidding based on such improvement. The saying is, you do not pay for synergies.

Third, beware of the winner's curse. If we all try to estimate the value of something, the one who guesses highest will be willing to pay the most, but the one who guesses highest probably overvalues the target. In many auction situations, the winners systematically overpay.

These assume the owners of the target firm want to sell at the highest price. When the owners or board members do not want to sell, we have a hostile takeover. Here, we see firms repeatedly raising their bids and often trying to deal directly with owners contrary to the wishes of the target's board and management. We also see a wide variety of legal strategies. We will talk about these briefly when we discuss corporate governance.

HOW ARE SYNERGIES CREATED?

While we emphasized the importance of synergies in assessing a diversification decision, common ownership can create additional value in two basic ways: economies of scope, and economies from internalizing some transactions or activities.

Economies of Scope

Sometimes we can efficiently share tangible resources across the businesses belonging to a company. Alternatively, we may be able to transfer functional abilities (e.g., in marketing new products) across different businesses. Finally, we might be able to transfer general management capabilities across businesses. For example, GE is an extremely diversified company with businesses ranging from power generation to television. GE appears to add value through its corporate management; many observers consider GE one of the best developers of management talent in the world. We also might gain economies of scope in more tangible ways, by combining research laboratories or other activities. When P&G (the maker of Crest toothpaste) acquired Gillette (the maker of Oral B), R&D scientists in the two product categories of toothpaste and toothbrushes got access to each other's laboratories to develop better products.

Internalization Economies

In addition to economies of scope, TCE economies may also justify bringing new businesses into the company. We discussed these internalization economies in the context of vertical integration. Many of the same arguments apply to diversification.

Internalization economies may be particularly valuable in specific contexts. For example, in many developing countries, we observe some exceedingly large and exceedingly diversified business entities. In India, they appear as large conglomerates like Tata that operates in everything from steel manufacturing to IT consulting. In Korea, they appear as industry collaborative groups called chaebols. In Japan, similar groups are called keiretsus. In other parts of Asia and much of South America, we see similarly highly diversified family businesses.

Some observers argue that these highly diversified businesses developed due to relatively inefficient or undeveloped markets for capital and labor. In a country with a well-developed capital market, a firm benefits less from transferring capital internally within a company relative to doing so in the marketplace than it would in a country that does not have an equally well-developed capital market providing investment funds. Likewise, in a country short on skilled labor and trained managers, a large company may train managers and employees, thus providing an internal labor market. Firms in countries with large pools of skilled labor and managers may benefit less from an internal labor market.

However, these benefits may also apply to a lesser extent in all economies.

Consider a company that needs capital. If it borrows the money, it has to provide a limited set of data to the lender and, as long as it fulfills a specified set of conditions, the lender generally cannot take the money back. The equity investor faces an even more difficult situation. The equity investor also has access to only a limited amount of information and has almost no ability to take the money back. Often the best a lender or equity investor wanting out of an investment can do is to sell the debt or equity at a loss.

Compare this to a division that needs capital in a corporation. The corporate office does not just have a limited set of information; it has the right to any information it wants. If it decides a project or division has a promising future, it can direct capital to it. Once it has allocates capital, it has the right to impose any review and control system it wants. If it decides that the division is not using the money well, the corporate office can do a wide variety of things to either improve the usage of its money or stop the spending. It has complete authority to take these steps. Corporate's greater information and control than outside investors mean corporate might sensibly fund projects that outside investors would not. In short, an internal capital market offers some advantages.

However, organizational factors may outweigh these advantages. Corporations often consider interdivisional equity in allocating capital—

they do not simply allocate to divisions with the most promising prospects. Likewise, corporate management may resist reneging on commitments it has made to the divisions.

Similar factors operate for labor markets. Firms have access to a substantial amount of information about their employees. They can talk to the employee's supervisors, coworkers, or subordinates. They have 100 percent access to all records regarding the employee's performance in the corporation. In contrast, with an outside hire, firms have very limited information, often relying on just a resume and references, both provided by the applicant.

After hiring an employee, companies may benefit by training and developing employees. Most satisfied employees do not search for other employment. Given the costs of changing jobs, internal development of employees often offers a better price–performance relation than hiring employees from the outside who can command a market price. Again, balanced against this, firms may not be sufficiently hard-nosed about internal selection and promotion decisions. Internal politics may exert an effect. In addition, at times (e.g., in a changing industry), the company may prefer to hire from outside to bring new perspectives to the firm.

Both the corporate office's understanding of the businesses and the likelihood that employee skills will transfer mean that these benefits appear more in corporations with related than unrelated businesses. Consequently, strategic relatedness helps.

LESS VALID REASONS FOR DIVERSIFICATION

Perhaps even more than vertical integration, observers often claim firms overdiversify. Some common motivations for diversification rest on questionable foundations.

Diversification often benefits the company's management more than the stockholders or employees. Stockholders can escape a declining industry by selling stock; they do not need the company to exit the industry for them. With the exception of top management, employees often do not benefit from a more diversified company. However, top management frequently does benefit from diversification—managers have more job security (and often higher compensation) if they lead a large company operating in a variety of industries than if they lead a smaller company in a stagnant or declining industry.

Second, companies diversify to grow. Very often, companies force growth. For example, you sometimes see companies in mature industries saying that they plan to grow by 50 percent in the next 5 years or even more. These kinds of statements or goals almost automatically translate into the company making acquisitions to increase size rather than because the growth makes good business sense.

Third, managers' egos and/or incentives sometimes drive diversification. The primary determinant of CEO compensation is firm size. Management has a strong incentive to grow the company even if it is not in (or is even explicitly against) the interests of the shareholders. Similarly, as we noted in the beginning of this chapter, even managers who are superb at managing one kind of business are not necessarily capable at managing a different kind of business. However, managerial overconfidence, driven by managers' past successes, may result in a company diversifying into a business it knows little about.

DRAWBACKS OF DIVERSIFICATION

Diversification has several inherent drawbacks.

First, diversification adds often substantial administrative costs. Large corporations frequently add layers of management or increase the size of corporate management to encourage the different businesses to talk to each other, share resources or information, and collaborate on new products or markets. Even if diversification has the potential to lower some costs by sharing common activities across businesses, this may not actually happen. Instead of centralizing some common functions such as HR, business units may each need their own HR department if their criteria for hiring and training new people differ from those of other units.

Second, diversification lowers the incentives for management. Even if a division manager has higher compensation than the manager would have as an owner/operator, less of that compensation depends directly on the performance of the division whereas almost all the wealth of an owner/operator often depends on the performance of the firm.

Third, diversification often results in managers using systems poorly suited for their particular business. Corporations generally impose similar systems across the company. In a diversified company, this means these systems may not be appropriate for some of the divisions, particularly if these divisions differ greatly from the others.

Fourth, large public corporations often subsidize poorly performing divisions, frequently because they cannot take an unbiased view of the division's performance.

Fifth, divisions in large diversified corporations often develop an "us-versus-corporate" perception. Division management thinks that corporate adds little but needlessly meddles in the division. The corporate managers may see division managers as uncooperative. Some level of this perception is normal but becomes dysfunctional at high levels.

MANAGING DIVERSIFICATION

Corporate management plays a critical role in managing diversification. What do they have to do to create value from diversification?

First, the corporate office has to manage the corporate portfolio: it has to decide the businesses the company operates, acquire (or internally grow) more units, divest other units, and so on. It also has to allocate resources among the different businesses. We sometimes use the term dominant logic to describe how corporate makes these decisions.

As we noted in our discussion on core capabilities in Chapter 5, dominant logic includes the mental maps of top managers combined with a wide variety of organizational processes that developed in the core business. How managers conceptualize the business and allocate resources to technologies, product development, advertising, and so on depends on the primary business of the company (often reinforced by past market successes) and their problem solving behaviors (subject to managers' cognitive biases and simplifications). The organization's processes reflect the dominant logic but the best processes for one kind of business often differ from those for another. Dominant logic is not a good or bad thing—it just is. Prahalad and Bettis claim that dominant logic provides managers with the repertoire of tools they use to identify, define, and make strategic decisions, but dominant logic can also constrain managers' thinking about how the company should diversify.[8]

Second, the corporate office has to manage and oversee individual businesses. Generally, corporate offices oversee the formulation of division business strategies, and usually must approve such strategies. The corporate office also has to monitor and control the performance of individual units through either strategic planning or financial control. Strategic planning and financial control each have their own advantages and disadvantages. While strategic planning involves strategy formulation by both corporate and business units, financial control involves strategy formulation primarily at the business unit level with corporate headquarters setting targets for performance. Consequently, compared to financial control, strategic planning supports greater linkages across businesses and potentially, a greater focus on medium to long-term strategic goals. However, these may come at the expense of divisional or business unit autonomy.

Third, the corporate office has to manage the linkages among businesses to ensure the different units appropriately share or transfer resources and information, and collaborate effectively (or not actively compete with one another). Transfer pricing, the terms on which the firm transfers goods or services from one unit to another, can strongly influence reported division profits and division behavior. Transfer pricing rules like at cost, cost plus, or market value each has advantages and disadvantages, including the signals they provide each unit on the value the company places on collaborating with other units within the company.

Finally, while we have emphasized the importance of corporate creating synergies in diversification, diversification is not an on/off switch. That is, instead of viewing companies as diversified (and therefore, worried about creating synergies between business units) or not diversified (and therefore, having no concern for synergies since the business has only one unit), it is more fruitful to see multibusiness firms as differing in their degree of diversification. In particular, firms can differ in their types of diversification, patterns of linkages across units, and in their preferred mode of diversification.[9] For example, firms may offer a single product, a dominant product, or a range of either related or unrelated products. The business units in some multibusiness firm may lie along the value chain (representing vertical integration), or all relate to a single core strength. Other firms may have direct relations among only a couple of business units (with the rest of the units operating independently of one another), or alternatively, have linkages among a majority of business units (with a minority of businesses operating independently of the rest). At the extreme, some conglomerates may have no linkages among most of their business units. Firms may also differ in how they implement diversification, for example, diversifying primarily through acquisitions or primarily through organic growth.

The role of corporate management in managing diversification differs across businesses with different degrees of diversification. While corporate management influences the creation of synergies in diversified firms with closely linked businesses, in firms with fewer linkages across business units (e.g., in conglomerates), corporate management's focus shifts from synergy creation to ensuring that business units have appropriate incentives, high levels of autonomy in decision making, and good strategic plans. Corporate management, in such companies, tends to emphasize competition rather than cooperation between divisions, often by providing strong incentives for improved divisional performance (e.g., through stock option plans linked to divisional—not company—performance), intense financial monitoring, and financial resources and/or specialized services such as legal or bookkeeping.[10]

SUMMARY

The key question, whether with vertical integration or diversification, is how a corporation adds value by operating businesses as a combination of units relative to each business operating independently.

We have discussed both valid and not-so-valid reasons for vertical integration and diversification. While transactions cost economics provides a valuable tool to predict when a business should vertically integrate or diversify, both strategic actions have other benefits, particularly related to managing risk, gaining additional control, and creating synergies. In addition, firms have alternatives to bringing a function into the company; these include things such as alliances, long-term contracts, and franchising.

While we discussed what corporate offices do to increase the chances of a successful diversification or vertical integration, the question of relative skill in new businesses is paramount. Even as we become experts in our normal business, our experience may not apply to new businesses.

FOOD FOR THOUGHT

1. In the 1950s, several large companies were conglomerates that diversified into a variety of industries. Around the 1990s, however, companies were exhorted to shun diversification and focus on their core businesses in order to achieve superior performance. Recently, the pendulum appears to be swinging back, with several large, successful companies such as Apple, Google, and Microsoft diversifying into a variety of new businesses. What do you think is causing the CEOs and senior managers of these companies to make the decision to diversify?

2. Berkshire Hathaway has been successful, in part, because of its buy-and-hold strategy; it has invested in a number of companies in a variety of industries for the long term. While this strategy has worked for the company, do you think it is replicable by other companies? What do you see as the downside of this strategy? What is your assessment of this company's future?

NOTES AND BIBLIOGRAPHY

1. Denrell, J. "'Experts' Who Beat the Odds Are Probably Just Lucky," *Harvard Business Review* 91(4) (2013):28–29.
2. Bower, J. L. "Not all M&As Are Alike—And That Matters," *Harvard Business Review* 79(3) (2001):92–101.
3. Prime, R. "When Two Vendors Are Better than One Gartner," *Information Age* (September 3, 2014), www.information-age.com/when-two-vendors-are-better-one-gartner-123458431/
4. Schumpeter, "Keeping It Under Your Hat," *The Economist*, April 16, 2016.
5. Dyer, J. H., Kale, P., and Singh, H. "How to Make Strategic Alliances Work," *MIT Sloan Management Review* 42(4) (2001):37–43.
6. Gulati, R., Khanna, T., and Nohria, N. "Unilateral Commitments and the Importance of Process in Alliances," *MIT Sloan Management Review* 35(3) (1994):61–69; Bleeke, J., and Ernst, D. "Is Your Strategic Alliance Really a Sale?" *Harvard Business Review* 73(1) (1995):97–105.
7. Porter, M. E. "From Competitive Advantage to Corporate Strategy," *Harvard Business Review* 65(3) (1987):43–59.
8. Prahalad, C. K., and Bettis, R. A. "The Dominant Logic: A New Linkage between Diversity and Performance," *Strategic Management Journal* 7(6) (1986):485–501.
9. See Rumelt, R. P. "Diversity and Profitability," paper presented at the Academy of Management Western Region Meetings, Sun Valley, Idaho (1977); Leontiades, M. *Strategies for Diversification and Change* (Boston, MA: Little Brown & Co., 1980).
10. Berg, N. A. "What's Different about Conglomerate Management," *Harvard Business Review* 47(6) (1969):112–190.

CHAPTER 9

International Strategies

As with the discussions of vertical integration and diversification in the last chapter, the underlying question in international strategy is, what additional value does the corporation create by diversifying geographically? In other words, why expand into foreign markets? While we will talk about international markets and geographic diversification, similar issues often apply to geographic diversification within a country.

In addition to the benefits that accompany any kind of diversification (e.g., economies of scale and scope, potential risk reduction, internalization economies), there are a number of additional reasons why companies might benefit specifically from geographic diversification. These include extending the life cycle of a product, optimizing the physical location of activities on value chain (e.g., locating manufacturing in places with low labor costs), new learning and adaptation capabilities potentially gained from foreign operations, transferring home office managerial skills across worldwide units, and making use of opportunities for arbitrage or cross-market subsidization.

Mirroring our discussion of vertical integration and diversification, when thinking about geographic diversification, we need to consider whether a company needs to bring activities in-house to benefit from geographic diversification. Consider, for example, expanding into foreign countries to obtain lower labor costs. Such expansion can provide lower-cost labor, but a firm might also obtain the benefits from lower-cost labor through contracts with companies in the target country. However, if the company's primary benefit comes from transferring knowledge across countries, internalization becomes more attractive.

Likewise, bringing foreign operations in-house can allow cross-market subsidization. Consider two competing companies (A and B) where A only operates in only one market while B operates in a dozen markets. B can use profits from 11 other countries to subsidize operations in A's market, potentially driving A out of business. After driving A out of business, B can increase prices and profits. Depending on how B does this, it can be illegal. United States law might see this as predatory pricing. Internationally, while generally frowned on under GATT and other trade agreements, B might meet legal requirements with a more temperate version of this strategy like accepting very low returns in the focal market (compensated by higher returns elsewhere) or manipulating costs through transfer pricing.

In addition, firms operating business units in different countries can move money around internally in ways outsiders have difficulty observing, often lowering the overall tax bill for the corporation. This has motivated the recent popularity in the use of tax inversions by large U.S. corporations where corporations establish legal headquarters in countries with particularly favorable taxes and laws, even though the actual headquarters remains in the United States.

MODELS AND TYPOLOGIES FOR ANALYZING INTERNATIONAL STRATEGIES

International strategies have an added layer of complexity that other discussions of diversification strategies do not have: they deal with the operation of a company in multiple countries. Before we delve into the different types of international strategies, let us look at patterns of geographic diversification across industries.

Why do we see some industries concentrated in some areas or regions of the world while other parts of the world lack similar concentrations of industries? For example, why do we see a Silicon Valley in California but not in Calais? Porter's diamond model of national competitive advantage (Figure 9.1) offers an explanation.[1]

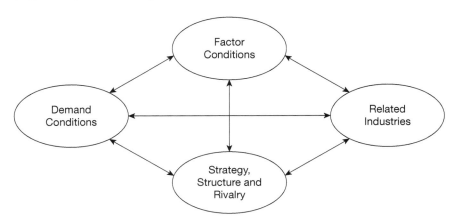

Figure 9.1 Porter's Diamond Model of National Competitive Advantage

The diamond identifies four things that lead to national competitive advantage: factor conditions; demand conditions; related and supporting industries; and firm strategy, structure, and rivalry.

Factor conditions refer to the factors of production: labor, land, infrastructure, and so on. Industries that develop in a country reflect the availability (or nonavailability) of these factors of production. Japanese firms, for example, pioneered the use of just-in-time systems partially to compensate for a lack of space and shortages of funds necessary to store large amounts of inventory. National disadvantages (e.g., the scarcity of a factor of production) can lead to national competitive advantage if two conditions are met. First, disadvantages need to give companies advance, accurate signals about circumstances that might apply in other countries. This forces companies in the home country to innovate in ways that accommodate those circumstances ahead of firms in other countries. For example, smaller residences in Japan led Japanese companies to develop smaller appliances; these smaller appliances suited emerging needs of customers (e.g., small appliances for a dormitory or an office) in other countries. Second, the region must have some advantages identified in the other parts of the diamond. For example, firms in the industry might face a high cost of labor (a factor condition) but benefit from the existence of related industries, favorable demand, and a good industry structure.

Demand conditions refer to what the customers within a firm's home country expect from the goods and services they buy. Sophisticated and demanding buyers force local firms to become innovative and produce high-quality products. This innovative capability lets firms compete better when they expand abroad.

Related and supporting industries refer to the presence or absence of suppliers or other related industries within a home country. For example, the presence of dye manufacturers supported the development of the pharmaceutical industry in Switzerland. Computer technology firms in the Silicon Valley can draw on a massive assortment of supporting firms that firms elsewhere cannot access as readily.

Firm strategy, structure, and rivalry refer to how aggressively firms compete with one another in their home country. While this may seem self-defeating in the short run, high home country rivalry forces firms to become more competitive, improving their abilities to compete when these firms expand abroad.

We next turn to the firm level of analysis and examine the types of international strategies firms can use.

A TYPOLOGY OF INTERNATIONAL STRATEGIES

Some characterize international strategies on two dimensions: national responsiveness versus global integration.

Companies pursuing nationally responsive strategies focus on responding to country-specific conditions often by offering products tailored for specific national markets. Naturally, this requires international differences in consumer tastes or some aspect of the value chain (e.g., radically different distribution channels). Alternatively, countries may differ due to differences in government regulations or legal frameworks. In this case, companies may pursue nationally responsive strategies by letting each unit decide how to deal with country-specific restrictions or policies.

Nationally responsive strategies appear in many industries. Differences in national taste force food producers and restaurant chains to offer different products and services in different countries. Likewise, firms must accommodate national differences in fashion, home furnishings, dishes, and many other products and services. Even with a common underlying technology, some firms will cosmetically tailor their products to satisfy local preferences, as mobile phone manufacturers do with mobile phones sold in different countries. Alternatively, regulated industries such as insurance and banking often require substantial adaptation to national (or even state) regulations.

Companies that pursue globally integrated strategies attempt to optimize production and distribution of similar products and services across countries. Thus, where companies low in global integration operate each national unit independently (i.e., treating the company as a collection or portfolio of different companies operating in different countries), com-panies high in global integration integrate and coordinate activities across countries. For example, such companies may centralize some activities such as manufacturing or R&D and/or use common systems or practices across different geographic units. Often, globally integrated companies develop internal value chains that help different components in different countries gain economies of scale and take advantage of local factor markets.

Global integration does not necessarily imply complete standardization across units; products and operations of the different geographic units of a company following a global strategy do not necessarily look exactly alike. A global mobile phone manufacturer might have very similar internal components globally, but adapt the cosmetic features of phones to local tastes. Global integration does not necessarily imply that the company competes on cost. Global integration tends to occur in industries with economies of scale, but such scale can exist with highly differentiated products. For example, the largest automobile manufacturers operate globally integrated production systems but often try to differentiate their products.

Large hotel chains like Marriott follow a global integration strategy. These chains provide global reservations and operational technology at the same time as they guarantee quality for their hotels around the world. In this case, the standardization changes customer experience in specific dimensions more than it does cost. Hotels in different countries may share some operational procedures or technology along with minimum service standards, but may also work hard to provide a customer experience that reflects the country.

Three factors determine whether companies emphasize nationally responsive or globally integrated strategies.[2]

The first imperative is strategic: where is the value added along the value chain? Industries that add value upstream (e.g., steel manufacturing) favor global integration. Industries that add value downstream (e.g., food retailing) favor national responsiveness.

The second imperative is political: the relative bargaining power of the company and the nations in which it operates. Countries often want companies to adopt nationally responsive strategies. National responsiveness often requires higher levels of local production and employment. Companies with more bargaining power relative to host nations (e.g., companies that use proprietary technology, economies of scale, or product differentiation; think Apple or Google) favor global integration strategies. Companies with lower bargaining power relative to host nations favor nationally responsive strategies.

The third imperative is the strategic predisposition of the company: companies may be ethnocentric (strategic decisions guided by the values and interests of the parent company), polycentric (strategic decisions guided by the values of the geographic units), regiocentric (strategic decisions guided by the blend of parent and geographic units), or geocentric (strong integration across geographic units).

Bartlett and Ghoshal use these two dimensions to identify four types of international strategies (see Figure 9.2).[3] Companies following these strategies differ not only in their relative emphases on national responsiveness and global integration, but also in the extent to which they centralize or decentralize key functions and allow central control over greater subsidiary autonomy.

1. International strategy. Companies following an international strategy emphasize neither national responsiveness nor global integration. These companies centralize some functions such as R&D while decentralizing others for limited local customization.

2. Multidomestic strategy. Companies following a multidomestic strategy emphasize local (i.e., national) responsiveness over global integration. These companies tend to decentralize key functions and promote geographic subsidiary autonomy, for example, by having each regional unit develop and market its own products. Geographic units may use common processes across nations for a few functions such as finance.

3. Global strategy. Companies following a global strategy emphasize global integration over national responsiveness. These companies

Figure 9.2 Typology of International Strategies

centralize activities by function, for example, locating manufacturing or R&D in a few centers around the world to take advantage of national differences in labor or materials costs and the availability of skilled labor. The use of such centers often leads to economies of scale. This strategy works best when consumers around the world demand standardized products and governments do not differ greatly in their regulatory approaches.

4. Transnational strategy. Companies following a transnational strategy try to gain the advantages of both national responsiveness and global integration. While it is not clear that firms have actually achieved transnational strategies, companies following this strategy might have a decentralized network of units linked to one another and to the parent by systems of information or knowledge transfer.

TOOLS FOR ANALYZING GLOBAL EXPANSION

Even within a strategy with specific levels of national responsiveness and global integration, firms must choose to operate in specific countries or regions. Ghemawat's CAGE (cultural, administrative, geographic and economic distance) framework provides a tool for answering this question of where to operate.[4]

The CAGE framework looks at the costs and risks associated with the distance between a company's home market and a particular foreign market. Distance includes both physical (i.e., geographic) distance, and cultural, administrative and political, and economic differences; different types of distance vary in their effects in different industries.

High cultural distance between two countries occurs when people in the two countries speak different languages, belong to different ethnicities, follow different religions and social norms, and have few connecting ethnic/social networks. India and China have greater cultural distance than India and Nepal. Cultural distance increases the difficulty of working together; cultures often differ in their ideas about power, authority, independence, and other factors critical to the operations of management systems. Cultural distance also matters more for firms in industries with high linguistic and cultural content. Advertising seldom translates across cultures. A TV program that viewers in one culture love may not connect with viewers in another culture.

High administrative and political distance between two countries or regions occurs when they lack a shared monetary or political association, when the governments of the two countries are hostile, and when the two countries differ in the strength of their legal and financial institutions. Firms from countries belonging to the European Union, for example, usually find it easier to expand within Europe than to expand into China. Administrative distance matters particularly in industries that governments view as strategically important. Chinese investments in U.S. tech companies, for example, have faced a pushback from U.S. lawmakers amid concerns related to national security, while Google and Apple services face constraints in China.

Geographical distance, as we might expect, refers to the lack of a common border between the home country and the foreign country, the absence or lack of transportation and communication links between the two countries, or the physical remoteness of the foreign country. Geographical distance matters particularly for industries that manufacture low value-to-weight products (e.g., cement), fragile or perishable products (e.g., glass or dairy), or industries where the company and its foreign operation need frequent communication (e.g., financial services).

Economic distance comes from differences in consumer incomes, resources, information, or knowledge. This distance matters particularly for firms in industries that manufacture high-value products or for firms in industries where labor costs are a significant component of the final product cost. Thus, for example, luxury goods manufacturers might not find expansion into sub-Saharan Africa attractive.

The CAGE framework complements other tools to analyze global expansion such as a country-portfolio analysis. A country-portfolio analysis plots a company's actual and potential markets on a grid, with a measure of GDP or per-capita income on one axis and a measure of product performance or consumer propensity to buy the product on the other. Larger bubbles represent more attractive markets. However, taking into account different kinds of distance may make some of these potential markets appear more or less attractive.

Consider, for example, a U.S. fast food company's decision to expand internationally. In his 2001 paper, "Distance Still Matters," Ghemawat suggests that, superficially, China or India may appear to be attractive markets due to their sheer size. However, accounting for CAGE factors may change our calculations. Specifically, the cultural distance between the United States and China—a particularly important factor when it comes to something like food preferences—is extremely large. The administrative distance between the United States and China is large as well, given that the two countries do not share a common currency, do not belong to a political union, and are political rivals. The geographical distance increases the cost of shipping perishable food items from the United States to China. Instead, the company might need a local supply chain in China, raising its cost of operations. Economic differences may raise additional difficulties; differences in consumer incomes may mean that reasonably priced items in the United States appear expensive to most customers in a different country. This kind of analysis may make the U.S. company rank Mexico—culturally, administratively, and geographically closer to the United States—as more attractive for foreign expansion than China.

In this context, KFC's successful expansion in China is informative.[5] KFC opened its first outlet in China in 1987 and expanded rapidly, becoming China's largest restaurant chain in 2015 with about 500 outlets. KFC's success derived partially from KFC's ownership by PepsiCo. PepsiCo cared more about Coca-Cola than about selling fried chicken. Thus, PepsiCo took a hands-off approach to KFC's China operations. Given a free hand, KFC China's executives developed a business model geared to China that included a menu with Chinese characteristics, designing a logistics network tailored to local conditions (e.g., renting temporary warehouses and reserving space on cargo airlines to circumvent traffic), training local employees, and emphasizing ownership rather than franchising. This worked because KFC China's executives had the freedom to deviate from the dominant logics of PepsiCo's executives; they could develop a dominant logic tailored to their particular environment.

BEHAVIORAL IMPLICATIONS OF THE DIFFERENT TYPES OF INTERNATIONAL STRATEGIES

To illustrate the behavioral implications of the different types of international strategies, consider Philips and Matsushita.[6] In the 1930s, in anticipation of World War II, Philips, a Dutch electronic products company, gave individual country organizations (later known as national organizations or NOs) substantial independence and autonomy. This multidomestic strategy succeeded initially; NOs not only customized their marketing for the countries they operated in, the autonomy given to each NO spurred innovation across the company. For example, Philips of Canada created the company's first color TV, Philips of Australia created the first stereo TV, and Philips of United Kingdom created the first TVs with teletext.

By the 1960s, however, the creation of the European Common Market lowered the benefits of this multidomestic strategy. New technologies required larger production runs than could be carried out by plants managed by individual NOs. In addition, low cooperation among the NOs meant that innovations created by one NO did not transfer effectively to other NOs. Since the NOs could choose what products they sold in their markets, some NOs even chose to manufacture and sell products based on technical standards created by Philips's competitors. Famously, North America Philips decided to manufacture a VHS videocassette under license from archrival Matsushita rather than adopt the technically superior V2000 format developed by another division of Philips. Together, these factors, combined with increased price competition from the Japanese, led to a decline in Philips's performance.

Over the next four decades, successive Philips CEOs tried to restructure the company to move power away from the NOs and toward global product divisions in an attempt to have more coordinated global product development and production; this, in turn, would lead to greater efficiency and make Philip's cost structure more comparable to that of Matsushita. These efforts succeeded only partially, mostly due to power struggles between the NO managers and the product division heads. In the 1990s, for example, many country managers resisted the CEO's initiative to reduce headcount, instead digging in their heels to save local jobs.

Matshushita faced the opposite problem. A thriving export business in the 1950s and 1960s morphed into a global strategy in the 1980s, with technology and innovation concentrated in Japan, and production, sales, and marketing done by overseas subsidiaries. Product divisions headquartered in Japan retained strong control over the subsidiaries, often with monthly face-to-face meetings, daily faxes, and nightly phone calls.

By the 1990s, however, price competition from cheaper Chinese and Korean manufacturers forced Matsushita to confront a fundamental problem: without innovation, Matsushita's future was bleak. Matsushita's CEOs tried to restructure the company to increase innovation (in an attempt to become more like Philips), moving power away from powerful product divisions to local subsidiaries. Like Philips's efforts, however, this restructuring met with limited success.

The cases of both Philips and Matsushita illustrate a single issue: the effects of the type of international strategy selected depends on managers' behaviors and incentives to take certain kinds of actions. Thus, while Philips' multidomestic strategy gave its NO managers complete freedom to make their decisions, thereby making each NO both innovative and extremely responsive to its local markets, it also reduced cooperation across divisions. Cooperation among NO managers would have benefited the company as whole; however, no single NO would capture all of the benefits from cooperation. Some NOs might even lose by cooperating with others (by being less responsive to the specifics of their markets). Given this, Philips had difficulty gaining synergies from its geographic diversification. As Cor Boonstra, one of Philips's CEOs, put it, the company needed to change from "a plate of spaghetti" to "a neat row of asparagus."

Matshushita, in contrast, had a successful global strategy primarily because it implemented decades of tight control of headquarters over subsidiary managers. This very control, however, left subsidiary managers reluctant to take independent, risky actions without headquarters approval. This deprived the company of much needed innovation when the environment changed.

OTHER BEHAVIORAL INFLUENCES ON GEOGRAPHIC DIVERSIFICATION

The interaction between geographic diversification and managers' behaviors and incentives flows both ways. As we illustrated with the Philips and Matsushita examples, international strategies influence managers' behaviors and incentives. At the same time, underlying national differences in top management influence the success of a company's geographic diversification efforts. Often, top management consists almost exclusively of individuals from the corporation's home country. Even when they try to understand national differences, foreigners seldom develop the depth of understanding of a locale that locals have. This can create continuing friction between corporate and national subsidiaries and result in corporate decisions that do not make sense for the divisions. The literature is replete with examples of terrible product decisions made by corporate managements that did not understand local norms, although some of these examples appear untrue.

The individual experiences and biases of top management also matter. A truly global perspective benefits from a top management that derives from multiple countries and has substantial experience in multiple countries. Inherently, someone who grew up in an area has a depth of understanding of the explicit and implicit rules and conditions that outsiders have immense difficulty matching. At the same time, however, increased diversity in top management backgrounds can make it more difficult to reach consensus and increase the potential for misunderstandings.

COSTS OF GEOGRAPHIC DIVERSIFICATION

As with product diversification, geographic diversification or expanding internationally has costs.

First, geographic diversification increases complexity. The company that operates in multiple areas must coordinate the activities of more units and people than it would if it only operated in one area. Furthermore, customer preferences, legal conditions, rules, customs, etc. differ across countries adding to the complexity. All this costs money and can make decision making more difficult.

Second, as a company diversifies internationally, overhead increases. Each national unit may have to develop locally appropriate procedures for activities such as hiring and training people (reflecting differences in across-country talent and law). This can increase expenses for the company as a whole.

Third, the systems and dominant logic that work well in one geographic region may not fit elsewhere. Companies want some coherence in systems and processes across their units, but that coherence and unity may not work well across diverse environments.

These issues often increase conflict between different units of the company and/or between geographic units and the corporate office. An "us versus them" mentality often sets in. Geographic units may try to influence corporate strategy in ways that either benefit the units specifically, or minimize any perceived harm caused to their units by corporate initiatives, even if this hurts the company as a whole.

Fourth, geographic diversification may expose the company to risks such as variation in exchange rates or political factors.

Finally, as with other kinds of diversification, geographic diversification may increase agency problems. Divisional managers rewarded for their unit's performance will push for policies that benefit their units rather than the company as a whole. In addition, managers of national subsidiaries rewarded with incentives based on national profits have little incentive to help other national subsidiaries.

SUMMARY

As with vertical integration and diversification, the key issue in geographic diversification is, how does the company add value by diversifying into different countries or regions? In addition to the benefits and costs associated with any kind of diversification, we also see some benefits and costs associated specifically with geographic diversification. These include the potential for cross-subsidization and currency or political risks.

We can analyze geographic diversification at different levels. At the national or industry level, Porter's diamond model helps us understand why some industries concentrate in certain geographic areas. At the firm level, we can identify four types of international strategies—international, multidomestic, global, and transnational—depending on the extent to which a company emphasizes national responsiveness and global integration. Within a firm, we can analyze the attractiveness of potential markets using a country-portfolio analysis or the CAGE framework.

In all of these cases, behavioral strategy underlies the strategic decisions that companies make. The value a company places on integration (e.g., by having the parent make all key decisions) versus responsiveness to national conditions (e.g., by decentralizing decision making to the geographic unit level) influences the choice of international strategy and how the parent and the geographic units influence one another, eventually determining the success of the company's geographic expansion.

FOOD FOR THOUGHT

1. A central concept in research on international strategy is the "liability of foreignness"—the additional cost to do business abroad that is incurred by a foreign firm due to its unfamiliarity with the foreign environment. How do you think firms can overcome the liability of foreignness?

2. Internalization theory, the parallel to transactions cost theory in the context of internationalization, suggests that when intellectual property rights such as patents and trademarks are weak, firms will tend to protect their intellectual property by internalizing the knowledge within the firm rather than licensing it to a local producer. In effect, internalization leads to larger, more multinational enterprises. Does this imply that small firms cannot expand internationally? What is the relation between size and international operations? How could new technology help small businesses expand geographically?

3. Most firms have limited resources. Therefore, many companies devote fewer resources to corporate social responsibility overseas than to corporate social responsibility in their home country. Is this fair? How should companies balance corporate social responsibility domestically and overseas? How responsible should multinational companies be for their foreign operations?

4. Multinational firms typically transfer people from their home office to different geographic locations to give transferees knowledge of the foreign locations. Firms assume such transferees will help the company make better decisions when they return to the home office. In practice, companies often fail to utilize the specialized knowledge of the transferee; they ignore the transferee's input. What causes this problem? How can companies overcome it? From a personal perspective, if you were transferred to a foreign location, how would you ensure your career stayed on track? How could you leverage your experience to advance in your company's corporate office?

5. What is your company's dominant logic? In a 2012 paper, Govindarajan suggests answering the following questions:[7]

    On a 1–5 scale (where 1= strongly agree, 2 = agree, 3 = neither agree nor disagree, 4 = disagree, and 5 = strongly disagree), rate the thinking of your company's key decision makers on the following statements, then add up the total of all 10 items.

    (i)   Rich countries are the most technologically advanced. So innovation and learning will move from rich countries to poor countries.
    (ii)   Sales of our existing products and services will increase as emerging economies grow and consumer incomes rise. We need only to be patient.
    (iii)   The best approach to emerging markets is to export stripped-down versions of existing products and services, and sell them at lower prices.
    (iv)   The bulk of the customers in poor countries have low per-capita incomes, low sophistication, and low affordability. We should be able to meet their needs with cheap products based on older technology.
    (v)   Poor countries today are where the rich countries were in their infancy. Poor countries will evolve in the same way that wealthy economies did. As they develop, poor countries will catch up with rich ones.
    (vi)   It is impossible to earn healthy profits in emerging markets.
    (vii)   The only competitors worth our attention are other multinationals.
    (viii) Products that address poor countries' special needs cannot be sold in rich countries because they are not good enough to compete.
    (ix)   We excel in product leadership and advanced technology— values inconsistent with the ultra low cost products poor countries require.
    (x)   Because we stand for premium products and high quality, we will undermine our global brands if we compete in low-cost markets. Worse, we risk cannibalizing our premium offerings.

    What is your company's score? If less than 30, you will under-perform in emerging markets. Your business needs an antidote.

NOTES AND BIBLIOGRAPHY

1. Porter, M. E. "The Competitive Advantage of Nations," *Harvard Business Review* 68(2) (1990):73–93; see also Porter, M. E. "Clusters and the New Economics of Competition," *Harvard Business Review* 76(6) (1998):77–90.

2. Chakravarthy, B. S., and Perlmutter, H. B. "Strategic Planning for a Global Business," *Columbia Journal of World Business* 20 (1985):3–10; Doz, Y., and Prahalad, C. K. "How MNCs Cope with Host-Government Intervention," *Harvard Business Review* 58(2) (1980):149–157; Heenan, D. A., and Perlmutter, H. B. *Multinational Organization Development* (Reading, MA: Addison-Wesley, 1979).

3. Bartlett, C. A., and Ghoshal, S. *Managing across Borders: The Transnational Solution* (Boston, MA: Harvard Business School Press, 1989).

4. Ghemawat, P. "Distance Still Matters," *Harvard Business Review* 79(8) (2001): 137–147.

5. Bell, D., and Shelman, M. L. "KFC's Radical Approach to China," *Harvard Business Review* 89(11) (November 2011):137–142.

6. Bartlett, C. A. "Philips versus Matsushita: The Competitive Battle Continues," *Harvard Business School Publishing*, (2009) Case # 9–910–410; see also Bartlett, C. A., and Ghoshal, S. "Tap Your Subsidiaries for Global Reach," *Harvard Business Review* 64(6) (1986):87–94.

7. Govindarajan, V. "Reversing the Curse of Dominant Logic," *Harvard Business Review*, https://hbr.org/2012/03/reversing-the-curse-of-dominan (March 2012).

CHAPTER 10

Organization and Strategy

Vision without execution is hallucination.

Thomas Edison

In Chapter 1, we noted that a company's intended strategy (what it plans to do), its emergent strategy (how strategy emerges or adapts from experience), and its realized strategy (what the firm actually does) often differ. These differences arise, in part, from differences in organizational structure and processes.

An organization's structure influences both strategy formulation and strategy implementation.

1. Organization structure influences how managers perceive the world, and the levers they have to adapt to that world. For example, managers in a firm organized by product tend to think about problems differently than managers in a firm organized by geography. Not only does organizational structure influence managers' cognition and perceptions, it also strongly influences the data available. The data available, in turn, strongly influence what questions managers tend to ask or answer.
2. Organization structure influences how managerial intention filters down to action. The organization structure and processes strongly influence the connections between intended and realized strategy.

If intended organizational strategies morph into something else during implementation, should companies even bother to come up with formal strategies or plans? The answer is yes. Almost all strategies and plans need adjustment in implementation. However, the strategy and plan provide some coherence in implementation.

WHY HAVE AN ORGANIZATION?

While some treatments in economics would see the organization simply as a nexus of many contracts, the theory and empirical evidence on organizations demonstrate that they have a variety of functions and processes independent of a contractual view. What do organizations do?

Organizations allow specialization, coordination, and motivation. In the previous chapters, we talked about coordination and motivation costs as two components of transaction costs—costs the organization takes into account while deciding whether or not to bring an activity in-house. Coordination and motivation, however, are not just costs. Combined with specialization, they determine how well (or badly) an organization carries out its activities. Let us look at the effects of specialization, coordination, and motivation on organization design more closely.

We all work in organizations filled with specialists. Functional categories define some specialties—accounting, sales, production, etc. Other specializations reflect factors such as knowledge of particular geographic regions, knowledge of specific technologies, connections with other important entities or individuals, etc. As soon as we start to organize by specialty, we hit coordination problems. In addition, we need to motivate people appropriately. People need reasons to do the right thing for the organization. Overall, well-designed organizations ensure that specialists coordinate their tasks and are motivated to act in a manner that enables the organization to achieve its desired outcomes.

Consequently, we want to design organizations that permit specialization in the building of capabilities even as they motivate individuals to work toward common goals. All of this must be done while still having the right information at the right place to identify problems, make decisions reasonably quickly, and keep costs within control. How do we do this?

Overall, you group employees together who must coordinate or interact frequently. Activities with substantial interdependence tend to end up in the same unit. This can create problems. Units often develop their own ideas of appropriate goals; they may work toward unit goals that do not align well with corporate or organization goals. In addition, grouping individuals by activities in the same unit may cause your company to miss economies of scale. Such groupings may not lead to efficient allocation of resources or learning. Finally, no matter what the design of the organization, organizations operate under standardized control systems that themselves reflect compromises among a number of things.

In other words, like almost any design, organizational design reflects a variety of trade-offs. If we took any single criterion to its logical conclusion, we would not end with an efficient or effective organization.

WHY HAVE AN ORGANIZATIONAL HIERARCHY?

Most organizations have hierarchical structures. In recent years, it has become fashionable to talk about a movement away from hierarchical organizations. Nevertheless, most of us work in hierarchies. Nonhierarchical organizations work very well for some purposes, but for many of the purposes we want, we use hierarchies. Why?

First, hierarchy helps with coordination. Suppose we have five individuals trying to coordinate themselves without hierarchy. Five individuals create nine potential interactions. Without formal structure, we have nine pairs of individuals trying to coordinate. A hierarchy with one supervisor and four subordinates has only four connections to coordinate.

Second, hierarchy generally invests one individual with the right to resolve disagreements. Without hierarchy, highly contentious decisions can drag on with no obvious path to resolution. An organization often does better with a questionable decision than no decision. Consider, for example, the launch of Proctor & Gamble's environmentally friendly laundry soap, Tide Purclean. When the product development team debated whether to use an orange colored bottle cap (consistent with Tide's signature color) or some other color (to signify environmental friendliness), the CEO, David Taylor, stepped in and told the team to go with orange, ending what could otherwise have been an interminable discussion.[1]

Third, hierarchy may allow modularization and decentralization. This has a parallel with programing or designing computer programs. At one point, people wrote complex parts of programs that interacted across various portions of the overall program in a variety of ways. In recent years, people have instead begun to develop modular programs—programs that we "plug-and-play." In place of designing one complex program that is hard to reconfigure, we try to simplify the connections between different parts of the program. This lets us develop better modules that can be adapted more easily to our requirements without having to redesign the system completely.

In organizations, this reduced interaction means that we can develop better procedures or operations in one part of the organization without changing all the other parts of the organization.

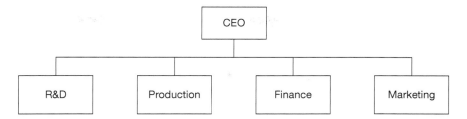

Figure 10.1 A Functional Structure

With these preliminary comments, we now turn to a number of basic organizational designs.

Most companies start with a functional organization—a hierarchy arranged largely by function (see Figure 10.1). The company has units addressing sales, purchasing, production, shipping, accounting, etc. Almost all small organizations use functional structures, although they may not have all the functions we listed above; individuals sometime handle multiple functions in small companies.

Large functional organizations can be effective, but only under limited circumstances and with limited efficiency. If an organization has a very simple set of products and relatively simple interactions between activities, then the organization can develop prespecified decision criteria to operate efficiently with a very large functional structure. For example, an oil refining company that does nothing but refine oil into a small set of fuels can operate with an exceedingly large functional structure. However, once the company begins to convert crude petroleum into a wide variety of products from fuels to plastics to drugs, a functional organization becomes unwieldly.

A functional structure benefits from specialization and economies of scale, since grouping people by the type of job facilitates learning within functions. However, a functional structure can lead to the development of a silo mentality, where people from one function do not talk to people from other functions, leading to coordination problems.

Functional structures may also slow decision making. Consider a situation when a disagreement occurs between low-level employees from different functions. If the employees cannot work out the problem themselves, in a large functional organization, the issue may go up the chain of command

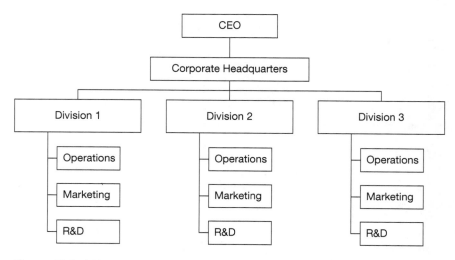

Figure 10.2 A Divisional Structure

a long way before it reaches an individual who supervises both functions and can therefore adjudicate fights between functions. This passing of the decision up the chain of command results in delayed decision making that lets coordination and other problems fester for a long time because no one has the authority to make a decision, at least at the level where these problems occur.

The next step up from a functional structure is usually a divisional structure (Figure 10.2). Divisional structures break the company up into categories (usually based on product or geography), and then operate the categories as separate businesses. We will talk about divisions as incorporating most of the important activities, although many companies use divisions for most activities while maintaining corporate units for others (e.g., for accounting or R&D).

For example, many organizations have divisional structures based on the products they sell, often with a division office or unit responsible for overall management of each product category. These division offices handle all the major activities related to their products including R&D, new product development, production, sales, and distribution of the product.

Alternatively, some organizations have geographic divisions. Here, each geographic area operates as its own business, and handles all functions within that business.

Divisional structures facilitate coordination of activities related to a product or region. Divisional structures facilitate diversification into multiple product lines or countries. In the divisional structure, divisional managers focus on managing their product or region while managers at the corporate office handle strategic issues such as the allocation of resources across divisions. This separation of strategic and operating control allows the company to respond effectively to changes in the external environment.

Divisional structures have some drawbacks. First, they reduce specialization and perhaps lose economies of scale. With every division managing each functional area separately, we may have small numbers of specialists at each division. The company may thus not achieve economies of scale or learning among divisions in the way they might in a larger group. For example, having each product or national division producing independently can result in many small production facilities making similar products. Having R&D at the division level can result in a lack of critical mass and diversity of skills necessary for substantial innovations.

Second, you have duplication. For example, some medical products companies have multiple salespeople calling on the same hospital to sell different divisional product lines. Having multiple sales people call on the same customer wastes resources and confuses the customer who seldom understands or cares about the company's internal divisions. In the worst case, geographic divisions may sometimes compete against one another for the same customer.

Third, divisional structures can lead to information processing problems. As we get more divisions, top management can have difficulty keeping on top of all of the divisions. Some very large American corporations literally have a hundred or more businesses. Obviously, corporate management cannot devote much time to understanding each of a hundred businesses.

At the extreme, divisional structures essentially become holding companies. Here, top management largely deals with divisions by looking at their strategic plans and at their financial performance. Top management allocates resource using largely financial criteria. This simplifies decision-making and reduces the need for corporate staff.

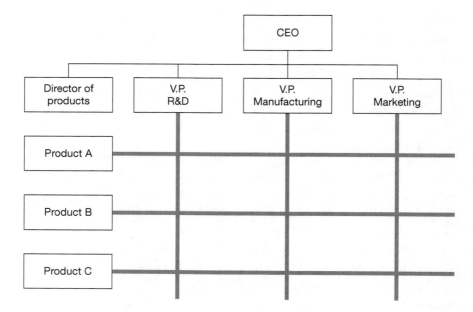

Figure 10.3 A Matrix Structure

However, such highly decentralized systems can miss opportunities in various ways. These kinds of structures may miss opportunities that arise from coordinating activities across the divisions. In addition, a lack of standardization in management systems across divisions can make it hard for corporations to compare performance across divisions. Divisional structures may create destructive interdivisional competition. Given the orientation of the headquarters toward financials, managers may focus on meeting the numbers in the short term rather than managing for the long term. At the extreme, this kind of structure raises questions about the value added by the corporation.

Given these problems, many organizations have moved to matrix structures (Figure 10.3). The matrix structure essentially says we need to pay attention to more than one structural dimension (e.g., products, functions, or regions). Frequently, one side of the matrix will be products and the other will be functions. In this case, the corporation wide functional groups may either operate functional activities (e.g., HR) for the divisions, or tell the divisions how to operate in functions by setting standards for training, recruitment, reporting systems, etc.

Matrix structures are not limited to products and functions. The sides of the matrix could be countries, regions, technologies, or almost anything else management wants.

Matrix structures offer some of the advantages of both functional and divisional structures; they potentially allow the company to handle complex coordination problems while keeping the benefits of specialization.

On the other hand, matrix structures often are time-consuming and confusing. Sometimes employees in a matrix structure find themselves caught in the middle when one side of the matrix demands something incompatible with what the other side demands. For example, a product line supervisor might order the employee to do one thing and a functional supervisor might order something else. A lot depends on who controls

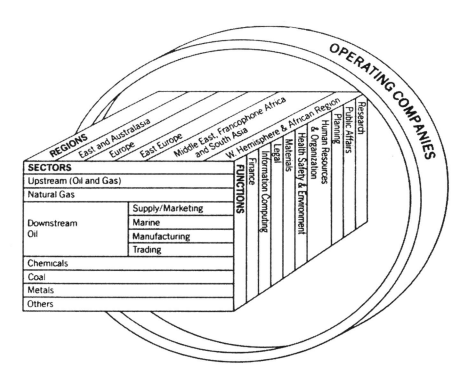

Figure 10.4 Royal Dutch Shell's Matrix Structure, 1994

© 2012 Robert M. Grant and Judith Jordan. Reprinted with permission from Wiley Publishers. Source: Grant, R.M., and Jordan, J. 2012. *Foundations of Strategy.* Chichester, U.K.: John Wiley & Sons.

individuals' careers. Some of these complex coordination problems appear inherent in highly diversified organizations.

Having said this, matrix structures remain popular. Some companies have actually moved to a three-sided matrix. The structure from Shell in 1994 even has four sides to it (Figure 10.4).

Shell is not unique. We have had students tell us their organization uses an organization structure that looks almost exactly like the Shell structure above.

ADDITIONAL NON-HIERARCHICAL VARIATIONS

Companies have tried other ways to handle the basic problem of specialization versus coordination. Probably the most common nonhierarchical ways are project-based or cross-functional team structures.

In a project-based structure, management puts together the employees with appropriate skills on a project-by-project basis. Often, this results in project teams including individuals from various functions or geographic areas or other subdivisions in the corporation.

In a cross-functional team structure, management creates groups that, as you might expect, include representatives from various functions to deal with something on an ongoing basis. While project-based groups generally have limited duration, some organizations rely heavily on cross-functional teams for continuing activities.

Both of these structures help companies with coordination. However, both structures can also create some serious difficulties for employees. Employees may be torn between acting in the interests of their home divisions and acting in the furtherance of the team's objectives. Employees may also lack the authority to commit their units to actions the team needs. With the exception of a few organizations designed largely to handle projects (e.g., construction firms), firms add cross-functional and project-based teams to a more conventional operating structure—organizations using one of the other designs for their primary structure often supplement the structure with project or cross-functional teams.

STRUCTURE IN GENERAL

Structure alone cannot solve strategy implementation problems for most organizations. The structure, systems, and culture of an organization must align. The 7-S framework emphasizes this point[2] (see Figure 10.5). In this framework, structure is one of seven inter-related components including strategy, systems, and shared values that work together to lead to organizational coordination and therefore, effectiveness.

We mention the 7-S framework because it highlights the need to align all the factors in the organization. Practitioners use various frameworks in this area, but the essential issue is the need to align all of these factors appropriately.

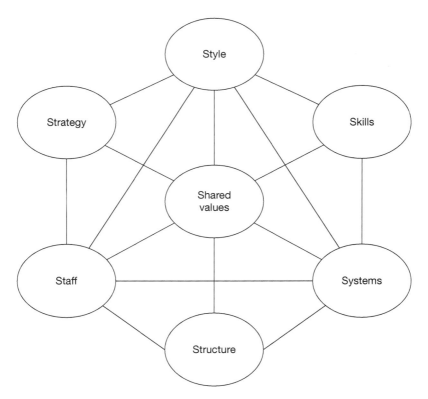

Figure 10.5 McKinsey's 7-S Framework

SYSTEMS

An organization's structure becomes realized through a set of systems.

Organizational systems determine where management focuses attention, the information management has available, the people who work in the organization, the training and incentives given to employees, etc. Organizations involve the interaction of many routines. For example, a company does not come up with new procedures every time it hires a new person. Indeed, you may want to think of an organization as an amalgam of routines that determine almost everything that happens in organization on a day-by-day basis.

Routines do not occur just in organizations. Most of you have a routine that governs how your morning operates. Most mornings, this routine saves you from thinking about what you do next. This routine would also help coordination by determining who uses the bathroom when, etc.

Routines have the same benefits in organizations. They reduce the cognitive effort employees have to exert when doing the tasks they do regularly. For example, you would not want the janitor to come in every night and try to figure out the best way to clean the building. This problem merits thinking about once or twice, but after that, following a routine makes sense.

Routines also allow coordination; if I know your routine, I can coordinate our activities. Often the routines themselves determine the coordination. For example, think about all the things that happen to have you in this class with a faculty member. The university needs systems that recruit and select students. It needs financial aid systems, student advising, student housing, course scheduling, room scheduling, assignment of faculty to classes, payment of faculty and staff, etc. All of these have to act predictably so that the other portions can count on their behavior. You cannot run a large organization without a plethora of routines.

Routines allocate management attention. Many organizations have routines that require management set goals for individuals or units. Management pays attention if the individual or unit does not meet those goals. Management focuses on places where the routine does not meet expectations.

Routines also influence the amount and type of information managers use to make decisions. If you have tried to do a project in a corporation, you know the data available largely comes from specific routines for specific purposes. Data that fall outside those purposes (i.e., data not collected by operating routines), often simply does not exist. Routines thus influence managerial decision making; they both allocate attention and determine what we can talk about sensibly and what we cannot.

Finally, routines influence the effectiveness of a company's strategy implementation. Routines influence implementation in a myriad of ways. They determine what the firm can and cannot do with reasonable amounts of effort. They determine if and how the organization will change.

Routines often have unintended outcomes. For example, routines can lead to what Levitt and March (p. 322) label "competency traps," wherein a "favorable performance with an inferior procedure leads an organization to accumulate more experience with it, thus keeping experience with a superior procedure inadequate to make it rewarding to use."[3] That is, routines can trap organizations into doing things that are inefficient or costly even when better procedures exist. Sometimes the cost of changing makes retaining an inefficient technology or process appear desirable. As another example, consider the routines associated with personnel evaluation. Since performance evaluation often depends on recent performance, HR routines may encourage or even force managers to indulge in short-termism, that is, overemphasizing immediate results.

Short-termism relates to risk preference. Organizational structures strongly influence managerial risk preferences.

RISK PREFERENCES

When would a manager take risks? Research indicates that managers have the same propensity to take risks as an average individual. Risk taking varies with the situation.[4] Individuals take more risks when faced with the prospect of losses, but become risk averse when most of the outcomes of a choice or decision involve gains, that is, above a reference point or desired outcome.[5] Stated simply, the prospect of losing something causes more pain than the prospect of gaining an equal amount.

This simple relation also holds for organizations.[6] The behavioral theory of the firm suggests risk taking by organizations depends on firm performance relative to an aspiration or target level.[7] Performance above an aspiration level means that the firm continues to work according to its established routines. If performance falls below an aspiration level, the firm seeks ways to raise performance above the aspiration level; these ways may involve risk taking.

A firm has targets or aspiration levels on many dimensions; firm behavior depends on which aspiration level triggers search. If managers perceive the problem of falling sales as a marketing problem, the organization will look for a marketing solution. If managers perceive the same problem as a quality problem, the organization may adopt a quality improvement program. However, firms do not react every time managers perceive a problem. Firms may use their slack—excess cash, say, or inventory—to buffer themselves against small problems.

Managerially, this implies substantial change occurs when a unit or organization persistently fails to meet goals (particularly when competitors appear not to have problems). Even when organizations try to fix a problem, the solution is likely a compromise, satisfying the interests of a number of stakeholders. Further, if the implemented solution appears to solve the problem, others in your organization will be unlikely to be interested in making further changes, essentially leaving well enough alone.

The incentive structure for most managers discourages risk-taking. Consider what happens if a mid-level manager takes a big risk. If the risk turns out well, the manager may get a promotion or a bonus, usually some fraction of the individual's salary. If decision turns out badly, the firm may fire the manager. In an extreme case, the manager may lose the ability to find employment in the industry in which the manager has worked for many years. It does not take a genius to see that most organizational incentive systems do not encourage risk-taking.

This does not apply to all managers. Traders in financial institutions often have incentive structures that encourage risk. Investment firms often retain a portion of positive financial returns but do not share in losses. The exceedingly high potential compensation for individual traders also encourages risk taking. A trader who can make millions in bonuses in a good year may not worry much about long-term results. A similar problem may occur at the CEO level where stock options result in CEOs gaining substantially if the stock price increases but losing little if the stock price declines. Many observers worry that the incentive structures of top management and traders often reward excessive risk-taking.

Finally, managers conceive risk differently than academics. Academics often talk about risk as a variance in outcomes or association of outcomes with the stock market. Academics tend to imagine a choice from which some random outcome occurs. Managers tend to define risk by the potential for outcomes to fall below a target or aspiration level or by the worst possible outcome.[8] Doing better than anticipated does not constitute a risk to managers, nor does uncertainty involving trivial stakes. This agrees with how we would see risks in day-to-day life. For example, we would not see buying a lottery ticket for $1 or the possibility of a promotion as risky. While many managers see risk taking as part of their job, they also report that the choices are not risky because they make sure the results turn out well.

FORMAL STRATEGIC PLANNING

In strategic management, a routine of particular interest is formal strategic planning.

In the early days of research on strategic management, scholars paid a lot of attention to the participants and processes of formal strategic planning. However, they did not find consistent results. This led to two changes. First, scholars started to look at strategic decisions (mergers, divestitures, etc.) rather than strategic planning processes. Second, people started to argue that the benefits of planning came not in the plan, but in the process of thinking through the strategic plan. This sounds good, although we have no direct evidence to support it.

Strategic planning is not a natural act for most managers. Most managers are firefighters or problem solvers. They move quickly from one issue to another. They seldom spend long hours worrying about any specific issue. They want to act. Contrast this with formal strategic planning where we ask managers to ignore immediate, tangible problems and to focus on more amorphous, longer term issues or scenarios. Some large companies like

Intel deal with this issue by having separate strategic planning departments insulated from day-to-day problem solving. However, plans largely driven by staff offices have additional problems we discuss below.

Based on work at the Ford Company, the U.S. military differentiates its planning into a variety of stages in the PPBS: planning, programming, and budgeting system. In the planning stage, the military tries to understand the potential challenges it will face, and develop general ideas about how to meet those challenges. In programming, planners attempt to understand how the organization will put those general ideas into practice in the next 2–5 years. Budgeting primarily deals with what the organization does in the next fiscal year.

For-profit planning may benefit from a similar distinction. Strategic analysis (the core of this text) differs from programming and budgeting activities. In strategic analysis, we ask the broad strategy questions—whom we compete against, what determines who wins, what should our broad strategy be? In programming and budgeting, we translate this general strategy into a series of coherent steps.

Unfortunately, most managers prefer programming, that is, solving tangible problems, to strategic analysis. Consequently, many corporate strategic plans are actually programs.[9] We dealt with one corporation that asked its divisions to identify how much they would sell to each of its major customers in each of the next 5 years. While perhaps important for programming, that is, trying to figure out how to allocate resources, develop necessary production capacity, etc., it does not address the broader strategic issues. Indeed, Richard Rumelt, in his book *Good Strategy, Bad Strategy*, argues that many companies do not even have strategies.[10] They may have buzzwords, they may have goals, they may even have programs, but they have never really thought deeply about the environment in which they compete, their competitors, and how they could realistically win.

Most managers prefer programming to strategic analysis. Programming deals with clearly defined, well-structured problems. Managers have great experience and many tools to address such problems. Strategic analysis, in contrast, is (or should be) an inherently uncomfortable activity; strategic problems are called wicked problems for good reason.

Strategic planning must connect to programming. Indeed, if strategic plans do not result in explicit action items with review cycles, managers will ignore the plans. Companies routinely develop plans that they largely ignore as the company manages to the budget. Some claim that's okay because the value of the plan is in the thinking; the process matters, not the actual decisions. This appears a bit facile.

STRATEGIC PLANNING CYCLE

Given managers do not have a natural tendency for strategic analysis, firms use formal planning processes to provide times when managers must do the analysis. Strategic planning follows a reasonably standard process in most companies. We will discuss a standard process for large firms. While smaller firms often use simpler procedures or even skip formal strategic planning, venture capitalists and equity investors often force smaller growth companies to generate strategic plans.

First, the corporate office develops some common guidelines. These guidelines often include the economic assumptions the divisions will use. Common economic assumptions make it possible to compare division plans. Often, the guidelines specify some major concerns or thrusts the corporate office wants to emphasize in the upcoming year.

Second, the business units develop plans for their businesses. They discuss these plans with the corporate office, usually leading to revisions. The corporate office tends to increase whatever targets the divisions propose.

Third, incorporating the business unit plans, the corporation develops a corporate plan. This corporate plan summarizes or aggregates the business unit plans and provides direction for corporate office activities.

Fourth, top management presents the strategic plan to the board. For the most part, board review is more symbolic than a real review.

Fifth, the company (often the divisions) develops a set of budgets for the next year for the divisions and the corporate functions. Ideally, but not always, these budgets align with the division plans. These budgets include the targets and the criteria that will guide operations and evaluation. In addition to the operating budget, firms often produce a capital budget specifying the allocation of capital to divisions. Annual capital budgets generally include the total funds allocated to each of the operating units as well as earmarked funds for a few large projects. R&D budgets operate similarly, although they come out of the operating planning system. Budgets provide the performance targets for divisional management.

Sixth, the organization operates by the budget, with periodic reviews of outcomes against budget targets.

Note that these steps apply to companies following a traditional waterfall model of strategic planning, where following a sequential (non-iterative) series of steps results in a strategic plan. Some observers consider the minimum viable product (MVP) model as an alternative to strategic planning.

The MVP model is an iterative process that involves producing and marketing the simplest products possible and consequently learning rapidly about customer preferences. For example, the founder of Dropbox, a file hosting company that allows users to share and synchronize files, used a basic 3-minute video as an MVP to test the market potential of the company's service. The video had the founder narrating while using the technology; this simple video demonstration increased the wait list of people wanting to sign up for the beta version of the product from 5,000 to 75,000 people overnight. A number of other internet-based firms have used the model to test and launch their products and services, often on crowdfunding platforms such as Kickstarter.[11]

MVP, as the words say, focuses on developing products, rather than full plans. Along the lines of the Dropbox example, the Lean Startup thread in the entrepreneurship prescriptive literature emphasizes MVP. MVP deals more with product development than strategic direction, but for an early stage company, development of the initial product is the core strategic issue. Such companies must choose the characteristics of their initial products, and the success of those products often determines the continued existence of the companies. The existence and success of Dropbox, for example, depended initially on the success of the file sharing and recovery product we know as Dropbox. Such firms do not have portfolios of ongoing products to manage. They also often face great uncertainty about how customers will respond to new products and what features customers want. Consequently, the MVP approach makes more sense at the strategic level for organizations in their early stages where the organizations face substantial uncertainty about basic product and strategic choices. Rather than lock into a specific strategy, MVP helps such firms learn about their markets and customers. However, even an organization that uses formal strategic planning can use MVP for product development, especially if the organization operates in a rapidly changing environment.

As a company grows, full reliance on minimally coordinated product development to determine the scope of the company can create substantial difficulties. Just because the company develops a good product does not mean the company should pursue the product. As we noted in the chapter on technology intensive industries, a firm that invents a product but lacks many of the necessary complementary assets often benefits from licensing or selling the technology rather than trying to exploit it in-house. Executives at a major oil company told one of the authors that they ask three questions about a new product: (i) is it technically feasible, (ii) do customers need or want it, and (iii) can our company do it better than competitors? Many entrepreneurial firms also need conventional strategic and financial plans (usually called business plans) to explain their businesses to investors and other stakeholders.

Irrespective of whether a company follows a traditional waterfall model, an MVP model, or something else, useful strategic planning requires certain things.

1. *Management must own and take responsibility for the strategic planning process.* One of us has had consultants in class who said companies had paid them to develop plans that the companies then proceeded to ignore. These consultants had coordinated heavily with company staff while developing the plans. This is insufficient. When managers take a strategic plan seriously, they stake their careers on these decisions about how to operate the division or the corporation. Line managers, who hold the real authority, will not stake their careers on plans that they have not been instrumental in developing. Line management must own the plan. Staff can help with analysis, but it cannot and must not be the staff's plan.

2. *The plan must involve analysis, not just extrapolation.* With Excel, we all can easily do projections. While useful for certain purposes, it is not strategic planning. Effective strategic planning usually includes serious analysis by having corporate staff review the plans. Top management then grills the divisions on their plans. This grilling improves the thinking in the plans and forces divisional

management to commit to their plans. To focus the discussion on the critical issues, many companies severely limit the amount of quantification available in strategic plans and require short statements of strategy.

3. *Planning requires data and rigor.* Ideally, initial stages of planning identify important issues that merit additional analysis and often data collection.

4. *Planning must lead to closure.* You must not draw out strategic planning ad infinitum. We know of one company that spent a year and a half developing a strategic plan. What a waste—in a year and a half, the analysis is probably obsolete.

5. *Planning must result in decisions—tough decisions.* When asked to advise a university planning committee on planning, one of the authors told the committee members that if they were not going to make tough decisions, if they would not decide to be good at X and not good at Y, they should not even bother planning. As we have discussed extensively earlier, to be good at one thing almost guarantees you not being good at something else. Attempting to be good at everything normally results in mediocrity.

6. *Planning must grow from a sophisticated understanding of the situation.* The first part of this text dealt with how you analyze the situation—understand the general environment, the industry environment, your abilities relative to the competition in that environment, etc. Without a sophisticated understanding of the problem, you cannot develop a good strategy. You need to be explicit about your assumptions and understanding of the situation. Nothing is less productive than having managers arguing because they make different implicit assumptions and do not even know that these different assumptions underlie their disagreements.

7. *Strategic planning must lead to targets.* Day-to-day, managers face a continuous stream of things to do. To force them to pay attention to the strategy, you need explicit strategic targets with deadlines and review sessions during the year. Performance on strategic targets must matter in managerial evaluation. An effective strategic plan should include a number of milestones, identification of individuals responsible for reaching the milestones, and specification of times when management will evaluate progress toward those milestones.

8. *The strategic plan must influence the budget and personnel evaluation.* Managers manage to the budget, so an effective plan must influence the budget. Where the budget influences personnel evaluation, and the progress toward strategic targets does not, managers have little choice but to emphasize the budget and ignore the strategic targets.

This does not mean that the strategy should be a straitjacket. Reality will differ from what you anticipated. Nevertheless, progress beyond our immediate concerns requires a mechanism that keeps strategic issues on the agenda.

Students face similar problems. Many of you have immediate concerns from your classes. Likewise, many have immediate concerns from your jobs. However, you also recognize that you need to make time for things like the development of your network, looking for a job, or maintaining your personal relations. If you do not systematically put these longer term activities on your agenda, immediate deadlines may overwhelm them.

CORPORATE GOVERNANCE

Corporate governance refers to the relations among various participants—typically the shareholders, the board of directors, and top management—in determining the direction and performance of companies.

Corporate governance depends heavily on the laws under which a corporation operates, and so varies across countries and even somewhat across U.S. states. To keep this section at a reasonable length, we will discuss U.S. history and laws. Note that while similar issues exist in many countries, the laws and their implementation differ internationally.

Discussions of corporate governments often emphasize whether the company's managers act largely in the interest of the shareholders or in their own interests. This concern follows directly from the basic assumptions of agency theory, the predominant theory that underlies most discussions of corporate governance.[12]

AGENCY THEORY

Agency theory assumes two central players: an honest, risk-neutral principal (usually the firm's shareholders, board of directors, or top management) and an amoral, risk-averse agent (the managers or employees of a firm). The principal must rely on the agent to make decisions on behalf of the principal, but the principal cannot tell if the agent acts fully in the principal's interest. Furthermore, monitoring the agent is costly. This is important because (the theory assumes), given a chance, agents will lie to the principal and act in their own interests. For example, agents might take less risk than the principal would like, and/or increase their own benefits excessively. Agency theory addresses how the principal can get the agent to act in the principal's interest.

The theory suggests that principals can use monitoring and incentives to control agents. The cost of using these two tools is called agency costs. The theory predicts that the contracting parties will incur agency costs up to the point where additional cost of incentives and monitoring exceeds the benefits. In simple terms, principals try to get agents to work in the principals' interest—but without spending so much that it is not worthwhile getting an agent in the first place.

Researchers have used agency theory to examine issues ranging from executive compensation to diversification. The widely diffused ownership that characterizes modern public corporations results in little oversight of managers by owners (shareholders), increasing the potential for agency problems; this is often termed the Berle and Means hypothesis.[13]

CORPORATE GOVERNANCE IN ORGANIZATIONS

Whether you deal with higher-level governance directly or not, corporate governance influences your organization and consequently, you. Some of you may deal with corporate governance issues relatively directly, for example, by preparing reports that go to the board or that react to questions from the board. Every employee experiences the outcomes of decisions influenced by corporate governance.

Regardless of whether you have a direct involvement in governance-related issues, you need to understand how this entity called the corporation operates from a governance standpoint. While governance varies somewhat across companies, we will address some commonalities now.

Let us differentiate between publicly and privately held businesses. In the United States, you can hold a company privately and not have to comply with a large set of regulatory issues. Such companies may have advisory boards or boards of directors, but powers and authority of the boards depend on choices by the owners—many such boards have little power. The owners, being small in number, may take a direct role in the company, often playing important managerial roles in addition to ownership.

Alternately, you can have a public company. Instead of relying on a very small set of owners, the company offers stock to the public. The first time this is done is referred to as an initial public offering or IPO. For entrepreneurial companies, the IPO lets early investors convert their illiquid ownership in the startup into cash or stock convertible into cash. Having stock issued to the public gives public companies access to investment capital that privately held companies do not have. At the same time, the public company faces state and federal regulations and laws that require certain forms of governance and provision of information to investors, including that the company have a board of directors. While boards of directors have a number of important roles, their most important role is determining the CEO of the corporation. Boards do not run or speak for corporations. CEOs do.

In addition to governance requirements, public companies face regulatory requirements that vary with the state of incorporation. Many corporations incorporate in the state of Delaware. One can see this from two different perspectives. First, because so many corporations incorporate in Delaware, Delaware has courts specifically created to address corporate issues. The judges on these courts deal with corporate law day in and day out. This results in more knowledgeable judges and more predictable administration of the law. Second, Delaware offers a set of guidelines and rules that particularly benefit corporate management and ownership. Because Delaware has almost no locally grown companies, it can increase state revenue by offering relatively low corporate tax rates. In many cases, Delaware law and jurisprudence appears to favor management over stockholders. Since management decides where to incorporate, many incorporate in Delaware.

Over the last two decades, the federal government's role in corporate governance has increased. Following accounting fraud in companies such as Enron and WorldCom in the early 2000s, the Sarbanes–Oxley act of 2002, among other things, requires top management certify the accuracy of financial information reported to the federal Securities and Exchange Commission, and specifies criminal penalties for corporate misconduct. Following the financial crisis of 2008, the Dodd–Frank Wall Street Reform and Consumer Protection Act of 2010 addresses a number of issues claimed to have led to the crisis. For example, the act permits shareholders to use a company's proxy solicitation materials to nominate their own individuals to the board of directors. The act also requires a company explain to its shareholders why it does (or does not) have CEO duality—a situation where the same individual serves both as the CEO and as the chairman of the board of directors. Recently, however, there has been some pushback against these regulations, with some legislators and companies suggesting that these regulations do nothing but increase red tape.

Given these debates on corporate governance, it is worthwhile clarifying some issues.

The most important issue is, who owns the company? Most might answer that shareholders own the company. Technically speaking, however, this is not correct. Shareholders do not really own corporations. Shareholders own shares in corporations, and holding of shares gives them specific but limited rights with respect to the corporation. Shareholders have the right to act in their own interest. Shareholders have the right to a limited set of public information. Shareholders have the right to vote for directors and share in the profits of the firm subject to decisions of directors. Finally, shareholders have the right to vote on some key strategic decisions. Specific implementation of these rights depends on the bylaws the corporation chose when it incorporated. Proxy statements and related shareholder votes routinely revise these bylaws, for example, on incentive plans for top management.

However, these rights fall short of what we would normally consider the rights of owners. The owner of a private company has the right to all information in the company and the right to make specific choices about the management of company. Shareholders do not have these rights with the exception of very clearly delimited domains. Especially with widely distributed shares (where no single shareholder owns a substantial portion of the stock), management runs corporations under the supervision, to some extent, of the board. In the modern corporation, control of the firm has passed from the principals (shareholders) to the agents (managers and directors or board members).

BOARD OF DIRECTORS

The board of directors stands between shareholders and management. Members of the board have a responsibility to act in the best interests of the corporation and its shareholders. However, the law does not clearly define the exact meaning of "best interests." With the exception of situations when a corporation is in the process of being sold, the board does not have to act in the short-term interest of the shareholders.

Board members have several duties:

- Board members have a duty of loyalty; they must put the corporation's interests ahead of their own. Violations of this duty are one of the clearest ways in which corporate directors can get into trouble.
- Board members have a duty of care; they must take appropriate care while performing their duties. Often, this means using outside consultants and recording discussions in the minutes of the board. Known as the business judgment rule, courts generally will not question a board's decision if the board has put in a reasonable amount of consideration. The judiciary is loath to second-guess boards and management even where management makes decisions that appear quite questionable. The business judgment rule means that, while investors sue board members with some regularity, with the exception of violations of the duty of loyalty, board members seldom pay any fines personally.
- Boards need to monitor the corporation's performance in light of the company's strategic plans. Boards also need to supervise the corporation's risk management, understand the corporation's financial statements and disclosures, and the company's internal controls.
- Boards have to evaluate and approve major transactions such as mergers and acquisitions, as well as establish monitoring and effective information systems to ensure compliance.

- Boards select the CEO, set goals for the CEO, and review CEO performance.
- Boards are supposed to develop and implement succession plans for the top management of the company (although some fail to do so).

While management runs the company, technically, their decisions are subject to advice and supervision by the board. Management speaks for the corporation; the board does not do so except under unusual circumstances. For the most part, boards react to managerial initiatives rather than taking the initiative. Boards depend on management for most of the information they have on the company.

There has been a continuing debate over corporate boards, their formation, their operations, and their effectiveness. While companies pay board members quite well for their efforts, historically, observers described boards as ineffectual; they simply did not do their jobs well. Boards often included people who brought no obviously relevant expertise to the company— actors, sports figures, and the like. Indeed, even more recently, one of the authors' friends who advises boards noted that board members sometimes sleep during meetings.

However, the biggest issues regarding board effectiveness come from two things: perceptions about the fairness of the governance or election process, and board oversight, particularly regarding top management compensation and risk taking.

Let us begin with the election process. For the most part, boards are self-perpetuating. The board nominates one candidate to fill each open seat on the board; with one candidate for a seat, the candidate automatically "wins" the election. While shareholders can nominate other candidates, historically this has been an expensive and difficult process, made somewhat easier by the provisions of the Dodd–Frank Act. However, almost all of the time, boards determine who will be on the board. Many corporations only elect a third of their members each year. This means that even if you go to the trouble of nominating your candidates, and succeed in getting them elected this year, you would have to repeat the process next year before you have a majority of your candidates on the board. As might be expected, boards tend to appoint directors that look like the current directors—largely Caucasian, elderly, and male.

While issues around the alignment of incentives between management and the stockholders appear frequently, they become highlighted when another company offers to buy the company in question. Almost universally, the other company offers more, and often much more, than the stock trades for prior to the offer. Despite this, boards and management often fight takeovers.

Top management and board members often have substantial interest in status quo—they receive compensation and prestige from the company's continued existence. The board members and senior managers of an acquired company seldom receive equivalent positions in the acquirer's structure. Consequently, top management and boards frequently attempt to prevent takeovers. Sometimes, such prevention acts in the stockholders' interest by increasing the amount offered for the company. Often it simply keeps current board and management in place.

CEO COMPENSATION AND RISK TAKING

A second major area of concern over governance relates to CEO compensation and risk-taking. The ratio of CEO compensation to the average compensation of corporate employees has gone from roughly 24 to almost 300 times over the last few decades. Observers concerned with income inequality, though not necessarily stockholders, find this troubling. Stockholders and their representatives complain when CEOs receive bonuses and stock options even when investors lose money. With some regularity, the business press reports on CEOs who receive bonuses (supposedly based on performance) despite stock prices declining 20 and 30 percent.

The empirical evidence is that despite billions of dollars in corporate incentive plans, CEO compensation has almost no correlation with stockholder returns.[14] The primary determinant of CEO compensation remains firm size. This means management has a strong incentive to grow the firm even when it will not increase stock price or stockholder returns.

Recent research suggests that the CEOs in the top 10 percent of CEO compensation, where compensation largely comes in "incentives," underperform the average of the stock market by 5–10 percent.[15]

In other words, the highest compensation goes with bad performance. When the stock market went down in 2006, CEO compensation remained stable with some industry-specific declines. In the run-up since, CEO compensation has skyrocketed. CEOs generally do not suffer much when the stock price declines, but benefit substantially when it rises.

Some observers blame CEO compensation for excessive risk-taking, particularly prior to the 2008 recession. The big money in CEO compensation usually comes from stock options. A stock option gives the CEO or manager the right to buy the stock at a given price (the strike price) sometime in the future. Options usually have a period they cannot be exercised followed by a period when the holder has the choice of exercising it. If the stock price falls below the strike price, the manager loses nothing. On the other hand, if the stock price rises above the strike price, top managers can receive substantial gains. If management shares generously in the upside, but does not bear the downside of firm outcomes, a rational manager should take substantial risks. Essentially, management can gamble with the stockholder's money, but the stockholder retains all the losses while the manager shares in gains. Under this structure, a rational manager should take extreme risks even if the risks have negative expected value from the stockholder standpoint.

We have a very difficult design problem. An incentive structure based largely on salary and bonuses tied to net income and such measures rewards the manager for past performance; this may result in a short-term perspective and insufficient risk-taking. An incentive structure based largely on options can provide management an incentive to take excessive risks. Research also shows that options have very different impacts on managerial behavior when they are not exercisable and when they are exercisable.[16] Boards have difficulty designing incentive systems that reward performance but discourage gambling. As we mentioned in our discussion of agency theory, firms can control management behavior either by providing the agent (the CEO) with the right incentives, that is, incentives that align the CEO's interests with those of the principal, or monitoring the agent.

Companies typically compensate top managers with a combination of salary, bonuses, stock options, restricted stock (that cannot be sold until a specified date), and stock ownership. In theory, the fixed component (salary) protects the manager from the downside of risk taking while the variable components (stock options etc.) let the manager share in the upside. Supposedly, this should align the interests of the managers with that of the owners. Many question how well this works in practice. For example, managers may choose to emphasize investments that increase stock price in the short run to benefit from stock options—irrespective of whether this benefits for the company in the long run.

In addition, major questions arise over the appropriate general level for CEO compensation.[17] Some could argue that CEO compensation provides extremely muted incentives; Milgrom and Roberts, for example, suggest that a CEO earning $1 million in salary and bonus for heading a $1 billion dollar company may get about 10–16 cents for every $1,000 created for shareholders.[18] Hence, extremely high levels of CEO compensation are appropriate. Others compare CEO compensation to the compensation of other workers, which makes CEO compensation appear quite excessive. In reality, however, CEO compensation depends less on an assessment of how much additional value the CEO could create for the company than on what other CEOs in the industry receive. Most boards have a compensation subcommittee that determines CEO compensation, usually based on advice of compensation consultants. However, the CEO often has a hand in picking compensation consultants. Some research finds (perhaps unsurprisingly) that companies that use compensation consultants appointed only by the board pay CEOs about 13 percent less than similar firms where the CEO hired a second set of consultants.[19]

In terms of monitoring, the management makes the key decisions for the company, theoretically with oversight from the board. While some firms fire CEOs for poor performance, the real question is, how long does a board tolerate poor performance? In theory, boards fire CEOs when the boards have lost confidence that the CEO can take actions to turn around the company. The percentage of forced departures of CEOs from their jobs at large global companies fell from 37 percent in 2004 to 14 percent in 2014. This may indicate improved governance as boards do a better job of recognizing the costs and consequences of CEO selection and succession planning. Alternatively, it may reflect a general increase in the stock market or boards retaining CEOs who deserve dismissal. CEOs are more likely to receive bonuses and retain their positions despite poor performance than lower-level managers.

One way to think about these issues is to compare corporate governance in the United States with corporate governance in other countries around the world. While corporate governance in the United States appears better than in countries where the government plays large roles in specifying firm behavior or where stockholder protections do not exist or are not enforced, comparing the United States to the United Kingdom (a country with a comparable free market, rule of law, and language) does not yield such a rosy picture. Directors, board members, and shareholders in the United Kingdom are more active than in the United States. Shareholders in Britain, for example, vote regularly on CEO compensation; while these votes are not binding, they pressure companies not to raise CEO compensation excessively. Recent changes to SEC rules have attempted to address some of the corporate governance issues we have discussed above; whether this results in the desired outcomes in the United States remains to be seen. Likewise, the benefits of corporate governance initiatives in other countries such as France or Norway, which specify certain quotas for women on the board, remain unclear.

A more philosophical way to think about these issues is to ask who has the most interest in a company? Is it the shareholders, who may sell their shares at any time? Is it the top managers, whose pay and reputation depends on the success of the company? Is it the company's employees, whose careers depend on the company's performance? Or is it the founders of the company and their families after them who often have both financial and emotional ties to the company? While this question is relatively easy to answer for small or newly founded companies, a clear answer for larger firms remains problematic.

More fundamentally, this brings us back to a question we raised at the beginning of this book: what is a company for? What are appropriate goals and objectives for a firm? Can we fault managers for not running their firms as effectively or efficiently as possible when we do not even know what this "optimum" might be? Stated differently, what are we trying to achieve through strategy: industry beating performance in all dimensions, industry beating performance in a few dimensions with industry average performance in others, simple firm profitability, longevity, or some combination of all of these and other factors?

SUMMARY

This chapter dealt with strategy implementation—how companies develop and implement strategies. Specifically, we looked at a variety of organizational structures (such as functional, divisional, and matrix) and systems, with a particular emphasis on routines such as strategic planning. The key issues here are (i) achieving a balance between specialization and coordination when designing structures, and (ii) integrating structures with the existing systems and routines of the company. When we look at strategic planning, the key issue here is one of ensuring that a company's strategic plans actually relate to strategy, and that the plans have the buy-in of people who will be implementing them.

The second part of this chapter examined corporate governance. While agency theory dominates discussions of corporate governance, stockholders face two problems. First, how do we ensure that boards of directors—a primary mechanism for monitoring management—perform their tasks effectively? Second, how do we address issues of CEO and top management compensation and, in particular, ensure a link between performance and compensation?

FOOD FOR THOUGHT

1. Some companies have attempted experimenting with doing away with hierarchy entirely, instead running themselves like a democracy, where each employee gets a vote on compensation and other corporate governance issues. In what kinds of companies do you think such attempts will be successful?
2. One study argues that, in the long term, Asian keiretsu or Indian conglomerates like Tata will show better performance than Western public companies because the former are basically family run (and hence, invest for the long term), while the latter are more focused on meeting the short-term earnings expectations of analysts and shareholders. Would you agree?
3. One suggestion to reduce excessive CEO compensation has been to pass legislation limiting the difference between the highest paid and the lowest paid employees of the company. What steps do you think companies might take in response to such legislation?

4. As we mention in the chapter, agency theory assumes two central players: an honest, risk-neutral principal and an amoral, risk-averse agent. To what extent do you agree with this assumption? Do you think this assumption itself might cause the agency problem? If business schools emphasized ethical decision making to a greater extent in MBA classes, do you think the severity of corporate governance issues would be reduced?

NOTES AND BIBLIOGRAPHY

1. Terlep, S. "P&G's CEO Holds to Fundamentals," *The Wall Street Journal* (November 1, 2016) B1.
2. Bryan, L. "Enduring Ideas: The 7-S Framework," *McKinsey Quarterly* (March 2008), www.mckinsey.com/business-functions/strategy-and-corporate-finance/our-insights/enduring-ideas-the-7-s-framework
3. Levitt, B., and March, J. M. "Organizational Learning," *Annual Review of Sociology* 14 (1988):319–340 (quote from p. 322).
4. MacCrimmon, K. R., and Wehrung, D. A. *Taking Risks: The Management of Uncertainty* (New York: Free Press, 1986). For a review of strategic decision making, see Bromiley, P., and Rau, D. "Strategic Decision Making," in S. Zedeck (Ed.), *APA Handbook of Industrial and Organizational Psychology* (pp. 161–182) (Washington, DC: American Psychological Association, 2011).
5. Kahneman, D., and Tversky, A. "Prospect Theory: An Analysis of Decision under Risk," *Econometrica* 47 (1979):263–291.
6. Bromiley, P. "Looking at Prospect Theory," *Strategic Management Journal* 31(12) (2010):1357–1370.
7. Cyert, R. M., and March, J. G. *A Behavioral Theory of the Firm* (Englewood Cliffs, NJ: Prentice-Hall, 1963).
8. March, J. M., and Shapira, Z.. "Managerial Perspectives on Risk and Risk Taking," *Management Science* 33 (1987):1404–1418; see also Shapira, Z. *Risk Taking: A Management Perspective* (New York: Russell Sage Foundation, 1994).
9. Mintzberg, H. "The Fall and Rise of Strategic Planning," *Harvard Business Review* 72(1) (1994):107–114.
10. Rumelt, R. *Good Strategy, Bad Strategy: The Difference and Why It Matters* (New York: Random House, 2011).
11. Ries, E. "How DropBox Started as a Minimum Viable Product," *TechCrunch* (October 19, 2011). https://techcrunch.com/2011/10/19/dropbox-minimal-viable-product/; see also Ries, E. *The Lean Startup: How Today's Entrepreneurs Use Continuous Innovation to Create Radically Successful Businesses* (New York: Crown Business, 2011).
12. Eisenhardt, K. A. "Agency Theory: An Assessment and Review," *Academy of Management Review* 14(1):57–74.
13. Berle, A. A., and Means, G. C. *The Modern Corporation and Private Property* (New Brunswick, NJ: Transaction Publishers, 1991).

14. Tosi, H. L., Werner, S., Katz, J. P., and Gomez-Mejia, L. R. "How Much Does Performance Matter? A Meta-Analysis of CEO Pay Studies," *Journal of Management* 26(2) (2000):301–339.

15. Cooper, M. J., Gulen, H., and Rau, P. R. "Performance for Pay? The Relation between CEO Incentive Compensation and Future Stock Price Performance" (2014), https://ssrn.com/abstract=1572085 (accessed October 1, 2014).

16. Souder, D., and Bromiley, P. "Timing for Dollars: How Option Exercisability Influences Resource Allocation," *Journal of Management* (forthcoming); Souder, D., and Bromiley, P. "Explaining Temporal Orientation: Evidence from the Durability of Firms' Capital Investments," *Strategic Management Journal* 33 (2012):550–569.

17. Kaplan, S. N. "Executive Compensation and Corporate Governance in the U.S.: Perceptions, Facts and Challenges," no. w18395 (Cambridge, MA: National Bureau of Economic Research, 2012).

18. Milgrom, P., and Roberts, J. *Economics, Organization, and Management* (Englewood Cliffs, NJ: Prentice Hall, 1992).

19. Chu, J., Faasse, J., and Rau, P. R. "Do Compensation Consultants Enable Higher CEO Pay? New Evidence from Recent Disclosure Rule Changes," https://ssrn.com/abstract=2500054 (accessed June 12, 2016).

APPENDIX
EXPERIENTIAL EXERCISES

RISK PREFERENCES

1. Your company has a choice of an investment with
   (a) an 85 percent chance to make $1,000,000 and a 15 percent chance of making nothing, or
   (b) receiving $800,000 with certainty.
   Which would you pick?

2. Your company has made a mistake that could potentially cost your firm $1,000,000. Your company has two potential ways out:
   (a) Option A has a 85 percent chance of losing the $1,000,000 and a 15 percent chance of losing nothing, or
   (b) Option B loses $800,000 for sure.
   Which would you pick?

3. Suppose your company had made a windfall gain of $1,000,000. Your company has a choice of investment options with this money. Your company could either choose
   (a) an investment with an 85 percent chance to make an additional $1,000,000 and a 15 percent chance of losing the $1,000,000, or
   (b) a safe investment that will guarantee your company an additional $800,000.
   Which would you pick?

4. Suppose your company had made a windfall gain of $1,000,000. Then, your company makes a mistake and has two potential ways out:
   (a) Option A has a 85 percent chance of losing the $1,000,000 and a 15 percent chance of losing nothing, or
   (b) Option B loses $800,000 for sure.
   Which would you pick?

FRAMING

5. Suppose your company is preparing for a flood that is expected to destroy your inventory on hand (worth $600,000) stored in a warehouse. Two alternative programs have been proposed.
   (a) If Program A is adopted, $200,000 of inventory will be saved.
   (b) If Program B is adopted, there is a one-third probability that all of your inventory will be saved and a two-thirds probability that all of your inventory will be destroyed.
   Which program would you prefer?

6. Now suppose your company is preparing for a flood that is expected to destroy your inventory on hand (worth $600,000) stored in a warehouse. Again, two alternative programs have been proposed.
   (a) If Program C is adopted, $400,000 of inventory will be destroyed.
   (b) If Program D is adopted, there is a one-third probability that none of your inventory will be destroyed and a two-thirds probability that all of your inventory will be destroyed.
   Which program would you prefer?

MARGINAL AND AVERAGE VALUES

7. Assume that you work for a company that currently, after accounting for the cost of capital, has a current return of 10 percent on $10 million of invested capital. You are asked to make a recommendation whether the company should invest in Project A, in Project B, in both, or in neither. Project A, after accounting for the cost of capital, has an expected discounted return of 10 percent on a $1 million investment. Project B, after accounting for the cost of capital, has an expected discounted return of five percent on a $1 million investment. Which project would you recommend?
   (a) Project A
   (b) Project B
   (c) Projects A and B
   (d) Neither project

8. Your company currently pays $1,000,000 in corporate income taxes on $5,000,000. You are considering an investment that should provide a net income of $500,000. What are your expected taxes after the project?
   (a) $1,100,000.
   (b) More than $1,100,000.
   (c) Less than $1,100,000.

FALLACIES AND COGNITIVE BIASES

9. Your company is considering the following two alternative strategies for R&D. Which of these two options seems more attractive?
   (a) Your company invests $10,000,000 in a new product; this investment cannot be recouped. There is a 51 percent chance that the new product will generate an additional $10,000,000 in profits, and a 49 percent chance that the investment will have to be written off.
   (b) Your company decides to invest $100,000 in each of a hundred new products; this investment cannot be recouped. Each new product comes with a 51 percent chance of generating an additional $100,000 in profits, and a 49 percent chance of being written off.

10. John, an older man, does not like women in technical fields. In evaluating women, would you expect that he will:
    (a) seek information that indicates deficits in their background and abilities,
    (b) seek balanced information regarding their background and abilities,
    (c) seek information that indicates positive features of their backgrounds.

11. You are considering two projects. A has extremely high potential for future returns. B has a lower potential for future returns. Which project do you think has a higher likelihood of being completed successfully?
    (a) A
    (b) B
    (c) Neither

12. Over the last few years, you have hired 20 new MBAs from a wide variety of schools. Most recently you hired two graduates from School A and both of them performed extremely well at your company. Therefore, you should try to hire more people from School A. Would you
    (a) agree, or
    (b) disagree?
    Why did you make this choice?

13. Bank A has made a great many loans over the years. Recently, it made a large loan to the developers of a sports stadium. The project was not completed and the bank lost all of the funds loaned. Now whenever a similar project is raised, someone is sure to point out the stadium debacle. Eventually, management decided that the bank should never make loans for stadium construction. Do you agree which this conclusion?
    (a) Agree
    (b) Disagree
    Why did you make this choice?

14. Joe has been extremely effective as a procurement manager, finding reliable, low-cost suppliers from around the world; this has really helped your company reduce its manufacturing costs. However, Joe will be retiring next year. Your ideal candidate for procurement manager will be someone whose qualifications are just like Joe's. Do you agree with this statement?

15. You have been involved in the approval of a 5-year project that was forecast to cost $10 million but would probably generate $3 million per year in profits on completion. Two years into the project, you now see that project will probably cost $15 million and generate only $2 million in profits. What should you do?
    (a) Push on—you have started and should finish.
    (b) Stop now—cut your losses.
    (c) Reevaluate the financial analysis and make a new decision.

BELIEFS AND PERCEPTIONS

16. You are the owner of a large restaurant. You are thinking of buying a small mom-and-mom restaurant for $100,000. Unfortunately, the owners of the smaller restaurant have been rather lax in their book keeping; their accounts are incomprehensible.
    (a) Your decision will be based largely on your guess as to whether the business with thrive or fail after it is bought by your company.
    (b) Your decision will be based largely on your guess as to how the small restaurant did last year.
    Would you be more likely to make your decision based on (a) or (b)?

17. Your company is trying to decide between two new product development projects. Project I deals with a completely new technology. The probability of success of the project is unknown; it may range from anywhere between 0 and 100 percent. Project II also deals with a completely new technology; however, here you estimate the probability of success as 50 percent. Which project would you prefer and why?

18. Suppose you must decide between two potential treatments for toxic chemical waste generated by your plant. Treatment A has been used extensively, and there is substantial information that indicates its success rate to be 50 percent. Treatment B is new, and there is little information underlying your environmental engineer's best guess that its chance of success is 50 percent. Which option would you prefer?

19. Since you store a lot of flammable chemicals, in addition to implementing pollution control, you also decide to purchase fire insurance. Unfortunately, this kind of insurance is very costly. Your insurance agent proposes an alternative to traditional insurance: For half the regular premium you can be fully covered if the fire occurs on an odd day of the month. He argues that this is a good deal because for half the price you are covered for more than half the days. Would you purchase this policy? Why or why not?

20. Your company requires customers go through a number of different steps to place an order. The order of these steps can be varied. Further, customers like some of the steps and dislike other steps. You should order the steps such that:
    (a) It does not matter—the sum of the steps is the same regardless of order.
    (b) The negative steps come early in the interaction giving time for positive steps to overcome them.
    (c) You should put the negative steps in the center of the ordering process and keep the positive steps at the beginning and at the end.

INFORMATION PROCESSING LIMITATIONS

21. As we discussed in Chapter 1, managers are subject to information processing limitations. In particular, many scholars note that managers do not attend to all information equally. Instead, they tend to focus on selective pieces of information, in particular, basing decisions on information that is either easily available or is particularly vivid or salient, and assuming that this information is representative of all the data available.

    For example, Dessaint and Matray find in a study that if a hurricane passes an area close to where a firm is located, decision makers begin to accumulate short-term liquidity for their firms.[1] Addoum et al. find in a 2015 study that when the frequency of bankruptcies increases, managers of firms from various sectors within a 100 mile radius from the bankrupt firm reduce their investment and indebtedness levels and hold more cash.[2]

    What implications does this kind of selective information processing have for firms' management of strategic risks, that is, risks that can threaten the firm's existence?

22. You are advising a bank on risk management practices. Would you recommend:
    (a) Identifying all possible risks, their likelihood, and potential impacts and building up from those risks to higher-level risks, or
    (b) Identifying major risks while ignoring many smaller issues.

23. In 1989, Eisenhardt used the term "high velocity" to describe many real world environments.[3] High velocity environments are characterized by rapid changes in technology, demand, competitors, and decision rules. Managers working in such environments are often stressed: they have to make strategic decisions under time pressure. The problem is that they face two conflicting pressures. On the one hand, accuracy (i.e., gathering and processing enough data) is key. On the other hand, making timely decisions is also critical. Hence, managers have to get the timing of their decisions just right: make decisions too soon (without sufficient data), and the firm could be rushing toward a costly mistake; make them too late (having waited to gather all the data you need), and you have given your competitors a head start in the changing environment.

    How do you think managers can make good decisions under time pressure? Should they evaluate a wide array of alternatives or look at a few alternatives in depth?

    If you chose the latter option (looking at a few alternatives in depth), how would you explain Toyota's position as perhaps the fastest and most efficient developer of autos using what is an apparently inefficient development process, wherein Toyota's engineers and managers delay decisions and give suppliers partial information while exploring numerous prototypes?[4]

24. Linda is a mathematics buff and an amateur astronomer. Growing up, she enjoyed playing chess and building her own computers. Which situation is more likely?
    (a) Linda is clerical worker.
    (b) Linda is a stock analyst.

25. You need to predict how a business unit will behave regarding a given set of potential customers. You can either:
    (a) Engage in a detailed analysis of the costs and benefits facing the business unit, or
    (b) Look at how the unit has reacted to similar opportunities in the past.
    Which would you prefer?

ANALYSIS OF RESPONSES

RISK PREFERENCES

Questions 1 to 4

Questions 1 to 4 incorporate several ways many people's judgments differ systematically from utility or expected value maximization.

Someone who is risk neutral (deciding on expected value) would choose 1(a) and 2(a). Someone who has a consistent sufficiently large aversion to risk would choose 1(b) and 2(b). However, very few individuals respond this way. Instead, Kahneman and Tversky (1984) find that a majority of respondents in their study chose the sure outcome (1b) in questions like the first question and the probabilistic outcome (2b) in the second question.[5]

Similarly, someone who is risk neutral (deciding on expected value) would choose 3(a) and 4(a) while someone who has a sufficiently large aversion to risk would choose 3(b) and 4(b). Adding a constant to all the outcomes does not change the difference in expected value between the two outcomes in questions 3 and 4. Again, similar to questions 1 and 2, very few individuals respond this way. Very often, the windfall gain changes preference; most people prefer 3(b) over 3(a) and 4(a) over 4(b).

Kahneman and Tversky built on their results to build a theory called prospect theory. In simple terms, the theory predicts that individuals will be risk averse in the face of gains (all potential outcomes above a reference point) and risk seeking in the face of losses (all potential outcomes below a reference point).

The interesting question is, while prospect theory can be used to explain individual decisions, can prospect theory also be applied to explain organizations' risk-taking in response to performance above or below a reference point? How does organizational decision making differ from individual decision making?

FRAMING

Questions 5 and 6

In their 1981 article, Tversky and Kahneman reported that a majority of respondents presented with problems similar to those in Questions 5 and 6 preferred Program A over Program B and Program D over Program C.[6] This pattern of responses reflects the effects of framing: the way people view problems influences the decisions they make.

As we noted in our analysis of Questions 1 to 4, people tend to be risk averse when facing positive outcomes and risk seeking when facing negative outcomes. However, whether people see an outcome as positive or negative depends on how the problem is presented.

Consider, for example, Question 5. In this question, both options have the same expected value. However, while option a (Program A) is presented as a "saving," option b (Program B) suggests a probability of destruction. Hence, for a majority of people, Program A seems more attractive than Program B.

A similar pattern holds for Question 6. In this problem, Program C tends to appear as less attractive than Program D even though, once again, the two programs have the same expected value. Program C is framed solely in terms of destruction while D appears to offer at least the chance of saving something.

How could you use framing to influence decision making in organizations? If, for example, the manager of a factory wishes to increase individual and team productivity by changing how incentives are framed, do you think he or she would get better results if bonuses are framed as losses or as gains?[7]

Alternatively, if you want to encourage risk-taking or change in your organization, you would want to define the situation as a negative, that is, frame the situation in terms of the harmful things that would occur if the company continues with business as usual. Framing the situation as a positive (e.g., suggesting that there is a chance that the organization will be just fine if nothing is changed) will weaken the case for change.

MARGINAL AND AVERAGE VALUES

Questions 7 and 8

For most purposes, analyses should use marginal rather than average values. For example, in calculating how much money you will net from an increase in pay, your additional income will be taxed at the marginal rate or rates (if it crosses limits for different rates) rather than your average income tax rate (which is generally much lower). If you are considering how to allocate resources to divisions, the issue is not how profitable is the division today, but rather the return from marginal investments in specific divisions.

In Question 7, both projects have returns well above the cost of capital and, according to finance theory, the firm should invest in both of them. The past returns of the firm are largely irrelevant. Indeed, sometimes very low risk cost-reduction investments in divisions with modest profitability can have much higher returns than much higher risk business expansion investments in divisions with higher profitability.[8]

In Question 8, the marginal tax rate is almost always above the average tax rate so the expected taxes should be above $1,100,000.

These examples may seem obvious, but the empirical evidence is that most firms use average tax rates in evaluating new investments, and routinely use average values when marginal would be appropriate for other purposes.[9]

Why do you think managers find average rates so much more compelling than marginal rates? How would you combat this problem?

FALLACIES AND COGNITIVE BIASES

Question 9

Question 9 raises an issue related to the one addressed in Questions 5 and 6. While a single investment with a 50 percent chance of success may be unattractive, for many people, multiple investments of the same kind may appear attractive. Samuelson (1963) illustrated this with a bet he offered a colleague: flip a coin, heads you win $200 and tails you lose $100. The colleague said that while he would not be willing to take a single bet because it would hurt more to lose $100 than to win $200, he would be willing to take a hundred such bets.[10]

The colleague's unwillingness to bet on a single flip of a coin illustrates something called loss aversion; consistent with prospect theory, people tend to find the prospect of losing something more painful than the happiness they would get from winning an equivalent amount. The interesting question then is, why would someone accept multiple bets when they find a single bet of the same kind unattractive?

Samuelson argued that this is due to the fallacy of large numbers. The law of large numbers states that for large samples, the expected value tends to approach the "true" value of the population. However, people tend to underestimate how large the sample actually is, and incorrectly apply the law of averages.

To illustrate this fallacy, consider the following example.[11] Suppose your company has a fleet of 100 cars. For any given car, on any given day, assume there is a 3 percent chance that it will be out of repairs. How many cars can you offer to customers in a day?

The obvious answer is 97. That is, on any given day, you can offer your customers 97 cars while keeping three in reserve to handle the possibility of breakdowns (and the subsequent loss of revenue that comes with not being able to offer your customers a car when they need it).

However, what if you are unlucky? After all, there is a chance that four, or five, or even six cars may be out of commission on any given day. In that case, how many cars should you reserve? Six? Seven? Or is that too much? Notice how your thinking about this problem may have changed at this point.

Mathematically, the likelihood of having more than four cars unavailable on any given day is 18 percent. The likelihood of having more than six cars unavailable is 3.1 percent, or about once a month. The likelihood having more than eight cars unavailable is 0.3 percent, or more than once a year. Reserving nine cars, or three times the number we started with, gets the risk down to 0.087 percent, or about one failure to rent a car to a customer every 3 years.

Going back to the fallacy of large numbers, many people may think that reserving three cars out of a fleet of 100 is sufficient because 100 is a large number. However, as we demonstrated above, 100 is actually not that large a sample; calculating the number of possible breakdowns (given a 3 percent chance of an individual breakdown) with a sample size of 100 may lead to unacceptable service.

In the light of this discussion, what do you think the fallacy of large numbers suggests about the efficacy of your company's risk management efforts?

Question 10

Question 10 illustrates something called confirmation bias. Confirmation bias occurs when people search for, interpret, or recall information that fits in or confirms what they already believe. Thus, if you believe that a certain person is a great candidate for a position, confirmation bias suggests that you will look for information that confirms your beliefs while ignoring information that disconfirms your beliefs. At an organizational level, if you strongly believe that expanding into a new geographic market or diversifying your product line in a particular direction is a great strategic move, you will gather information that supports your position while discounting information that suggests the opposite.

Can you provide examples where you or your friends might be subject to confirmation bias? How might you combat this?

Question 11

The answer is neither—you have no information about success probabilities. However, we often generalize from a positive impression in one dimension to positive impressions on other dimensions, or from negative impressions in one dimension to negative impressions in other dimensions. That is, we often generalize where the data do not support generalization.

For example, we might have a generally positive impression of someone or something. We then tend to evaluate them positively on dimensions on which we have no evidence. If we like a candidate's position on the policy most important to us, we tend to assume we will like the candidate's positions on other policy areas. If you think an employee is smart or friendly, you may assume the employee has abilities for which you have no evidence. This is called a halo bias. The halo bias works in both positive and negative ways; if you think a CEO is cold and unfeeling, you might view his emphasis on automation as a precursor to layoffs.

This can also align with generalizing from a specific property or trait of an individual to other properties or traits. If you have a single positive experience with customer service at say, Amazon, you will be likely to view the whole company as well run in other dimensions. If you find an employee has been padding his expense reports, you will be more likely to question the accuracy of all of his other reports.

Questions 12 and 13

These examples demonstrate two potential pitfalls.

Decisions regarding frequency depend on memory. That is, instead of a fair balancing of past experiences, people often judge essentially probabilistic matters by trying to remember similar instances.

This creates several systematic biases.

More recent events will have excessive influence. In the hiring question, you are likely to overweight your experience with the two most recent hires from that company and underweight any earlier negative experiences with other people from School A that you have hired in the past.

We also tend to generalize from excessively small samples. Two good individuals does not necessarily mean the program or average graduate is good—you could easily get lucky on two hires. Any MBA program has some excellent graduates.

In addition, more memorable instances will have greater influence than less memorable, but memorability does not equate to frequency. If you give people a list of obscure men and famous women and then ask if there are more men or women on the list, people will tend to say women because they can remember the names of these women. In problem 13, our bank may have made many similar loans to developers of sports stadia that turned out well, but the stadium that failed is the most memorable.

Question 14

Problem 14 illustrates anchoring bias: relying too heavily on the first piece of information that you come across when making decisions. In this example, the first pieces of information you have about the procurement manager's position are Joe's characteristics and effectiveness. Hence, you may rely too heavily on this information by looking for a candidate just like Joe, potentially missing out on more effective candidates who may not resemble Joe at all.

Anchoring also works in numerical issues. We anchor on last year's budget and adjust from there. Even artificial numbers can form anchors and influence decisions. For example, many companies use anchoring (and the often insufficient adjustment that people make from the anchor price) to determine their posted prices. Car dealers list high sticker prices; getting a couple of thousand dollars off the list price then makes customers feel they have got a great deal. Retailers like Kohl's list sticker prices followed by the discounted price; looking at the prominently displayed sticker price followed by the discounted price makes customers feel good about buying clothes from the store.

Question 15

We are all familiar with commitment bias. Commitment bias occurs when individuals become more convinced about their position once it has been publicly stated. When faced with increasingly negative outcomes from their decision, these individuals may choose to escalate their commitment rather than change course.

While we often see this in major publicly funded construction projects (e.g., a California high-speed railway from Los Angeles to San Francisco that continues to increase in cost and construction time even as its supporters remain committed to construction), it also occurs in all kinds of activities. Indeed, some evidence suggests that negative interim feedback can actually increase people's commitment to a course of action, a phenomenon called escalation of commitment. Commitment bias can also relate to the sunk cost fallacy—emphasizing the amount invested (and already lost) rather than doing a calculation of the returns expected based on the remaining investment and outcomes.

BELIEFS AND PERCEPTIONS

Question 16

You have equally insufficient information to make either prediction. If you preferred option (a), you agreed with the majority of respondents in Heath and Tversky's 1991 study.[12] Heath and Tversky posed a similar question to respondents asking them whether they would prefer to predict the price of a randomly drawn stock the next day, or guess the price of the same stock the previous day. In each case, a correct answer would win the respondent the same amount of money. Most respondents preferred to predict a future price than guess the past price. People, in other words, believe they have some ability to predict the future; hence, betting on the future rather than on the past is more attractive for most.

Question 17

This question is based on a problem devised by Ellsberg (1961).[13] Ellsberg proposed the following thought experiment.

You have the following information: Urn I contains 100 red and black balls, but in a ratio entirely unknown to you; there may be from 0 to 100 red balls. In Urn II, you confirm that there are exactly 50 red and 50 black balls. An observer—who, let us say, is ignorant of the state of your information about the urns—sets out to measure your subjective probabilities by interrogating you as to your preferences in the following pairs of gambles:

1. "Which do you prefer to bet on, Red_I or $Black_I$? Or are you indifferent?" That is, drawing a ball from Urn I, on which "event" do you prefer the $100 stake, red or black: do you care?
2. "Which would you prefer to bet on, Red_{II} or $Black_{II}$?"
3. "Which do you prefer to bet on, Red_I or Red_{II}?"
4. "Which do you prefer to bet on, $Black_I$ or $Black_{II}$?"

The typical response was "indifferent" to both questions 1 and 2. For questions 3 and 4, however, the majority preferred to bet on Red_{II} rather than Red_I and on $Black_{II}$ rather than $Black_I$.

This pattern of responses is termed the Ellsberg paradox. The paradox states that people prefer known risks to unknown risks, even if the known risk gives you a low chance of winning while the unknown risk could guarantee a win. That is, people prefer to take risks in situations where they know the specific odds rather than take risks in situations where the odds of success are unknown, even if these odds may result in better outcomes. If you preferred Project II over Project I, you have demonstrated the paradox.

Questions 18 and 19

People often show a preference for betting on known risks (and avoiding ambiguity) rather than unknown risks, a preference for betting on skill rather than chance, and a preference for certainty (even if the certainty is illusory).

Curley et al. (1986) posed a question similar to Question 18 to respondents and found that, in general, while making a decision, people prefer to avoid ambiguity.[14] Since Treatment A has a known probability of success, most people prefer it over Treatment B, where the likelihood of success is ambiguous.

A preference for ambiguity avoidance goes hand in hand with a preference for certainty—and if certainty is not possible, for perceived certainty or pseudo-certainty. Question 19, similar to the one posed by Kahneman and Tversky in their 1984 study, illustrates this preference. Kahneman and Tversky note that various kinds of insurance policies—health, home, etc.— are probabilistic in that they reduce the likelihood of some hazard rather than eliminate the hazard altogether. As Kahneman and Tversky note "An insurance policy that covers fire but not flood, for example, could be evaluated either as a full protection against a specific risk, (e.g., fire) or as a reduction in the overall probability of property loss" (pp. 345–346). As an extension of this, an insurance policy that covers fire on odd days reduces the overall probability of loss; however, most people would find this policy unattractive since they would prefer the pseudo-certainty of being fully protected.

All of these problems have a strong bearing on how top managers make decisions. March and Shapira observed in their 1987 study that though many top managers essentially made bets on uncertain business decisions, they preferred to think of themselves as reasoned risk takers and resisted the analogy between games of chance and business decisions.[15]

Question 20

The peak-end rule states that when people assess the pleasure or pain associated with an event, they tend to focus on the peak intensity and the endpoint, ignoring other parts of the events. For example, Kahneman et al. (1993) note that when subjects were exposed to two unpleasant experiences (in the first, immersing one hand in water at 14°C for 60 seconds, and in the second, immersing the other hand in water at 14°C for 60 seconds and then keeping the hand in the water for 30 seconds longer while the temperature was raised to 15°C), they preferred the latter experience.[16] Even though both experiences were painful, the pain in the second experience was greater than the first since it lasted 30 seconds longer. However, subjects preferred the second experience over the first since the second experience ended more positively, with people experiencing comparatively less pain toward the end.

A number of studies finds that the peak-end rule applies to real life. For example, Dixon and Verma (2013) find that people are more likely to repeat their purchase of season subscription ticket packages for classical music if the package ends on a high note with say, an exciting or a popular concert.[17] Similarly, in a longitudinal field experiment conducted at a commercial bank, Haisley and Loewenstein (2011) find that gifts to customers increase deposit balances, survey response rates, and customer satisfaction compared to the no-gift control condition.[18] Further, the sequence of gift giving (increasing or decreasing) matters. While decreasing gift value has a negative effect on deposit balances, improving gifts over constant gift sequences has a positive effect.

In Problem 20, the peak-end rule would imply option (b). Customers would prefer ending their order placement experience with a positive rather than a negative experience.

INFORMATION PROCESSING LIMITATIONS

Question 21–22

Managers' information processing limitations suggest that they can only pay attention to a few things at a time. When managers may try to pay attention to everything, they often neglect things that really matter. For example, in our 2016 article, we discuss how many managers, while trying to manage risks at the firm level through a process of enterprise risk management (which involves identifying all risks facing a firm, classifying them by their probability and impact, and determining which actions to take to mitigate or control them) turn risk management into a massive paper processing exercise.[19] Countrywide Financial, for example, was praised by the Institute of Internal Auditors in 2007 for its comprehensive risk management program, which involved 45 risk management professionals, supplemented by 112 internal auditors, who assessed 530 risk matrices, 9,500 risks, and 27,000 controls. Within a year, however, Countrywide had gone bankrupt and was acquired by the Bank of America due to its risk-taking in the subprime lending market. Given managers' information processing limitations, it may be more effective for firms to manage their strategic risks by (among other things) focusing on a few critical risks and setting appropriate incentives.

Question 23

This problem adds a twist—the effect of time pressure—to the topic of managers' information processing limitations. Payne et al., in their 1996 study, identify three alternatives for information processing under time pressure: spending less time processing each item of information (i.e., accelerating information processing), becoming more selective in information processing, or focusing on more important or more negative information about alternatives.[20] Based on a series of experiments, these authors conclude that decision makers face a trade-off between accuracy and time pressure: "decision makers who are more motivated to be accurate can sometimes make decisions that are not adaptive for the tasks or environments they face" (p. 151). Note that Eisenhardt (1989) finds that fast decision makers in high velocity environments use more information, not less, develop more (not fewer) alternatives, and use a two-tiered advice process where conflict resolution and integration among strategic decisions and tactical plans critically influence the pace of decision making.[21]

Question 24

If you picked (a), you are guilty of base rate neglect. The number of clerical workers is orders of magnitude greater than the numbers of stock analysts. Consequently, it is much more probable that any individual will be a clerical worker than a stock analyst.

People routinely ignore base rates. Thus, they react to individualizing information more than they should. For example, in judging borrowers, lenders will emphasize their impressions over credit scores. Likewise, in the context of firms' management of strategic risks, managers may pay more attention to easily available or vivid information (e.g., the recent occurrence of an earthquake, hurricane, or bankruptcy of firm in a geographically close location) while disregarding the frequency of occurrence of these events. This, in turn, may cause managers to neglect preparing for risks that are less vivid but are more likely to occur and cause significant damage to the firm. Consider the amount of energy that goes into worrying about shark attacks or terrorism relative to the energy that goes into worrying about the immensely greater number of people who die in car accidents.

Question 25

In Question 25, option (b) implies relying on routines to make a decision. The immense majority of the time, what happens in organizations derives from routines. The best predictor of organizational (and individual) behavior is almost always how the organization or individual behaved on previous days.

Organizations could not function if most things were not routine. Every employee cannot stop to figure out the best way to do every job every time a job appears. In addition, coordination requires predictability. Thus, you do not want the cleaners to spend time every day figuring out the most efficient way to clean. Likewise, consider all the things that must come together to get you in a course with an instructor. All of these things cannot mesh if they are not highly predictable. Routines give predictability.

We also use routines in our personal lives. Anyone living with someone else generally has a routine about how things go in the morning. Such a routine saves thinking and facilitates coordination.

There are times when we probably must consider the full incentives facing someone or an organization but they generally apply where the organization has identified the event as extraordinary or has a specific routine for evaluating the incentives associated with the event.

NOTES AND BIBLIOGRAPHY

1. Dessaint, O., and Matray, A. "Do Managers Overreact to Salient Risks? Evidence from Hurricane Strikes," *Journal of Financial Economics* (Forthcoming). https://ssrn.com/abstract=2358186 or http://dx.doi.org/10.2139/ssrn.2358186
2. Addoum, J. M., Kumar, A., and Le, N. "Contagious Negative Sentiment and Corporate Policies: Evidence from Local Bankruptcy Filings," August 28, 2014, Paris, December 2014 Finance Meeting EUROFIDAI—AFFI Paper, https://ssrn.com/abstract=2490742

3. Eisenhardt, K. M. "Making Fast Strategic Decisions in High Velocity Environments," *Academy of Management Journal* 32 (1989):543–575.

4. For a full description of this process, see Ward, A., Liker, J. K., Cristiano, J. J., and Sobek, D. K. "The 2nd Toyota Paradox: How Delaying Decisions Can Make Better Cars Faster," *Sloan Management Review* 36(3) (1995):43–61.

5. Kahneman, D., and Tversky, A. "Choices, Values, and Frames," *American Psychologist* 39(4) (1984):341–350.

6. Tversky, A., and Kahneman, D. "The Framing of Decisions and the Psychology of Choice," *Science* 211(4481) (1981):453–458.

7. For one way of handling this problem, see Hossain, T., and List, J. A. "The Behavioralist Visits the Factory: Increasing Productivity Using Simple Framing Manipulations," *Management Science* 58(12) (2012):2151–2167.

8. This example is from Shapira, Z., and Shaver, J. M. "Confounding Changes in Averages with Marginal Effects: How Anchoring Can Destroy Economic Value in Strategic Investment Assessments," *Strategic Management Journal* 35 (2014): 1414–1426.

9. See Graham, J.R., Hanlon, M., Shevlin, T., and Shroff, N. "Incentives for Tax Planning and Avoidance: Evidence from the Field," *The Accounting Review* 89(3) (2014):991–1023.

10. Samuelson, P. A. "Risk and Uncertainty: A Fallacy of Large Numbers," *Scientia*, XCVIII (1963):108–113.

11. This example is from Dspeyer, "The Fallacy of Large Numbers," *LessWrong* (August 12, 2012), http://lesswrong.com/lw/e24/the_fallacy_of_large_numbers (accessed January 28, 2017).

12. Heath, C., and Tversky, A. "Preference and Belief: Ambiguity and Competence in Choice Under Uncertainty," *Journal of Risk and Uncertainty* 4 (1991):5–28.

13. Ellsberg, D. "Risk, Ambiguity, and the Savage Axioms," *Quarterly Journal of Economics* 75 (1961):643–669.

14. Curley, S. P., Yates, J. F., and Abrams, R. A. "Psychological Sources of Ambiguity Avoidance," *Organizational Behavior and Human Decision Processes* 38(2) (1986):230–256.

15. March, J., and Shapira, Z. "Managerial Perspectives on Risk and Risk Taking," *Management Science* 33(11) (1987):1404–1418.

16. Kahneman, D., Fredrickson, B. L., Schreiber, A., and Redelmeier, D. A. "When More Pain Is Preferred to Less: Adding a Better End," *Psychological Science* 4(6) (1993):401–405.

17. Dixon, M. J., and Verma, R. "Sequence Effects in Service Bundles: Implications for Service Design and Scheduling," *Journal of Operations Management* 31(3) (2013):138–152.

18. Haisley, E., and Loewenstein, G. "It's Not What You Get but When You Get It: The Effect of Gift Sequence on Deposit Balances and Current Sentiment in a Commercial Bank," *Journal of Marketing Research* 48(1) (2011):103–115.

19. Bromiley, P., and Rau, D. "A Better Way of Managing Major Risks," *IESE Insight* 28 (2016):15–22.

20. Payne, J. W., Bettman, J. R., and Luce, M. F. "When Time Is Money: Decision Behavior Under Opportunity-Cost Time Pressure," *Organizational Behavior and Human Decision Processes* 66(2) (1996):131–152.

21. Eisenhardt, K. M. "Making Fast Strategic Decisions in High Velocity Environments," *Academy of Management Journal* 32 (1989):543–575.

GLOSSARY

Agency costs: The costs of monitoring and providing incentives to agents.

Agency theory: Theory underlying most discussions of corporate governance. The theory addresses how the principal (usually shareholders, the board of directors, and top management) can get an agent (usually managers or employees of a firm) to act in the principal's interest by providing appropriate incentives and monitoring.

Agent: One of the two central players in agency theory. Usually refers to the managers or employees of a firm.

Ambidexterity: Companies simultaneously or sequentially pursue their original or dominant business models and new ways of doing business.

Backward integration: A buyer becomes their own supplier by manufacturing a product that they previously used to purchase from outside the firm.

Balanced scorecard: A strategic management system, originally designed by Kaplan and Norton, that allows managers to work backwards from their desired outcome to identify intermediate factors that influence the outcome, and then convert these factors into measurable and meaningful goals.

Bargaining power: The extent to which buyers or suppliers can negotiate with a firm for better prices or terms.

Behavioral approach to strategy: Recognizes that the way people think and interact with others are critical aspects of the strategic problem solving process.

Benchmarking: The process of comparing an organization's performance on a few key indicators to its competitors' performance on those same indicators.

Berle and Means hypothesis: Suggests that modern corporations are particularly prone to agency problems because widely diffused ownership results in little oversight of managers by firm shareholders.

Brand equity: The value of a firm's brands.

Business judgment rule: A presumption that, in making a business decision, management and board members have acted in good faith and have put in a reasonable amount of consideration into the decision.

CAGE framework: A framework that looks at the costs and risks associated with the distance between a company's home market and the foreign market it is considering expanding to; CAGE refers to the cultural, administrative and political, geographical, and economic distance between the home country and the foreign country.

Capabilities: Things that a firm does well. Two categories of capabilities include core and hygiene capabilities.

Capability-destroying changes: Changes that involve moving from one fundamental technology to another. The change often destroys the capabilities that an organization has built using the previous technology.

Capability-enhancing changes: Technological and other changes that build on the organization's current technology and result in an improvement in the organization's current products.

Capital requirements: The capital required to start up a new business in an industry.

Causal diagrams: A tool to clarify causal links. Managers develop explicit diagrams that reflect how they believe the business factors interact. This makes causal assumptions clear and offers the potential for empirical estimation of some important connections.

Competitive rivalry: How hard the companies in an industry compete with each other.

Complementors: A component of the value net analysis. Complementors are firms that supply complementary products (that are typically bought with the original product) to customers, or to whom suppliers could sell complementary products.

Coordination costs: A component of transactions costs that stems from the need to coordinate actions between specialized agents.

Core capabilities: Abilities that allow a firm to win. Core capabilities differentiate a firm from its competitors.

Core rigidities: Core capabilities that made an organizational successful in the past, but now prevent it from changing in needed ways.

Corporate governance: Refers to the relations among various participants—typically the shareholders, the board of directors, and top management—in determining the direction and performance of companies.

Corporate social responsibility: Contributions the company intends to make both to its stakeholders and to society in general.

Cost leadership: A firm strategy that relies on offering a product at a low price.

Country-portfolio analysis: A tool to analyze global expansion. Plots a company's actual and potential markets on a grid, with a measure of GDP or per capita income on one axis and a measure of product performance or consumer propensity to buy the product on the other.

Decline: Stage of the industry life cycle where demand begins to go down.

Differentiation: A firm strategy that relies on a firm's product or service being priced at a premium because of its higher perceived value to the customer.

Disruptive innovation: Innovation or technology that fundamentally alters the nature of the product or service offered by firms in an industry.

Diversification: Addresses issues related to what businesses a company should be in.

Divisional structure: An organizational structure that breaks the company up into categories (usually based on product or geography). The company operates, to some extent, as if the categories were separate businesses.

Dominant design: Generally accepted industry standards that define what a product should look like and what its core features should be.

Dominant logic: A common, institutionalized way of thinking about a business, built into the mental maps of top managers of a firm.

Duty of care: Board members have to take appropriate care while performing their duties for example by using outside consultants and recording discussions in the minutes of the board.

Duty of loyalty: Board members are supposed to put the corporation's interests ahead of their own.

Economies of scale: A benefit of large-scale operations. The cost per unit of a product declines with the number of units produced per time period.

Exit barriers: Financial and other costs that stop a firm from leaving an industry or market.

Focus or niche: A firm strategy that targets a given set of customers or offers a narrow range of products to achieve either low cost or differentiation.

Forecasting: A set of tools used to help firms plan for an uncertain future. Includes numeric techniques, limit analysis, trend correlation, and scenario analysis.

Forward integration: A situation where a supplier becomes their own customer.

Franchising: Involves a contract between a franchisor who normally owns the concept or production system, and a franchisee who normally invests to produce or market the franchisor's product, often in a given area.

Full integration: A firm takes over all of the suppliers or all of the customers for a given activity in backward or forward integration, respectively.

Functional structure: An organizational structure arranged largely by function.

Globally integrated strategies: Strategies that focus on operating the different units of a company in a unified way, emphasizing their connection with the company as a whole.

Global strategy: A strategy that emphasizes global integration over national responsiveness. This strategy works best when coordination across units is relatively easy, and consumers around the world demand standardized products.

Goals and objectives: Things that the organization, the unit of the organization, or an individual is supposed to accomplish.

Growth stage: Stage of the industry life cycle that is characterized by innovation along a defined trajectory and rapid growth in sales.

Harvest: A strategy that recognizes the best use of a business is as a source of cash flow.

Holding companies: A divisional structure where top management largely deals with largely independent divisions by looking at their strategic plans and at their financial performance.

Hold-up problem: After a contract has been written, the company that is not investing in a specific asset may attempt to renegotiate the contract on more favorable terms, putting the firm dependent on this exchange in a very weak negotiating position.

Incremental innovation: Innovation that results in minor changes in a product.

Industry life cycle: The stages an industry goes through with the passage of time; these stages usually include introduction, growth, maturity, and decline.

Innovation: The creation of something new and its transformation into a form that can be sold on a market or can influence something that is sellable on the market.

Intangible resources: Resources or assets that are not physical in nature, for example, brand reputation.

Intellectual capital: A variety of information-related things that provide benefits to the firm. Includes patents, know-how, complex business systems, and data on customers.

Introduction or birth stage: The first stage of the development of an industry, characterized by the entry of one or multiple firms into a given kind of business.

Invention: The discovery or creation of something new; the invention itself, however, is not generally suitable for selling.

Key success factors: The primary drivers of firm performance.

Knowledge management systems: Systems that attempt to inventory what people have solved or know and provide that inventory to others within an organization.

Last man standing strategy: The largest or the lowest cost firm is able to sustain a reasonable profit level despite industry decline.

Learning or experience curves: Decline in price per unit of a product with an increase in cumulative production or the total number of units produced.

Macro-environment: Situational factors that tend to influence a large number of firms within and across a variety of industries.

Matrix structure: An organizational structure that combines elements of both functional and divisional structures.

Maturity: Stage of the industry life cycle where sales growth slows to a replacement rate. Usually characterized by increased price pressures on firms.

Minimum efficient scale: Minimum size at which a company can compete effectively. Below this level of output per time, production is not economic for a firm.

Minimum viable product model: An iterative strategic planning process that involves identifying the riskiest assumption that managers are making while formulating a plan, testing this assumption with the smallest experiment possible, and then revisiting the plan based on the data gathered from the experiment.

Mission or vision: Statement containing basic ideas about what a company wants to achieve.

Motivation costs: A component of transactions costs that stems from aligning the interests of agents with those of the firm.

Multidomestic strategy: A strategy that emphasizes local (i.e., national) responsiveness over global integration. Companies following this strategy tend to decentralize key functions and promote subsidiary autonomy on a geographic basis.

Nationally responsive strategies: Strategies that focus on responding to cross-country differences and similarities.

Natural monopoly: A situation where serving the market with one company is much more efficient than serving the market with multiple companies.

Network effects or positive externalities: The value of a product to a person increases with the number of people using that product.

Opportunity cost: The value of a resource if it is used in some other way, including the value if the resource is sold on the open market.

Outsourcing: Having another company (at home or abroad) perform activities that were previously carried out in-house.

Partial or tapered integration: A firm produces part (but not all) of its needs for a given input or handles the next activity down the value chain for part (but not all) of its output.

Pestle analysis: A tool to analyze the macro-environment. Acronym for political, economic, sociocultural, technological, legal, and environmental factors.

Porter's five forces framework: A tool for analyzing a specific set of factors that determine the profitability of an industry. These factors include the threat of new entrants, intensity of rivalry, threat of substitute products, bargaining power of buyers, and bargaining power of suppliers.

Porter's diamond model of national competitive advantage:
A framework used to analyze why we see some industries concentrated

in some areas or regions of the world while other parts of the world lack similar concentrations of industries. The framework identifies four factors: factor conditions, demand conditions, related and supporting industries, and firm strategy, structure, and rivalry.

Primary activities: Activities on the value chain that directly contribute to the creation and sale of a product to a buyer, such as inbound logistics, operations, outbound logistics, marketing and sales, and service, in the case of manufacturing firms.

Principal: One of the two central players in agency theory. Usually refers to the firm's shareholders, board of directors, and top management.

Programming: Organizational processes that deal with clearly defined, well-structured problems.

Project-based structure: An organizational structure where management puts together the employees (from various functions or geographic areas or other subdivisions) with appropriate skills on a project-by-project basis.

Satisfice: When faced with complex, real-world problems, people make do with a good enough solution.

Scenario analysis: A forecasting tool that requires managers to imagine causal worlds consistent with a set of parameters.

Stakeholders: People and organizations involved in the firm. Includes owners, managers, employees, customers, suppliers, and the community or society the firm operates in.

Strategic groups: Groups of firms that compete more directly with one another than with other firms within the same industry.

Substitutes: Alternatives to a firm's product or service.

Substitutors: A component of the value net analysis. Consists of competitors, either existing or potential, from whom customers could buy their products or to whom suppliers could sell their products.

Support activities: Activities on the value chain that either add value themselves, or that add value in combination with other primary or support activities.

Switching costs: The costs to a buyer of switching to a new product. Switching costs could be monetary and/or relate to the time and effort the buyer has to put in before they can use the new product.

SWOT: Decision making tool based on an analysis of a company's strengths, weaknesses, opportunities, and threats.

Synergy: A combination of two businesses results in additional value being created over above the value created when the two business units are independent of each other.

Tangible resources: Assets or resources that are physical in nature, for example, the number of plants or buildings owned by a firm.

Threshold or hygiene capabilities: Abilities that are essential for a firm to compete, but which do not differentiate the performance of the firm from its competitors very much.

Transactions cost economics: Compares a set of costs and benefits associated with doing a particular transaction in the market to the costs and benefits of doing that transaction inside the organization.

Transnational strategy: A strategy that attempts to emphasize both national responsiveness and global integration.

Value chain: A tool to analyze the value a firm creates, by viewing the firm as a sequential process of value-creating activities or subsystems.

Value net: A tool to analyze an industry. Value net suggests a possibility of a win–win strategy among the players in an industry in addition to the win–lose strategy that is implicit in Porter's five forces analysis.

Value–price–cost: A framework to map firms' strategies based on the extent to which the strategies target value or cost.

Value strategy: A firm strategy that combines elements of both cost leadership and differentiation.

Vertical integration: A company undertakes to do something in-house that might otherwise have been purchased from a supplier or handled by its customers.

Virtual corporation: A company that has almost no physical assets or physical locations and operates largely by coordinating and integrating the efforts of a variety of independent individuals or corporations.

INDEX